CHARLESTON

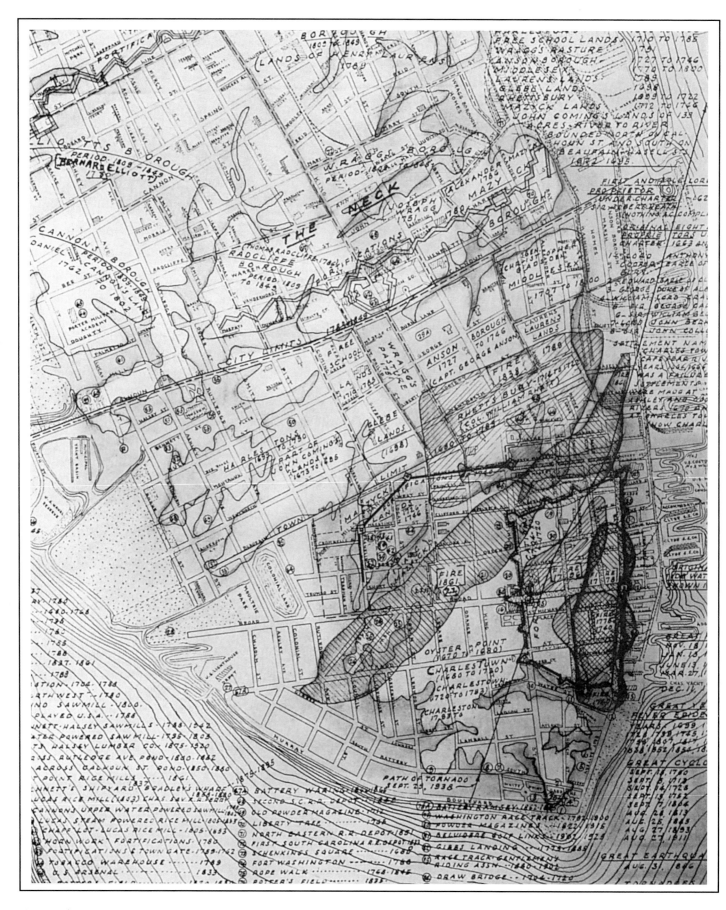

In 1949 after fifteen years research, Alfred O. Halsey completed "Historic Charleston on a Map." Superimposed on a City Engineer's map of 1946 are original high tide water lines, fortifications, boroughs, great fires, public buildings, and a wealth of fascinating information at a glance from the Carolina's sailing in 1669 to the tornado of 1938. Courtesy of Alfred O. Halsey, Jr. The map is sold at the Thomas Elfe Workshop.

CHARLESTON
CROSSROADS OF HISTORY
By Isabella G. Leland & Robert N. Rosen

American Historical Press
Sun Valley, California

Previous page
Henry Jackson's 1816 view of Charleston is from the site of Bennett's millpond in the foregrounf. The two large houses on the left still stand on Calhoun St., and near the center is the tower of St. Paul's Church, now the Episcopal Cathedral of St. Luke and St. Paul. The pond was filled in 1875, and for many years was the site of the Charleston Museum. Courtesy of The Gibbes Museum

© 2003 American Historical Press
All Rights Reserved
Published 2003
Printed in the United States of America

Library of Congress Catalogue Card Number: 2003096191
ISBN: 1-892724-37-5

Bibliography: p. 167
Includes Index

CONTENTS

Preface

Isabella G. Leland published *Charleston: A Crossroads in History* in 1980. It was the first general history of the city in many years. When I wrote *A Short History of Charleston* (1982), I relied on Ms. Leland's excellent work. Thus, it was a great honor for me to have been asked by the publisher to update her work and to provide a chapter on events since the original publication. Writing about Charleston from 1975 to 2003 is not without its difficulties. It is always a challenge to historians to evaluate the events of their own lifetime, to try to be impartial, and to discern which events have historic significance. I was privileged to participate in some of the events described in my chapter, having served as Assistant Corporation Counsel for the City of Charleston under Mayor Riley and having served as General Counsel for the Charleston County School District since 1982. Having also been actively involved in politics, I have been both friend and foe to some of the people described in this chapter. Nevertheless, I have made every effort to set down an accurate history of these very important years in Charleston's history.

I want to express my appreciation to numerous people who assisted me in my work: My dedicated Legal Assistant, Claudia Kelley, was a great help in bringing this work to fruition. My childhood friends, Michael Levkoff and Barbara Baker, were kind enough to take the contemporary photographs which appear in this book. Bill Murton and Ellen Dressler Moryl also provided important photographs. I also wish to thank Philip Overcash with the City Planning Department and especially Nancy Taylor for their research assistance and Charlton deSaussure and Alex Moore for reading the manuscript and offering their suggestions. Special thanks to those who graciously gave permission to use their photographs and paintings: John Doyle, Rob Hicklin of Hicklin Galleries, the *Post and Courier*, and the City of Charleston. I especially want to thank Yvonne Fortenberry, the Director for the City of Charleston Planning Department for her assistance.

In an effort to present a balanced view of recent history, I sent letters out to various community leaders, historians and political and civic leaders. I want to thank Mayor Riley, David Rawle, Franklin Ashley, Jack Bass, Molly Fair, N. Steven Steinert, Mayor John Bourne, Ernie Passailaigue, Marvin Delaney, and others who were kind enough to have given me their perspective. I also want to thank my wife, Susan, for her continued editorial assistance.

Robert N. Rosen

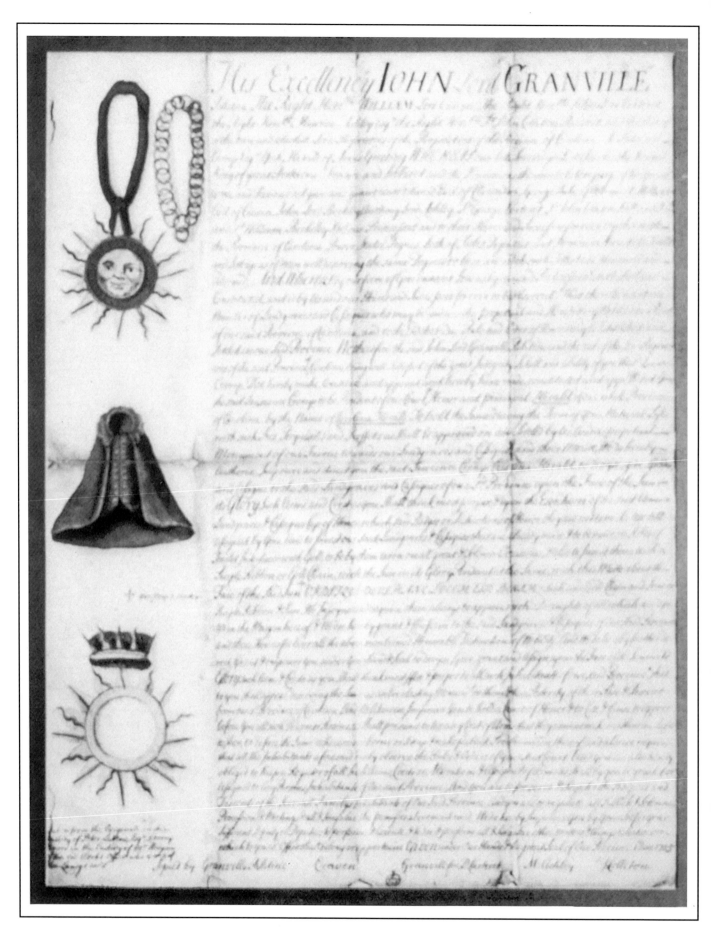

Lords Proprietors' appointment of Laurence Cromp as Carolina Herald gives instructions to devise and engrave on the "Sun in its Glory" arms and crests for the proposed Carolina nobility of Landgraves and Cassiques. This was to be worn on a purple ribbon or gold chain, and would bear the motto "Videtque Deus Hanc Lucem Esse Bonum (Gen. 1:4). It also provided for a Cap of Honor and "Robes of Scarlet Interfaced with Gold" for great and solemn occasions, as shown in the margin.

"Hiddy Doddy Comorado"

1521—1670
Indians, Spanish and French

In Jacques Le Moyne's Brevis Narratio describing the French expeditions, he explains that the river was so "large and magnificent" that Ribault named it Portus Regalis, or Port Royal. Frightened by the ship, the Indians ran away leaving behind a lynx's whelp they'd been roasting, and the French named the spot Lynx Point (Prom. Lupi). Courtesy of Carolina Art Association

John Locke's connection with Carolina was not only as author of the Fundamental Constitutions, he also took a deep interest in the settling of the colony. Many of the letters in the letter book of the Shaftesbury collection are in his handwriting. Courtesy of South Carolina Historical Society

All odds were against her survival when the little settlement that was to become Charleston was planted, as they called it in 1670, on the Ashley River in the colony of Carolina.

Founded as a business venture by absentee landlords, her site selected by an Indian chief, for over sixty years Charles Town remained a lonely outpost between hostile nations: Spain at St. Augustine and France on the Mississippi; open to year round attack from pirates and Indians, her economy requiring a large African work force that outnumbered her white population and presented a constant threat.

More than three hundred miles south of the James River, with only Indian trails through the wilderness, and Hatteras projecting into the ocean between, communication between Carolina and her sister English colonies was frequently more dangerous and took longer than with England. For many years her settlers were restricted to distances within reach of the fortifications of Charles Town, and in case of alarm withdrew from outlying plantations and parishes to the safety of her town wall. When this no longer was necessary, the unhealthiness of the plantations forced planters to continue to move to town from May through October, so population of the surrounding coastal plain, known as the Low Country, and Charles Town were for the most part the same. Her culture, economy and political leadership were based on her wealthy merchants and planters. Development was from Charles Town outward, but always with the port town at the center. There was one government for province, town and church encouraging the Carolina concept of the entity of the State and its absolute sovereignty; an idea which evolved into States Rights, then Nullification and ultimately Secession. City-

state of the province, seaport, trade town, capital and social center, Charles Town *was* Carolina until long after the Revolution. Forced to rely on their own resources for protection, Charlestonians became self-reliant and aggressive, producing national leaders far out of proportion to their population. It was their tenacious hold on the strategic position at Charles Town that secured England's frontier against France and Spain.

Spain and France both failed in their attempts to establish a foothold in this part of North America. Early in the sixteenth century, Lucas Vasquez de Ayllon landed with some 500 Spanish settlers to found San Miguel on Winyaw Bay near present day Georgetown. Within two months he was dead of fever and the survivors of his expedition abandoned the settlement without a trace. Twenty years later, Hernando de Soto explored western Carolina, enslaving Indians along his way. In Aiken County he forced the elegant little Queen of Cofitachiqui to act as his guide as he moved towards Georgia.

The French attempts later in the century fared no better. Jean Ribault's refuge for Huguenots near Port Royal lasted only briefly, and the French Protestants would only survive as settlers a hundred years later under English rule.

Spain's efforts in the Fort Royal area to establish Fort San Felipe, Fort San Marcos and the neighboring small town of Santa Elena were all unsuccessful. She withdrew from Carolina as a result of Sir Francis Drake's burning St. Augustine, and was not disposed to see the British succeeding where she had failed. Philip II warned the English that if they settled in Carolina, Spain would cut off their heads as she had done to Ribault and the French.

Ignoring this threat, Charles I of England, basing his claim on John Cabot's explorations in 1497, granted his Attorney General Sir Robert Heath a tremendous area in the New World, including most of present day North Carolina, South Carolina, Georgia, and part of Florida, and extending from the Atlantic to the Pacific.

Jean Ribault left two stone columns bearing the arms of France near Port Royal, and when Rene de Laudonniere returned with a group of French in 1564, he found the Indians were worshiping the one remaining column as an idol with offerings of food and weapons. Jacques Le Moyne de Morgues, a French artist accompanying Laudonniere, made forty-two paintings of New World scenes, from which engravings were published after his death by Theodore de Bry. Courtesy of South Carolina Historical Society

In 1630 another group of Huguenots set out for Carolina under Heath's charter in a ship named the *Mayflower*. Like her namesake ten years before that was chartered for Virginia, but carried the Pilgrims to Massachusetts, this *Mayflower* was blown off course also, and the Huguenots destined for Carolina landed in Virginia instead. This left Carolina still unsettled, and paved the way for revocation of Heath's grant.

When Charles II was restored to the throne, eight of his supporters persuaded him to name them Lords Proprietors of an even larger tract of land that extended from Virginia to below St. Augustine. The names of these Lords Proprietors are commemorated as place names in both Carolinas: Edward Hyde, the Earl of Clarendon; George Monck, Duke of Albemarle; the Earl of Craven; Sir George Carteret; Sir John Colleton; Lord John Berkeley and his brother Sir William Berkeley; Anthony Ashley Cooper, later to become the Earl of Shaftesbury. Five were members of the Council for Trade, six on the Council for Foreign Plantations, and six were involved both in the Royal African and Hudson's Bay Companies.

They hoped by offering generous land grants, a religious freedom second only to Rhode Island, and a share in the government, to attract experienced colonists from older settlements, and to line their own pockets from the resulting trade and land rents.

Lord Anthony Ashley Cooper and his secretary John Locke, drew up a set of Fundamental Constitutions for the colony which provided for an elaborate feudal society, including titles of Cassique and Landgrave, and a lower echelon of leetmen tied to the land like serfs. Never accepted by the colonists, the Constitutions were envisioned by the Proprietors as a future goal, and they set up a temporary government under a Governor and Grand Council, who, with a certain number of deputies elected by the freeholders, would act as a Parliament. Twenty years later the elected members of Council would sit as a separate Commons House of Assembly in a bicameral legislature.

West Indian planters in overcrowded Barbados immediately saw Carolina as an opportunity to put their experience to work on undeveloped mainland acres and at the same time avoid their destructive island hurricanes. The offer of religious tolerance not only attracted disgruntled Barbadians, but continued for fifty years to draw religious dissenters from all over Europe.

Two hundred wealthy Barbadians sent Captain William Hilton on an exploratory voyage from Cape Fear to Port Royal. His reports were distributed at the Carolina Coffee House in London in much the same way that Welcome Centers in modern South Carolina hand out promotional literature. With raves about the fertility of the soil, flora, and fauna, Hilton declared "The Ayr is clear and sweet, the Countrey very pleasant and delightful: And we could wish, that all they that want a happy settlement, of our English Nation, were well transported hither."

From a short-lived Barbadian colony at Cape Fear, another exploratory voyage made in 1666 proved significant for the future Charles Town. Twenty-one-year old Dr. Henry Woodward, young ship's surgeon, interested in learning Indian culture and language, accompanied Captain Robert Sandford. Woodward agreed to participate in one of the country's earliest exchange student programs, remaining at Port Royal while the nephew of the Cassique (chief) returned with Sandford. Woodward was received with "high Testimonyes of Joy and thankfullness," given a corn field, and the young Indian's sister to "tend him & dresse his victualls and be careful of him that soe her Brother might be the better used." Sandford met an old friend, the Cassique of Kiawah, who had traded at the Cape Fear settlement, and the Cassique immediately started a sales campaign that was to continue until he had sold the English on his site at Kiawah, describing it as having "a broad deepe entrance, and promising a large and plentiful entertainment: and trade"—a true red carpet reception.

Back in England Sandford predicted Carolina's potential commerce would make King Charles the "universall Monarch of the Traffique and Commodity of the Whole World." Settlers were attracted by enthusiastic broadsides and pamphlets, and the following August, 1669 three ships, the *Carolina, Albemarle,* and *Port Royal*, commanded by Captain John West, sailed from Gravesend, carrying eighteen months provisions, twelve cannon apiece and Indian trade goods including glass beads, hatchets, hoes, knives, sizzard (scissors) and ten striped suits (gifts for Indian chiefs). Their destination was Port Royal; their first landfall the island of Barbados, but they were to encounter storms, death, thirst and shipwreck, and only the *Carolina* would survive the voyage. The wrecked *Albemarle* and *Port Royal* would be replaced by *The Three Brothers* and a sloop. The only encouraging feature of their stormy island sailing came when they put into the island of Nevis to fill their water casks. Here, by a strange coincidence, they picked up Dr. Woodward, whose addition to the expedition may well have been the thread on which the colony's future survival hung. When the English failed to return to Port Royal, Woodward had written a Spanish missionary, and was serving as post surgeon at St. Augustine in 1668 when pirate Robert Searle rescued him, and was working his way back to England as ship's surgeon, when shipwrecked on Nevis, oddly enough, the same day the *Carolina* left England.

The Three Brothers vanished in a storm, not to reappear for two months, and it was some two weeks after leaving the islands, and miles off course, that the *Carolina* and the sloop sighted the mainland at Sewee (Bull) Bay near today's McClellanville. Friendly Seewee Indians carried them ashore through the shallow water, and exchanged deer skins for their beads and knives.

Women in "roabs of new mosse which they are never beholding to ye Taylor to trim up" brought them water, nuts and unfamiliar root cakes, and they got the bad news that a fierce tribe of Westoes, with the reputation of maneaters, had burned and destroyed settlements along the coast from Port Royal to Kiawah. The ubiquitous Cassique of Kiawah arrived and this "very Ingenious Indian & a great Linguist" sailed with them to Port Royal, where the Indians joyfully shouted "Hiddy doddy Comorado Angles Westoe Skorrye," which they loosely translated as "English very good friends, Westoes are naught."

The Cassique of Kiawah convinced them to take a look at his real estate before committing themselves. The sloop was sent to "View that Land soe much Comended by the Casseka." When it returned bringing a favorable report, a vote was taken, "The Governor adhearing for Kayawah & most of us being of a temper to follow though wee knew noe reason for it." Those holding out for Port Royal were "looked upon straingely." Already they had become true Charlestonians, looking down their noses at anyone who might even consider living elsewhere!

Shortly thereafter they hauled anchor and sailed up the coast to Kiawah.

At Kiawah village site this smooth water jar was found inside a complicated stamped bowl. The bowl may have held leaves of the yaupon plant from which Black Drink, used in ceremonies of many Southeastern Indians, was derived. Courtesy of Institute of Archeology & Anthropology, University of South Carolina

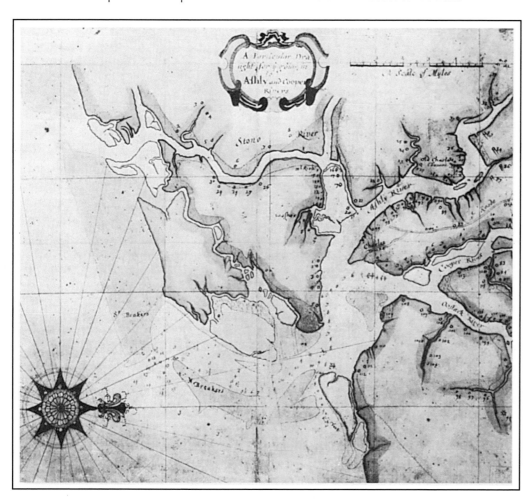

This map inset by Maurice Mathews c. 1685 shows "Ye Roade," the Indian Broad Path winding through the peninsula Charles Towne and branching approximately where present-day Broad and King Streets intersect. One branch went to Landgrave Joseph West's property on the Ashley River between today's King and Legare Street, the other towards Mathew's lot, about where Granville Bastion later stood. Courtesy of Library of Congress

Aerial view of posthole outline of Kiawah ceremonial area is revealed by excavation. In center are postholes of rectangular, square and round sheds, and open burial pits. An excavated posthole pattern shows a smaller compound area to the north, an outer palisade ditch outline that is not excavated, and a circular posthole pattern of a corner bastion at the west corner. The square grid is a pile of construction materials for the Tri-Centennial Commission's Pavilion constructed on top of the ceremonial center. Courtesy of Institute of Archeology & Anthropology, University of South Carolina

The one-room-to-a-floor Pink House at 17 Chalmers Street, built about 1717, was one of the "groggeries" which, together with sailor's boarding houses and dance houses, gradually occupied Chalmers Alley and Union Street. By 1810 they were "inhabited by courtesans, thieves and cutthroats of the vilest character, which rendered it a dangerous undertaking to traverse them after nightfall." Courtesy of Historic Charleston Foundation

Chapter One

"The Ayr Is Clear and Sweet, The Countrey Very Pleasant"

1670—1719
Proprietary Colony

In April of 1670 the *Carolina* and an accompanying unnamed sloop sailed up the Kiawah River and turned into a creek running through the marsh on its west bank, sufficiently upriver to be out of sight from the harbor, and not far from the Kiawah village. About 150 cramped, weary men, women and children disembarked, and stumbled up the low bluff. They named the site Albemarle Point, after the eldest of the Proprietors.

The *Carolina* passenger list shows that most of these first arrivals were English, with a few Scots and Irish, and possibly one or two Huguenots. Some were well educated and from well-to-do families, but not many of them were themselves wealthy, and the list included sixty-two indentured servants. In August at least one Black man was brought from Virginia, and Nathaniel Sayle returned from Bermuda the next month with three slaves belonging to his father, Gov. William Sayle. They were John Sr., Elizabeth and John Jr. Within a year blacks numbered approximately twenty.

Constructing shelters, enclosing ten acres and building palisades and moats for defense exhausted the settlers, leaving little energy for putting in crops. Many of these early settlers were tradesmen and knew almost nothing of farming. Food was scarce, and although the situation was not as bad as the "starving time" in the Jamestown colony of Virginia, by the end of June daily rations were down to a pint of dried peas per man, with enough left for only a few weeks. Their friendly Indian neighbors welcomed the protection of the English against the fierce Westoes, and provided the new colonists with much needed food. The Council wrote the Proprietors that Henry Woodward, thanks to his stay with the Port Royal Indians, had "been exceeding useful to us in the time of the scarcity of provision, in dealeing with the Indian for our supplyes who by his meanes have furnished us beyond our expectations." Without the corn, peas, fruit, and venison bought from the Indians, the colony might not have survived until the *Carolina* returned from Virginia with cows, hogs and eight months' supply of food.

Joseph West asked Lord Ashley to send indentured servants from England. He complained that those from Barbados needed a carrot before their noses to induce them to work—only in their case they "are so much addicted to Rum" the carrot had to be a bottle. Charges were made that Surveyor General Florence O'Sullivan professed much but performed nothing, and "all lands that he hath pretended to lay and run out is verie irregular." Irish soldier of fortune O'Sullivan, described as an "ill-natured buggerer of children," occasioned more controversy by his bad disposition than his moral character, and finally (could it have been to get rid of him?) was put in charge of a signal gun near the river mouth on the island that ironically bears his name today— he being one of the few of the first settlers so commemorated.

Before the year was out twelve cedar plants—"the first fruits of that glorious province"—were on the way to Lord Ashley. After planting peas, Indian corn, beans, turnips, and potatoes "to provide for the belly," they then experimented with cotton, indigo and tobacco, but soon found cattle, naval stores and deerskins most profitable. Skins and some furs were first procured from the small coastal groups making up the Cusabo confederation, but in 1674 Woodward made a daring expedition to the Westo village on the Savannah River, where the chief's house couldn't hold all the curious who came to see this strange white visitor, and "the smaller fry got up and uncovered the top of the house to satisfy their curiosity." Woodward's expedition resulted in trade with the Westo, who were supplied with arms and served as a buffer for the colony until 1680.

By mid February of the first year two shiploads of over a hundred Barbadians "were (weary) of the Herycane" arrived, and rich New Yorkers came to escape "their taxes and hard winters," beginning a trend that would accelerate in the twentieth century!

Lord Ashley wrote confidentially that he didn't want more settlers unless they were well-to-do and would give the Proprietors a return on their investment. He told them to call the settlement Charles Towne, reminding them that the river had some time ago been named the Ashley by Captain Sandford and that he wished them to use that name instead of the Indian name Kiawah. He ordered that a permanent town site be selected on high ground and sent over a plan known as the *Grand Modell* giving lot sizes and street widths, intending to "avoid the undecent and incommodius irregularities which other English colonies are fallen into for want of an early care in laying out the Townes."

In 1672 it was ordered that lots be surveyed and streets marked out across the river on a peninsula known as Oyster, or White Point, and within ten years of their arrival the move across the river had been made. Secretary John Dalton considered the new site "as it were a Key to open and shutt this settlement into safety or danger; Charles Towne (i.e. Albemarle Point) indeed can very well defend itselfe and thats all, but that (*new* Charles Town) like an Iron gate shutts up all the Townes that are or may be in those Rivers; besides it has a full view of the Sea being but a league or a few Miles from the mouth of the river and noe Ships can come upon the coast but may be seen from thence and may receive the benefitt of a Pilott from that Towne…It must of necessity be very healthy being free from any noisome vapors and all Summer long refreshed with a continued coole breathings from the sea."

Dalton prophetically foresaw a fishing industry, merchants' warehouses, and a profitable trade, and in 1860 Charleston was, indeed, an iron gate, and "coole breathings" from the sea still make her summer heat bearable. In 1682 the province was divided into three countries—Berkeley (including

Charles Town) extending from Seewee River on the north to Stono River on the south, Craven to its north, and Colleton from the south to the Combahee River. A fourth county, Granville, was established a little later from the Combahee to the Savannah River.

Thomas Ashe arriving on the *Richmond*, found Charles Town "very commodiously situated from many other Navigable Rivers that lie near it on which the Planters are seated. The Town is regularly laid out into large and capacious Streets, which to Buildings is a great Ornament and Beauty. In it they have reserved convenient places for Building of a Church, Town-House and other Publick Structures, and Wharfs for the Convenience of their Trade and Shipping."

The intersection of the modern Broad and Meeting Streets was set aside for public buildings and the Anglican church of St. Philip's was soon standing on the southeast corner—a "large and stately" black cypress building on a brick foundation, enclosed by a white palisade is the only description that has come down through the years. Today this intersection is called the Four Corners of the Law, God's law represented by St. Michael's Church, and man's by County Court House, City Hall and Federal Post Office. The old streets of Church, Tradd and Elliott present no problems for Charlestonians accustomed for generations to thoroughfares designed for drays or carriages, but could in no way be called "large and capacious" by today's standards.

Samuel Wilson advised prospective settlers he would be at the Carolina Coffee House in London at eleven of the clock every Tuesday with information on sailings and the latest progress report on Charles Town: "About a hundred Houses are there Built and more are Building daily by the Persons of all sorts that come there to Inhabit, from the more Northern English Collonys, and the Sugar Islands, England and Ireland; and many persons who went to Carolina Servants, being Industrious since they came out of their times with their Masters, at whose charge they were Transported, have gotten good Stocks of Cattle, and Servants of their own; have also Built Houses, and exercise their Trades; and many that went thither in that condition, are worth several Hundreds of Pounds, and live in a very plentiful condition, and their Estates still encreasing."

Promotional literature described Carolina as an earthly Eden, and to people knowing nothing of the country, it seemed credible. John Hash, one of a number of disgruntled settlers who ran off from Albemarle Point told authorities at St. Augustine that having heard "glowing tales" about Carolina, he had emigrated "to improve his fortune," but had decided to return to England "in view of the suffering he had to endure." To the forty-five French Huguenots who arrived in 1680 aboard the *Richmond* suffering in a New World was far preferable to the "hot persecuting time" at home. Charles II backed their voyage, hoping they would provide the wine, olive oil and silk England had to import from other countries. They brought cocoons with them, but the silkworms hatched out on the voyage, and with no mulberry leaves to feed on, all died. Silk was actually produced for many years, but other more profitable and easier industries took the place of these three.

The hardworking Huguenots were nonetheless a valuable addition to the young colony, and became prominent in business, politics and cultural life. By the eighteenth century a number who had arrived practically penniless were able to lend large sums of money to less substantial citizens.

Early in the 1680s five hundred English dissenters arrived, many settling south of Charles Town in Colleton County. They

were brought by some of England's richest and most prominent dissenters: Benjamin Blake, Daniel Axtel and Joseph Morton. Lord Cardross and a company of Scots settled Stuart's Town at Port Royal, to be destroyed by Spanish three years later.

Congregationalists from New England founded the town of Dorchester near the head of the Ashley River and remained there for about sixty years, then moved in 1752 to Medway, Georgia. The Rev. William Screven left the Puritan colony of

A view of the rebuilt and stabilized fortification ditch and parapet of 1670 is on the right, and the 1780 redoubt is on the left at Albemarle Point. In the background to the left is Old Town Creek, and beyond that is the point of land on which Governor West built a plantation for the Lords Proprietors in 1671. Courtesy of Institute of Archeology & Anthropology, University of South Carolina

Sir Nathaniel Johnson, shown in his armor, was governor from 1702-1708 under the Lords Proprietors. This painting is by an unknown artist. Courtesy of Carolina Art Association

Henrietta Johnston's portrait of Col. William Rhett gives no indication of Rhett's militant character. Receiver General for the Lords Proprietors, Vice-Admiral of the colonial navy, Surveyor and Comptroller of His Majesty's Customs, and Lt. General and Commissioner of fortifications, Rhett is remembered best for his capture of pirate Stede Bonnet in 1718. Courtesy of Carolina Art Association

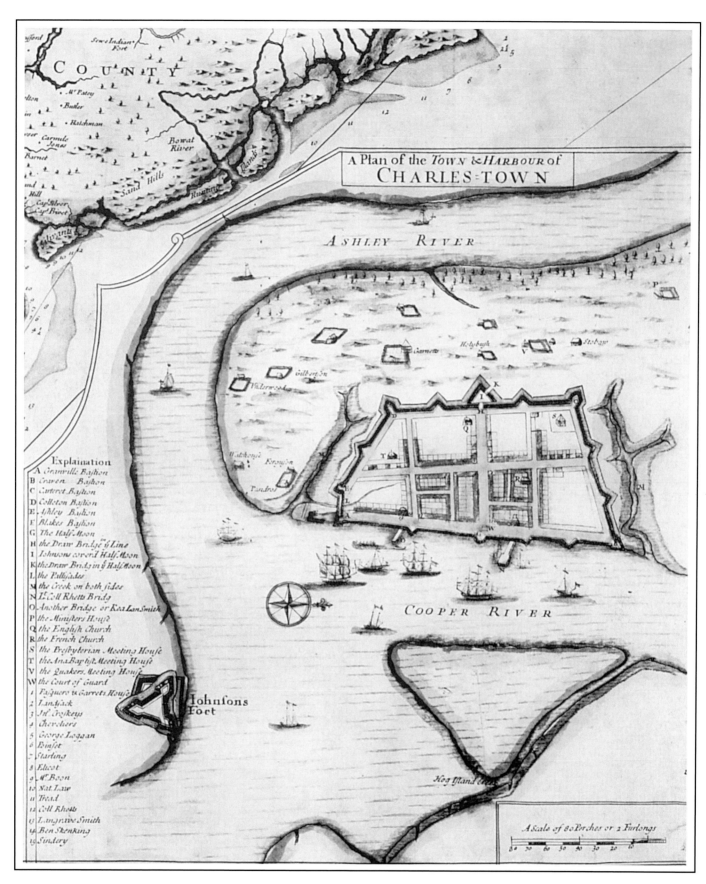

A Plan of the *Town* & *Harbour* of
CHARLES-TOWN

COUNTY

ASHLEY RIVER

COOPER RIVER

Johnsons
Fort

Hog Island Creek

A Scale of 80 Perches or 2 Furlongs

Explaination
A Granville Bastion
B Craven Bastion
C Carteret Bastion
D Colleton Bastion
E Ashley Bastion
F Blakes Bastion
G The Half Moon
H the Draw Bridge & Line
I Johnson covered Half Moon
K the Draw Bridge in ye Half Moon
L the Pallisades
M the Creek on both sides
N Lt. Coll Rhetts Bridg
O Another Bridge or Rea Lan Smith
P the Ministers House
Q the English Church
R the French Church
S the Presbyterian Meeting House
T the Ana Baptist Meeting House
V the Quakers Meeting House
W the Court of Guard
1 Fulquers & Garrets House
2 Landyack
3 Jno Croskeys
4 Cheveliers
5 George Loggan
6 Bonsot
7 Starling
8 Elicot
9 Mr Boon
10 Nat Law
11 Trad
12 Coll Rhetts
13 Langrave Smith
14 Ben Skenking
15 Sindery

This first real map of Charles Town was drawn by Edward Crisp about 1704 and probably published c. 1711 when the town fortifications and Fort Johnson were completed. It shows a walled city, with creeks to the north and south, a few houses outside the walls, including a Quaker Meeting House, four houses of worship and residences within the fortifications, and a lively trade represented by shipping in the harbor. Courtesy of Library of Congress

Mulberry still stands on a high bluff overlooking the west branch of the Cooper River, and is an unusual Jacobean style house with four small square towers at the corners. It was built by second Royal Governor Thomas Broughton, son-in-law of Sir Nathaniel Johnson, about 1714. The slave street pictured here has disappeared. Courtesy of Carolina Art Association Thomas Coram

Right:
Drawn by James Moxon in 1671 by order of the Lords Proprietors, this is one of the earliest maps using the name Carolina in its title. It includes an inset on the left showing Oyster Point and the first settlement of Charles Towne. Courtesy of Library of Congress

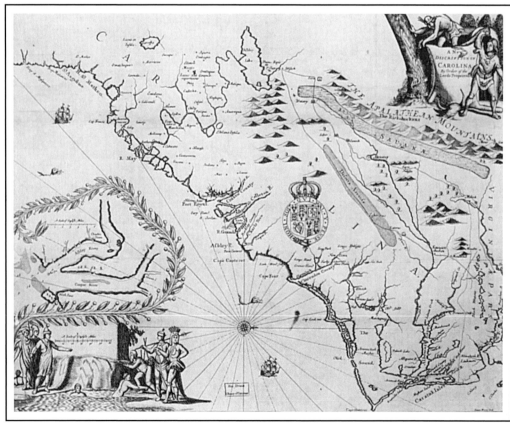

Kittery, Maine, with his AnaBaptist congregation, eventually becoming the nucleus of the First Baptist Church in Charles Town.

By 1700 some two thousand dissenters of a variety of beliefs had been attracted by the Proprietors' publicity campaign. By far the most influential group, however, and outnumbering all other immigrants in the first ten years, was the Church of England Barbadians. Col. James Moore, Arthur and Edward Middleton, Benjamin Scheckingh, Robert Gibbes, Ralph Izard, Captain George Chicken, and Thomas Smith (son of the Landgrave), were among those who settled in the neighborhood of Goose Creek, a tributary of the Cooper River. They played a strong role in determining policy for almost fifty years, and were bugbears not only of the dissenters, but of the Proprietors as well, who wrote new Governor Ludwell in 1693: "Beware of the Goose Creek men."

In 1692 about twenty new arrivals sailed into the harbor on the privateer *Loyal Jamaica* and gave surety for their good behavior, apparently until the validity of their Royal commission could be determined. These included Thomas Pinckney, Robert Fenwick and Daniel Horry, names to become well-known in the colony—but they went down in literature as the Red Sea Men, for legend associated them with tales of gold seized there in pirate raids.

By 1703 Governor Sir Nathaniel Johnson reported the total population was approximately 3800 whites, 3000 black slaves and 350 Indian slaves. Five years later these figures were 4080 whites, 4100 black slaves and 1400 Indian slaves, the sharp increase in the last figure due to the recent successful Indian wars.

There are many stories as to how rice was introduced into the colony, including one that attributes it to a woman. Another theory is that a sea Captain Thurber from Madagascar brought Dr. Woodward a packet of seed rice in 1685. However it arrived, by 1691 the Assembly had granted patent rights to Huguenot Peter Jacob Guerard for a pendulum husking engine, and five years later rice was so valuable that it was one of the commodities used to pay quit rents, and merchants were having difficulty finding enough ships to export their bumper crop.

With rice production a serious problem arose. In the early years indentured servants, and Indian and black slaves worked together, but indentured servants could be depended on only until their time was up, and Indians frequently escaped into the forest. Both succumbed to debilitating and often fatal fevers to which Africans had more resistance. Today we know this was because of the sickle cell trait many Africans carried, as well as an acquired immunity to malaria and yellow fever, both of which had been endemic in West Africa for generations. Because rice cultivation required a large force, by 1698 the Assembly became concerned that "the great number of negroes which of late have been imported into this Collony may endanger the safety thereof."

Soon blacks outnumbered whites, a trend that was to continue. The colonists continued the insidious practice of Indian slavery also, which at first had involved purchase of captured enemy Indians, excusing the practice on the dubious humanitarian reasoning that a gentle death in the cane fields was preferable to the torture they would otherwise suffer. Before long unscrupulous traders sold off their Indian allies to the sugar islands as well. Naturally, this practice resulted in frequent minor wars and skirmishes, aggravated by thefts of Indians' corn and livestock, and the murder and rape of their wives and daughters. Ten years after the first landing, a war broke out with the Westoes and in three years they were nearly exterminated, and Governor Archdale piously attributed the hand of God to "thinning the Indians to make room for the English."

As far as war was concerned the closing years of the seventeenth century were comparatively peaceful, but now a series of natural disasters occurred. "The whole country is full of trouble and sickness, " Affra Coming wrote her sister in England, and if God had thinned out the Indians, it now seemed he was also rapidly decimating the settlers. Smallpox raged from 1697-99; in 1698 a fire left most of the original town in ashes; plague broke out among the cattle; an earthquake shook the area, and the next year the first siege of yellow fever occurred, leaving at least 160 dead in Charles Town, new arrivals who had not undergone the "seasoning, " as well as "seasoned" settlers, including half the members of the Assembly.

"The dead were carried in carts, being heaped up one upon another Worse by far than the great Plague of London, considering the smallness of the Town." Among the deaths was that of Jonathan Amory, Receiver for the Public Treasury, extensive landowner and merchant, who had immigrated from Jamaica. Amory's daughter Sarah married Arthur Middleton, and they were progenitors of generations of that family who became leaders not only of their state, but the nation as well. His son Thomas went to Boston, declaring he found the climate of Carolina unhealthy, and disliked having to be constantly in arms for fear of Indian, Black, French, or Spanish attack. Here he married the daughter of the proprietor of the Bunch of Grapes tavern, and in turn they were the ancestors of the "Episcocrat" Amorys of New England.

A few months later "The swelling sea rushed in with amazing impetuosity, and obliged the inhabitants to fly for shelter to the second stories of their houses," sinking all aboard a ship of refugees just arrived from the colony of Darien in Georgia. Among the few survivors were the Reverend Archibald Stobo and his wife who happened to be ashore where he was preaching a sermon at the Congregational Church. Seeing the hand of God in his providential rescue, Rev. Stobo was called by the church and became significant in the establishment of the Presbyterian church locally.

John Lawson arrived in 1700 to gather material for his *New Voyage to Carolina*, in which he wrote: "The Town has very regular and fair Streets, in which are good Buildings of Brick and Wood, and since my coming thence, has had great Additions of beautiful, large Brick-Buildings, besides a strong Fort, and regular Fortifications made to defend the Town." He described Charlestonians as being rich by trade to Europe and the West Indies so that they could afford to "have Tutors amongst them that educate their Youth a-la-mode." He found a French church, and several dissenters' meeting houses "who all enjoyed at this Day an entire Liberty of their Worship."

Charles Town was market town for the colony and the skins in her waterfront warehouses came from as far away as the Mississippi. The production of rice increased from 330 tons shipped in 1700 to five or six times as much by 1713, and the plantation system rapidly spread up the rivers as planters moved to fertile lands along the waterways and banked and ditched the inland swamps. Parliament provided bounties on naval stores and trade with the West Indies expanded, including Indian slaves, staves, hoops, shingles, beef, rice, pitch, tar, and even myrtle berry candles, in exchange for rum, sugar, molasses, and blacks. Indian slaves, skins, pitch, tar, and a little rice went to Boston, Rhode Island, Pennsylvania, New York, and Virginia.

Trains of Indian carriers wound through Charles Town's streets on their way to wholesale merchants on the Bay, roistering sailors engaged in their favorite sport of beating up the watch, and pirates flashed gold doubloons in waterfront taverns. In 1699 for the first time Charles Town's exports exceeded imports in a favorable balance of trade that was to continue for the next twenty years.

Governor Sir Nathaniel Johnson ordered Col. William Rhett to strengthen the fortifications "with bastions flankers and half moons ditched and pallasadoes and mounted with eighty three guns," and city gates with moat and drawbridge were erected at the present Four Corners of the Law. A strong triangular fort of twenty-two guns was built at Windmill Point (later named Fort Johnson) on James Island "within carabine shott of which all must pass by." Sir Nathaniel also authorized a little eight-gabled powder magazine just within the northern wall. Gunpowder, including that paid as tax by ships entering the harbor, was stored here, with several feet of sand as safeguard between the vaulted ceiling and red tile roof.

These precautions were taken not a bit too soon, for in 1706 five French privateers loaded with Spanish troops appeared off the port demanding surrender of the town within an hour. Sir Nathaniel, as legend has it, had the French messenger blindfolded and led round his wall. The blindfold was removed at each bastion where the officer saw "a splendid body of soldiery." What he didn't realize was that the same soldiers were rushed ahead in time to meet him at each stop. The militia rallied to Charles Town's defense despite a raging smallpox epidemic, and they and a makeshift fleet under Col. Rhett routed the enemy forces.

On the domestic front Sir Nathaniel was less successful— he tended to equate dissenters with Spanish heretics and passed an act barring them from the Assembly. He established the Church of England as the state church, refusing to recognize marriages as legal unless performed by Anglican ministers. Chief Justice Nicholas Trott further enraged the dissenters by saying they never did any good in the Assembly and never would.

Joseph Boone sailed to England to protest this discrimination and hired a number of pamphleteers, including Daniel Defoe, author of *Robinson Crusoe*, who penned a diatribe on "high church tyranny" practiced in Carolina. Queen Anne declared Sir Nathaniel's act void, and a new act was passed in 1706 resulting in the formation of ten parishes, their names taken almost directly from those in Barbados. In Charles Town was St. Philip's, and six others were in Berkeley County: St. Andrew's, St. Thomas's, St. John's, St. James' Goose Creek, St. Denis' and Christ Church; two in Colleton: St. Paul's and St. Bartholomew's; one in Craven: St. James' Santee.

Although Landgrave Smith's brother was quoted as saying the new church act of 1708 "was only fit to wipe his Arse with-all," and Mrs. Boone stated it was a great pity that Mr. Trott had not been hanged seven years past, religious disputes lessened. The bitterness generated by the church controversy shifted to other issues.

One question that continued to break the colony into factions was the Indian trade. Settlers continually encroached on Indian lands, forcing them to buy goods they could only pay for with slaves or skins. Traders illegally sold rum to Indians, and then seized their families and sold them while

A portion of the old town wall was uncovered in 1965, when excavations were being made under the old Exchange building at Broad and East Bay. Just inside this spot stood the Watch House where Stede Bonnet's pirate crew was imprisoned in 1718. Courtesy of Author's collection

the men were away hunting. From September 1710 to April 1715 there were complaints ranging from theft to murder against 23 traders, and on Good Friday, April 15, Yemassees attacked St. Helena's and St. Bartholomew's parishes and terrified the province. The light of burning plantations could be seen from Charles Town's walls. Women and children fled from St. Paul's parish and St. James' Goose Creek to the safety of Charles Town, and even the French of St. James' Santee to the north panicked.

Benjamin de la Conseilliere was sent to Boston to trade deerskins for muskets, powder and shot; Arthur Middleton returned from Virginia with 118 volunteers, while a hundred white men and a company of Tuscarora came from North Carolina. Colonel Maurice Moore marched into the heart of Cherokee country with three hundred men, including a company of Black slaves and some of Charles Town's most experienced Indian fighters, to negotiate with the Cherokees. For a time it was touch and go as to which side this proud tribe would take, and emissaries of the Creeks and Yemassees had all but persuaded them to massacre the English, when unaccountably the Cherokees fell on the Creeks and Yemassees instead. Subsequently, they formed an alliance with the English. Once again it was the Indians who played a major role in Charles Town's future.

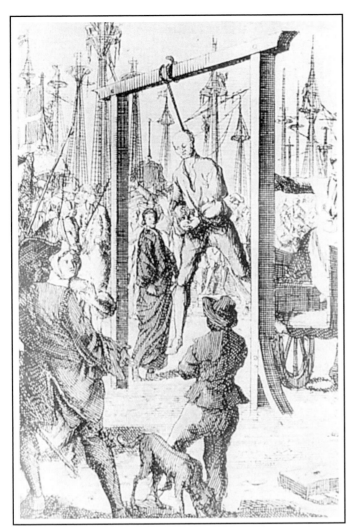

"Gentleman pirate" Stede Bonnet, wigless, and clutching a small bouquet, swings as the tumbrel moves away in this old illustration of his hanging at White Point in Charles Town. Courtesy of Charleston Post-Courier

Charles Town had hardly recovered from the Yemassee campaign when a new danger appeared from another direction. Pirates had been welcome customers in early days when gold and silver were scarce. Many came from a background of privateering against the Spanish, and Charles Town merchants winked at their freebooting and cheerfully accepted their free spending. Besides, they had a Royal precedent; not only had Charles II knighted buccaneer Henry Morgan, but he had also made him Deputy Governor of Jamaica.

Their welcome cooled, however, when the pirates began to show less discrimination and attacked the slow merchantmen laden with cargoes of rice, skins and naval stores. Often the inbound rum, slaves and sugar never arrived at the Cooper River wharves that were their destination. Charles Town was conveniently located between two favorite pirate haunts—the West Indies and their North Carolina hideouts, and Governor Robert Johnson, son of old Sir Nathaniel, wrote London that "Hardly a Ship goes to Sea, but falls into their hands."

In 1718 the notorious Blackbeard captured nine ships with a number of colonial leaders aboard, including Samuel Wragg, member of the council, and Wragg's four-year-old son William. Blackbeard promised to send their heads to Governor Johnson unless he received a chest of medicines. After ransoming Wragg and his companions, Governor Johnson

sent a letter to the Board of Trade requesting that a man-of-war be sent to protect Charles Town, but this was ignored. As ships were preparing to clear the port with their cargoes, Charles Town heard that a pirate ship was rendezvousing at Cape Fear, and the Governor and Council took matters into their own hands.

Col. Rhett was hastily commissioned to fit out two sloops with guns and men and sent to Cape Fear. After a five-hour gun battle, Rhett returned triumphantly, having captured pirate Stede Bonnet, whose name was known from Jamaica to Newfoundland. Bonnet, the "gentleman pirate" was a native of Christ Church Parish, Barbados, and had been a major in the militia there. He plundered cargoes he could have produced on his own estate in Barbados.

One historian explains: "This humor of going a-pyrating proceeded from a disorder in his mind, which had been but too visible in him some time before this wicked undertaking; and which is said to have been occasioned by some discomforts he found in a married state." Bonnet had been in on the Wragg episode with Blackbeard, and Rhett and his prizes arrived in Charles Town "to the great joy of the whole Province."

Bonnet and his crew were hanged at White Point and buried below low water mark in the marsh. Their bones may rest today beneath some downtown mansion, as the city long since grew beyond the old low water marks, and tradition gives the location as near modern Meeting and Water Streets.

Again Johnson begged the Lords of Trade for a man-of-war, but before his letter was well on the way, he received word that the notorious pirate Moody was offshore with two hundred men and a vessel of fifty guns. This time Johnson himself led the attack, and a desperate four hour gun battle followed. The sound of cannon reverberated across the water to anxious Charles Town, and her wharves and waterfront were crowded with citizens straining to see what was going on just out of eyeshot. The vessels were captured and the pirate turned out to be dangerous Richard Worley instead of Moody. A few days later word came that Moody had taken the King's pardon at New Providence, and when a force dispatched by Governor Spotswood returned to Virginia from doing battle at Ocracoke with Blackbeard's head hanging from a bowsprit, Charles Town knew that the last major pirate threat to her shipping was gone.

Once again Charles Town had stood off an enemy through her own resources and initiative, and once again not a barrel of powder or pound of lead had come from the Proprietors, who continually alienated Carolinians by vetoing laws essential to their economy and development. At length, exasperated by these absentee lords who were obviously mainly interested in their own profits, the Commons House in 1719, declared itself "a Convention, delegated by the People, to prevent the utter Ruin of this Government, if not the Loss of the Province, until his Majesty's Pleasure be known," and petitioned King George to assume control. Since Carolina's strategic position made it imperative that she not fall into the hands of the French or Spanish, the Board of Trade advised her protection.

On May 22, 1721, Charlestonians again lined the waterfront and upper windows on the Bay, and small boats scurried in the Cooper River as HMS *Enterprise* arrived with flags flying, bringing Sir Francis Nicholson, first of their Royal governors. To the booming of cannon, this time in celebration, he received an extravagant reception, including a petition of welcome signed by over five hundred delighted citizens.

Mr. Miles Brewton's House at 27 King Street, built c. 1769, was commandeered as headquarters by commanding officers of two occupying armies. The chevaux-de-frise on the fence is said to have been placed there after an attempted slave uprising in 1822. Courtesy of Historic Charleston Foundation -photograph by Robert C. Cleveland

Chapter Two
"Fairest and Most Fruitful Province"

1720–1766
Charlestown

Charlestown began the period of Royal Government not only with a new ruler, but a new spelling of her name, and the frontier village gradually started to assume the aspect of a town. When Nicholas Trott failed in an attempt to retain his position as Chief Justice, and Col. Rhett died of apoplexy, the last of the Proprietary faction fell apart. However, it wasn't until eight years later that the Crown finally bought out the Proprietors, after an abortive attempt on their part to resume control.

In 1723 Anglicans held Easter services in St. Phillip's, "a large, regular and Beautiful Building, exceeding any that are in his Majesty's Dominions in America." On their way to church they could hear the French liturgy through the windows of the Huguenot church on the corner of Queen Street. Many of the French congregation lived up the Cooper River, and it was difficult to row their heavy plantation barges against the tide, therefore they began to time their services so they could come to town on the ebb and return home with the flood.

Churchgoers might also have admired the tall brick house at 71 Church Street that Robert Brewton had recently built in a style that was practical in combatting Charlestown's hot summers. It was built with its narrow end to the street and a single room in width, so the breeze could blow through and lessen the heat that the Rev. Mr. Dehon said "tried a man's soul like a furnace." This fashion, known as the Charleston single house, became so popular that a later visitor exclaimed in surprise that Charleston was "built sidewise!"

The sense of security increased with the establishment of Georgia in 1733, and creeks and marshes to the west were filled in, and Church, Meeting and King Streets were extended. Just across the bridge over Vanderhorst Creek (today's Water Street runs along this former creek bed) well-to-do merchant George Eveleigh's fine cypress-panelled home was taking shape. For some years Col. Rhett's house stood at the head of an avenue leading westward to the chief road out of town, known as the Broad Path, an old Indian trail running through the wilderness. Now the suburbs of Ansonborough was laid out to the north of Rhettsbury, on land that Naval Captain George Anson was said to have won at cards with Thomas Gadsden.

Immigration was on the increase. John Moultrie, whose sons would soon play leading roles in history, arrived. His namesake John would become Tory Lt. Governor of Florida, while William's name would be perpetuated in Ft. Moultrie on Sullivan's Island. From Ireland came John Rutledge, whose sons John and Edward, would sign both the Constitution and the Declaration of Independence. From the Scots-Irish who moved into the back country were to come John C. Calhoun, Andrew Jackson, Andrew Pickens, and Langdon Cheves.

Some years later Abbeville County would be settled by poor German immigrants and the French, the latter nostalgically naming their settlements New Boardeaux and New Rochelle. Among these French would be the grandfather of James L. Petigru. Most of these arrivals entered through the port of Charlestown, and Scots-Irish Robert Witherspoon, who arrived as a child in 1732, has left a vivid account of his family's brief stay in town. He wrote that each member over fourteen received an axe, broad hoe, narrow hoe, and provisions including corn, rice, meat, rum, and salt, before they journeyed to the Willamsburg area to live in earth houses "rather like potatoe hooses," in a wilderness where the howling of wolves terrified him at night. His sister Sarah died before they left Charlestown, and he recalls that hers was the first burial in the "Scotch Meeting House grave yard."

Ethnic organizations were established to provide temporary help for these settlers. The St. Andrew's Society was available if a poor Scot lost his job, or a widow needed funds to return home. One man even applied for aid because bears had destroyed his crop. A group of French Huguenots who met at Pointsett's tavern agreed to contribute two bits or fifteen pence a week towards a relief fund for needy members of the French community, and were nicknamed the Two-Bitt Club, forerunners of the South Carolina Society. The English St. George's Society held an elegant organizational supper at Mr. Robert Raper's. The Friendly Society organized as a mutual fire insurance group in 1736, but apparently was put out of business by the great fire four years later.

It took a few years for the young colony to mature, however, because early Carolinians were a hodgepodge mixture including adventurers, runaways, and felons plus Indian and black slaves. Runaway slaves and footpads lurked on the outskirts of town waiting to relieve unwary travellers of guns, money, and even shoes and hats.

The *Gazette* warned that miscegenation was spreading worse than smallpox, and that "Certain young men of this Town are desired to frequent less with their black lovers the open Lots and the Chandler's House on the Green between the old Church street and King's Street." The paper recorded a duel over "a certain Sable Beauty." The rector of St. Bartholomew's reported that with few exceptions every bride of his parish had been pregnant, and "I was obliged sometimes to call for a chair to make the women to sit down in the time of Marriage because they were fainting away."

Gentleman played cards and billiards, met at taverns to smoke their pipes, dine and discuss the latest news from London. One of the favorite meeting places was the tavern on the northeast corner of Broad and Church, variously named Shepheards', Swallow's, City, and the Corner. Its long room served as Courtroom for several years, and here in 1735 the *Gazette* advertised there would be a public ball. Charlestown's first theatrical season opened here the same year with the performance of Thomas Otway's "The Orphan or the Unhappy Marriage." This was such a success that by the following season Charlestown had built the New Theatre on Dock

Street, where the first play was Farquhar's bawdy *Recruiting Officer*. This was a favorite with eighteenth century actresses because the roles included a "breeches part"—where the actress wore a British uniform, giving her an opportunity to show off her figure!

A local newspaper had made its appearance when Benjamin Franklin sent Thomas Whitmarsh in 1732 to publish the *South Carolina Gazette*. In his first issue Whitmarsh invited letters to the editor, provided "they forbear all controversies both in Church and State," at once provoking a suggestive correspondence between a sixteen-year-old "Merry Girl," and a number of gentlemen, becoming a kind of "Dear Thomas" column, until Whitmarsh advised "it wouldn't be over prudent in us to insert all that comes to our Hands."

When Whitmarsh succumbed to "stranger's fever," Franklin replaced him by Huguenot refugee Louis Timotheé, former librarian of the Philadelphia Library Company. A few months later he Anglicized his name to Lewis Timothy, and when he died of what the *Gazette* mysteriously called an "unhappy accident" in December of 1738, his widow Elizabeth with six children and "another hourly expected," became the first woman publisher in the colonies.

Elizabeth soon established her son Peter in the business, and he was among the seventeen founders of the Charlestown Library Society, whose avowed purpose was to prevent their descendants from sinking into "the gross ignorance of the naked Indian." The charter group included nine merchants, two lawyers, one schoolmaster, one peruke maker, one physician, two planters, and printer Timothy. By 1750 doctors and lawyers predominated in its membership of 128. They

soon had "a pretty well chosen library" bought by private subscription. Their society became a cultural center of the province, and from its members came the impetus for the establishment of the College of Charleston, Charleston Museum and Gibbes Art Gallery. Today scholars from throughout the country, as well as descendants of its founders, continue to visit its tall-ceilinged rooms at 164 King Street for research, to borrow the latest novels, follow national news in *Time* and the *Wall Street Journal*, and catch up on local gossip.

When evangelist George Whitefield visited Charlestown he was scandalized to find "the people seemed wholly devoted to pleasure," and Anglican minister Alexander Garden complained that "the gentlemen planters are above every occupation but eating, drinking, lolling, smoking, and sleeping." The gallons of punch consumed each day required importation of lemons and limes in such quantities that shopkeepers became known as lemon-traders. Dr. David Ramsay lamented that "drunkenness may be called an endemic vice of Carolina."

The Rev. Francis Le Jau, minister to the Goose Creek Men, found "the Indians I have conversed with do make us ashamed by their life, Conversation and Sense of Religion quite different from ours, ours consists in words and appearance, theirs in reality." He stoutly defended, however, his fellow cleric the Rev. Atkins Williamson from the charge that he had baptised a bear! Second Landgrave Smith, on the other hand, declared that the event was "so publickly known that no man doubted the truth of the Occasion," and said he himself had heard Governor Moore offer to swear to it. All agreed, nonetheless, that the befuddled Rev. Williamson was "too great a Lover of Strong Liquor." He was, unfortunately, not an ex-

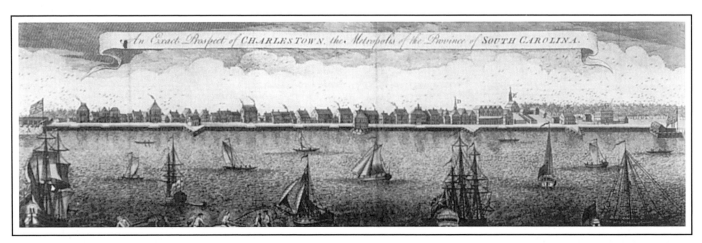

Above:
In this engraving from the London Magazine, 1762, is shown a view of 1739. The British ensign flies from Granville Bastion on the left and Craven to the right. The Watch House is at C, the Independent Meeting spire at D, and St. Philip's at E., and "everything conspires to make this town the politest, as it is one of the richest in America." Courtesy of South Carolina Historical Society

Right:
In 1730 Sir Alexander Cuming took five warriors and two Cherokee chiefs to England where they declared, "We look upon King George as our brother and will carry the chain of friendship to our people." This contemporary print identifies each Indian and is a copy of one in the British Museum. Courtesy of Carolina Art Association

ception to the quality of many of the Anglican clergy who were sent to the colonies in early days. Frequently they were the dregs of the church in England, not only drunkards and lechers, but sometimes even men who falsely represented themselves as clergy. After the organization of the Society for the Propagation of the Gospel, which sent missionaries to the colonies, the calibre in general improved.

The Grand Council had found it necessary to forbid "haunting of punch houses during the time of divine service," and in 1712 everyone was required to attend church on Sunday or be fined. Governor Glen posted sentries at the town gate to prevent "all Loose and Idle Persons from going a Pleasuring" during church services. The first recorded law of the Provincial Assembly in New Charles Town was an act for the observation of the Lord's Day, and Charleston is still struggling to enforce its modern equivalent, the state Blue Laws.

It was said of Carolinians that their religion rested as lightly on them as they sat their horses, however, as Swiss-born John Tobler remarked, "although as everywhere, the wicked outnumber the godly, there are nevertheless among these people various beliefs, many righteous souls." Although he undoubtedly exaggerated when he stated that "The inhabitants are all genteel," he was correct in that some were "quite elegant, and have a high degree of intelligence." He thought Charlestonians "very obliging and kind to strangers and poor people," the same report that Robert Witherspoon made on his arrival.

When fifteen-year-old Eliza Lucas arrived from Antigua she found Charlestown "a neat pretty place. The inhabitants polite and live in a very gentile manner; the streets and houses regularly built; the ladies and gentlemen gay in their dress," and declared that for its size Charlestown had as many agreeable men and women as anywhere in the world. When her father Lt. Col. Thomas Lucas was called back to become governor of Antigua, young Eliza remained to care for her sickly mother and take charge of Lucas' Carolina plantation, where she experimented with both silk and indigo. Thanks to Eliza, her neighbor Andrew DeVeaux, and the encouragement of Moses Lindo, the Inspector General for local indigo, this dye became one of Carolina's leading exports.

When Eliza married widower Chief Justice Charles Pinckney, her father gave him all the indigo then "on the ground." Pinckney saved it for seed and gave a quantity to other gentlemen, and so it spread over the area, until nearly 140,000 pounds were exported by 1747. In addition, Eliza found time to produce raw silk for three dresses. Today one of these, a gold brocade is on display in the Smithsonian Institution, and a dove gray with gold dots and a honeysuckle design is in the old Powder Magazine on Cumberland Street.

A wagon trade developed in the 1750s as the back countrymen began to bring pork, wheat and flour to town, and return home with manufactured goods. Dr. Alexander Garden, a physician (no relation to the Reverend Mr. Garden) wrote the Royal Society in London that horse-powered rice pounding machines had been invented that could pound as much rice in a day as it took sixteen Blacks to do by hand.

Charlestown had come a long way from the days of bartering glass beads with the Seewees in 1670. By 1750 she was the fourth leading port in the American colonies, and her commerce was building the great fortunes of not only the state, but the country.

One of the wealthiest men in the country, Arthur Middleton's son Henry, owned 800 slaves and about twenty plantations comprising a total of 50,000 acres, in addition to

his house in Broad Street. He started landscaping the world famous Middleton Place Gardens at his country seat on the Ashley River about the same time that his neighbor John Drayton was building a magnificent Palladian style mansion, Drayton Hall, downriver.

With the highest per capita income in the country, Charlestown became the social and political as well as economic capital to which all new roads led, and wealthy planters added townhouses to their plantation holdings. In the eighteenth century, Charlestown society was not closed, and merchants making fortunes in rice and indigo put their money into plantations, becoming members of the landed "gentry."

Huguenot Judith Giton arrived penniless in 1685, and she and her husband, weaver Noe Royer, cut trees and cleared land. Judith wrote her brother that since leaving France she had suffered "disease—pestilence—famine—poverty—hard

Huguenot Thomas Legare's 90 Church Street in the foreground was one of the few houses on the east side of Church to survive the fire of 1778. The next house has been the rectory of St. Philip's Church since 1908, and not only was the residence of Aaron Burr's daughter Theodosia and her husband Governor Joseph Alston, but John C. Calhoun drafted the Nullification Papers in its drawing room in 1832. The three might be called variations on the theme of the Charleston Single House. Courtesy of Charleston County Parks, Recreation & Tourism

In 1734, Charles Shepherd began renting out the second floor longroom in his tavern. This became known as the Court Room, and the following year was the site of Charlestown's first theatrical performance. The actress playing the part of Monimea was a great local success and continued to be known in Charlestown by the name of this role. Courtesy of the Charleston Library Society

Monimia and Matthew Sully are central figures in this mural of historic personalities identified with the Charleston stage. It is hanging in the Footlight Players Workshop at 20 Queen Street.

Longtime director Emmett Robinson painted the majority of the figures, and local artist Alfred Hutty did twelve of the heads. Courtesy of Footlight Players, Inc.

azure blue satin window curtains, rich blue paper with gilt, mashee borders, most elegant pictures, excessive grand and costly looking glasses." In his report to the Lords Commissioners of Trade and Plantations Governor Glen estimated Charlestonians comprised a little over one-sixth of the province, yet they lived better than any other Carolinians. He saw so many luxuries imported, Dutch linens, Flanders lace, French chintz, East Indian brocades, "every valuable and every triffling thing," that he was concerned lest it unsettle the balance of trade. But "as they thrive," said he, "they delight to have good things from England."

With wealth came time for additional leisure activities, and development of the arts. Charlestonians sat for pastel portraits by Henrietta Johnson, wife of the rector of St. Philip's, and to Jeremiah Theus, who described himself as "Limner of Charlestown." Simon Theus had been among the Orangeburg Swiss, and his son Jeremiah advertised that he would not only draw portraits, but "likewise Landskips of all sizes, crests and Coats of Arms for Coaches or Chaises," and would make plantation calls.

Music and dancing lessons also were regularly offered and the St. Cecelia gave fortnightly concerts for its members. In 1712 a semipublic school with private financing opened, and tutors, schoolmistresses and masters advertised their services. The Reverend Alexander Garden bought two black slaves for the Society for the Propagation of the Gospel, and began training them to become schoolteachers for Indian and black children. By 1744 this school had sixty pupils, and continued to be operated by the rector of St. Philip's until one of the black teachers died and the other "turned out profligate."

Wealthy Charlestonians usually sent their sons abroad to England for their formal education, after which they often made the "Grand Tour" of the continent before returning home. Young Peter Manigault wrote his mother from Paris that he had stayed at an inn, that though not as good as her kitchen, had fewer Cock-Roaches in it!

Cockfighting was a popular sport, and in 1734 there appeared the first account of a horse race, with the prize to be a saddle and bridle valued at £20. The following year the York course was laid out, and owners invited to enter their horses for a purse of £100, and races were run each spring. In 1754 the New Market Course opened just a mile beyond the town limits, under the direction of Mr. Thomas Nightingale, a Yorkshireman, and soon race week became the highlight of Charlestown's social season.

As population increased, so did the congregation of St. Philip's, and it was decided to divide the parish. The part south of Broad Street became the parish of St. Michael's, and in 1752 Governor Glen laid the cornerstone of a magnificent new church on the former site of St. Philip's. The ceremony was accompanied by great festivities including discharge of cannon from Granville's bastion and a large dinner with innumerable toasts at Mr. Gordon's tavern, eliciting a bill for "Glass Broak" from the proprietor.

Samuel Cardy, Irish immigrant, was hired as contractor at £25 a month—no record of an actual architect being found in the church records. The fine cabinetmaking firm of Elfe and Hutchinson carved bannisters for the arcade and clock level; Jeremiah Theus left off portrait painting to gild the large copper covered cypress ball atop the spire—a feature that was to cause later generations to identify this rather social church as the one with the highball on top!

Gabriel Manigault provided shingles for the steeple, James

labor" and for six months hadn't tasted bread, "working the ground like a slave." In 1699 widowed Judith married Pierre Manigault, who had taken in boarders on his arrival, built a distillery and cooperage, and at his death left a fortune to their son Gabriel, who became one of the richest of colonial Carolina merchants and at the time of the Revolution lent the state $220,000.

Nathaniel Russell came to Charlestown as a young man of twenty-four to seek his fortune, and became a merchant on the Bay, later building one of the finest Federal style mansions in the city. One of his daughters married into the Middleton family, the other became the wife of Episcopal Bishop Theodore Dehon.

As the demand for slaves to cultivate rice and indigo increased, so did the fortunes of the trading firm of Austin and Brewton, and Miles Brewton imported Ezra Waite, civil architect from London, who described himself in the *Gazette* as having "27 years experience, both in theory and practice, in noblemen and gentlemen's seats." Waite stated that he "did construct every individual part and drawed the same at large for the joiners to work by, and conducted the execution thereof" for Mr. Brewton's house on King Street, still owned by his descendants and one of the most magnificent of Charleston's mansions.

In 1773 Josiah Quincy of Massachusetts would describe his dinner at Mr. Brewton's: "The grandest hall I ever beheld,

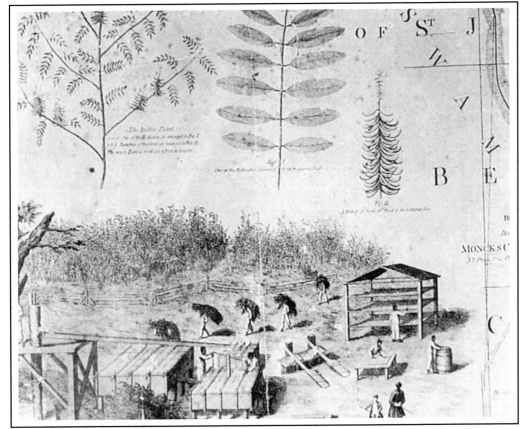

Botanical illustration for the "Indico Plant" and a panorama of processing in the corner of a map show plantations along the Cooper River. Courtesy of Collection of the Charleston Museum, Charleston, South Carolina

Laurens'company the HL hinges for pew doors, Zachariah Villepontoux floated brick down from Parnassus Plantation on Back River, and Humphrey Sommers subcontracted the roof slating. From Robert Pringle and Company came rope for a derrick, carver Henry Burnett added the Corinthian entablature of the arcade and eight cherubim on the keystones, as well as Ionic capitals in the interior, and the pulpit with "1 Pine Apple" as its finial.

On December 27, 1758, the Ancient and Honorable Fraternity of Free and Accepted Masons processed from their lodge room at "Brother John Gordon's" to St. Michael's for a meeting, but the first church services weren't held until three years later. Original pewholders included a cross-section of the community: Cardy, Elfe, Theus, Thomas Nightingale, Miles Brewton; Job Colcock, auctioneer; watchmaker Stephen Lee; General Arnoldus Vanderhorst; Thomas Lynch and Thomas Heyward Jr., later to become signers of the Declaration of Independence; Henry Laurens and Henry Middleton, future Presidents of the Continental Congress; Eliza Lucas Pinckney, and Lady Mary Middleton, Henry's wife, and daughter of the third Earl of Cromartie.

"A fine peal of bells" arrived from England, and rang for the first time September 21, 1764, and soon became the voice of Charlestown: calling to worship, crying alarms, tolling in sorrow, striking terror in troublous times, and pealing in triumph and joy—part of the lifeblood of generations of Charlestonians. They rang the political pulse of the town, celebrating the birthday of "our most gracious sovereign, King George III" on June 4, 1765, and the following October expressing opposition to the Stamp Act.

They rang so vehemently for fires in 1832 that two of the smaller bells cracked; they rang evening curfew and called out the guard, and brought tears to the eyes of the honor guard in 1862 when Confederate dead returned to Charleston just at sunset, and "St. Michael's rang the old air of

'Home, Sweet Home.'" They still celebrate Carolina Day every June 28, with a half hour of old tunes, including "Carolina," "Taffy Was a Welchman," and "Three Blind Mice." Today St. Michael's is the oldest church building in the city, and has an active congregation of over a thousand communicants.

On the opposite corner a fine new State House was under construction, and up the street the new Independent Meeting House, and the "great street that runneth past the Meeting House" soon became known as Meeting Street. In 1731 a frame building just south of Tradd on Meeting held the Scots Kirk, the first (Scots) Presbyterian congregation of today. Sephardic Jews had organized Kahal Kadosh Beth Elohim in 1749, meeting for worship in a small wooden house on Union (now State) Street, and Quakers came together in a meeting house on King Street. St. John's Lutheran church on Archdale Street resembled the large white wooden churches of Germany.

Charlestonians continued the interest in gardening that Thomas Ashe had remarked in 1682 when he found them beautifying their gardens with "such herbs and flowers which to the smell or eye are pleasing and agreeable." Governor Nicholson contributed to Mark Catesby's wilderness expedition that provided the groundwork for his *Natural History of Carolina, Florida and the Bahama Islands.* Europeans were amazed at the "wild spontaneous flowers of this country," and the Beauty Bush and sweet flowering bay took their places in town gardens next to periwinkle, daisy and snapdragons, grown from "divers sorts of best garden seeds" from Samuel Eveleigh's shelves and Mr. Charles Pinckney's new store on the Bay.

John Watson, gardener and seedsman on Trott's Point advertised tulips, hyacinths, lilies, anemones, ranunculus, and double jonquils—garden seeds and tools, fruit trees and asparagus roots and that he "continues gardening in all its branches." Bignonia from the West Indies climbed on garden walls above four o'clocks, called "afternoon ladies" because

"Step lightly down these terraces, they are records of a dream," poet Amy Lowell wrote of Middleton Place. Henry Middleton, one of Carolina's largest landowners, ran the central axis of his world-famous gardens through the hall of his residence, across a parterre and terraces, and between two lakes in the shape of outstretched butterfly wings. Only the steps of his home remain, having been burned on Washington's birthday, 1865. The present Middleton Place house to the left was one of a pair of matching flankers.
Courtesy of Middleton Place Foundation

of their habit of blooming in the early evening. A half lot on Tradd Street was advertised for sale with over ninety orange trees that had been bearing for several years. An Ashley River plantation was available with fruit trees, asparagus, a kitchen garden, a nursery with grafted pear and apple trees, thousands of orange trees, and several lemon and lime trees.

Governor Glen reported 296,000 oranges exported from November 1747 to November 1748. Mrs. Martha Logan's garden calendar was reprinted in the local almanac almost every year from its initial appearance in 1751 until 1818.

Elizabeth Lamboll had a "large and handsome flower and kitchen garden upon the European plan" at the southwest corner of King and Lamboll streets, her house is the present 19 King Street. Dr. Garden, who had arrived from Scotland in 1752, had a house on Tradd Street as well as a botanical garden at Otranto on Goose Creek, and he corresponded with Bartram in Philadelphia, Benjamin Franklin, and with the famous Swedish naturalist Linnaeus, who named the gardenia for him.

Several other local physicians were pursuing scientific experiments. Dr. John Lining made the first scientific weather observations from his house on Broad Street, near the foot of Union, and also corresponded with Franklin, several times "making Dr. Franklin's experiment with a kite, for drawing the lighting from the clouds."

Chalmers Street, one of Charleston's few remaining cobblestone thoroughfares, is named after its well-known resident Dr. Lionel Chalmers, who published a treatise on the influence of the weather on disease. One of his lighter observations on Charlestown's heat was that he "had seen a beefsteak of the common thickness so deprived of its juices when laid on a cannon for the space of twenty minutes as to be overdone."

Charlestown continued to have her share of disasters. In 1728 a summer drought was followed by an August hurricane that damaged fortifications, houses and wharves, and drove twenty-three ships ashore. Not long after a yellow fever epidemic struck that was so severe that there were scarcely enough living to bury the dead. Charlestown joined Georgians in a campaign that was known as the War of Jenkin's Ear, begun when a Spanish captain cut off the ear of British naval officer Captain Jenkins.

Black slaves for some years had outnumbered whites, and their continued desertions to Florida, encouraged by the Spanish, alarmed Lt. Gov. William Bull and the legislature. There were rumors of a conspiracy of Carolina Blacks to force their way out of the province and escape to St. Augustine. On Sunday, September 9, 1739, about twenty slaves broke into a store at Stono Bridge, murdered the two storekeepers, leaving their heads on the front steps. In this uprising, known as the Stono Rebellion, the slaves killed some twenty whites, while twice as many blacks lost their lives. The result of the uprising was the slave law of 1740, which tightened restrictions, and imposed a prohibitive tax on new slave imports which cut importations for several years.

November 18, 1740, "a Most terrible Fire" started in a "Sadler's House in Broad Street" and raged for six hours down the area between Church and East Bay as far as Granville Bastion, destroying "the most valuable part of the Town on account of the Buildings and Trade." The loss was estimated at some three hundred houses and over a million and a half dollars in today's currency. Parliament allocated 20,000 pounds sterling to help rebuild the town.

The great hurricane of 1752 hit after the hottest summer Charlestonians had ever felt. The night of September 14 the

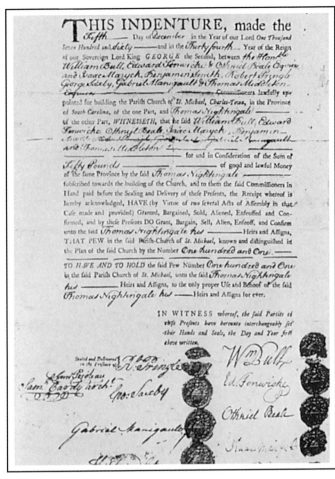

wind blew with increasing violence all night, and next morning at nine o'clock the tide began pouring in, and soon was ten feet above the record high water mark. In two hours all the ships in the harbor were blown ashore, one driven down Vanderhorst Creek to Meeting Street. The Sullivan's Island Pest House containing fourteen occupants washed up the Cooper River. People fled to the upper stories of their houses, and many "being up to their necks in water," waited for death because there were still two hours before high tide. Unexpectedly the wind suddenly shifted and the water fell five feet in ten minutes. "For about forty miles round Charlestown, there was hardly a plantation that did not loose every outhouse upon it, and the roads, for years afterwards, were incumbered with trees blown and broken down."

The storm had severely damaged the fortifications and William Gerard de Brahm was employed to raise the sea wall four feet above the high water mark of the hurricane of 1752. This fortified a line that ran from Granville's Bastion to Broughton's, at the approximate corner of South Battery and Church Street, and from there it was continued westward to the neighborhood of Gibbes Street.

When the French and Indian war broke out, it was known in Charlestown as the Cherokee War, and plans were drawn up for a tabby hoornwerk to be built on either side of the town gates—tabby being a strong building substance made from burning oyster shells—and lines were projected to protect the peninsula. Soldiers, including Francis Marion, William Moultrie, and Andrew Pickens, were members of Col. Thomas Middleton's Carolina Regiment, and received the training in Indian fighting that they would apply in the Revolution ten years later; however, Charlestown herself did not suffer in this war.

19

Upon the fall of Charlestown, General William Moultrie was parolled to Snee Farm, Christ Church Parish. While there, Lord Charles Greville Montagu attempted to persuade Moultrie to quit his country. Moultrie replied, "The repossessing of my estate, the offer of the command of your regiment, and the honour you propose of serving under me, are paltry considerations in the loss of my reputation. No. Not the fee simple of that valuable Island Jamaica should induce me to part with my integrity." Courtesy of South Carolina Historical Society.

Chapter Three

"They Shot the Breeches off His Back"

1765–1800
Rebellion

The close of the French and Indian War found Charlestown prosperous; trade in rice and indigo was expanding and the back country was rapidly becoming settled. The power of the Assembly continued to increase, and the successful outcome of campaigns against the Spanish, Indians, and pirates, plus the rebellion against the Proprietors all had strengthened Charlestonians' confidence and sense of power.

An English bounty on indigo, the increase in African slave imports, and permission to ship rice direct to Spain, Portugal, and the Mediterranean made such fortunes that the thriving port hardly felt the restrictions of the Navigation Acts which so enraged New England. The smuggling that occurred in the North was not only absent here, but Hector Berenger de Beaufain, collector of customs for twenty-four years, was so popular that a monument was erected to him in St. Philip's church, and even a street was named for him. On September 3, 1768, Peter Timothy wrote Benjamin Franklin, "I do not suppose there is a Colony on the Continent in so flourishing and promising a Situation as South Carolina at present. Private and public Works are every where carrying on with Spirit."

Boundary Street (now Calhoun) was laid out from Scarborough (Anson) to King. Harleston Village was surveyed with its streets given patriotic names of Gadsden, Lynch and Rutledge, and Beaufain, Montagu, Wentworth and Bull after Royal officials. Thomas Gadsden's son Christopher was building a mammoth wharf on the Cooper River at his suburb of Middlesex, and William Gibbes was extending the longest wharf into the Ashley River just opposite his residence on South Bay. Timothy reported "all White-Point, which for many Years was almost a desolate Spot, is lately almost covered with Houses, many of them very elegant."

When the Stamp Act was passed in 1765 in an effort to have the colonies assume part of the expense of their protection, it raised a political dilemma that divided most families in Carolina. William Bull supported the King, opposing his nephews Stephen and William Jr.; William Henry Drayton first supported the Stamp Act, then turned into a violent revolutionary, but his cousin William, Chief Justice of Florida, remained loyal to the King. Gabriel Manigault supported the rebels generously with his money, but Gabriel Jr. remained a Loyalist; Thomas Heyward Jr. signed the Declaration, his father Daniel was a Tory. Col. William Moultrie's brother John continued to serve as Royal Lt. Gov. of Florida.

The Commons House of Assembly adopted resolutions opposing taxation without representation, and appointed Thomas Lynch, Christopher Gadsden and John Rutledge delegates to the Stamp Act Congress in New York, to meet that October. When Captain Gadsden's Artillery Company heard of their arrival in New York they "fired three vollies of small arms, upon the joyful news."

When the *Planter's Adventure* from London dropped anchor under the guns of Fort Johnson on Friday October 18, it seemed suspicious that she didn't come up to town and discharge, and rumor had it that a stamp distributor was aboard. There were muttered threats and speculation that the ship carried the stamps themselves. The next morning Charlestonians received a shock as they rounded Broad Street and saw two figures swinging from a gallows in the center of the street opposite Mr. Dillon's tavern at the corner of Church. Horror turned to chuckles when closer examination showed them to be effigies—one of the devil and the other labeled "Distributor of Stampt Paper." A notice warned of dire consequences to anyone who might pull them down.

St. Michael's bells rang muffled all day and that evening the figures were removed and placed in a wagon, and a procession of at least two thousand, it was said, proceeded through town, accompanied by the tolling of the great bell of St. Michael's. The figures were burned on the green to the west of town, where a coffin labeled "American Liberty" was buried.

Rumors continued to fly, including the suspicion that the stamps were in Henry Laurens' Ansonborough house. A mob burst into his garden, demanded the surrender of the stamps and put a cutlass to Laurens' throat. Only Laurens' bearing and his recognition of the disguised ringleaders kept them from entering his house, and they satisfied themselves by searching the outbuildings and helping themselves to his imported wine. Proceeding to Chief Justice Skinner's they were received with bowls of punch, and he joined them in drinking "Damnation to the Stamp Act."

The next day a notice was posted to the effect that the stamps were at Fort Johnson, ending further searches. When Saxby and Lloyd, the stamp agents, agreed not to distribute the odious stamps until a reply to the Stamp Act petition returned from London, St. Michael's bells clamored unmuffled once more. Ships ran up their colors, and the *Gazette* reported that the largest crowd ever assembled with "bells, drums, hautboys, violins, hurrahs," and cannon firing, escorted the two officials from Mr. Motte's wharf to the corner of Broad and Church—not for hanging fortunately—but for refreshments at Mr. Dillon's!

The Act went into effect the next day, and Lt. Gov. Bull wrote the Lords of Trade that "the courts of common law, admiralty and ecclesiastical jurisdiction are all silent; no grants of land are passed; all the ships remain in the harbor as under an embargo; every transaction requiring stamps is at an end." The excess of ships depressed freights so much that Laurens declared the rice planters had turned the tables on their British owners. Rawlins Lowndes, Daniel Doyley, Benjamin Smith, and Robert Pringle secured appointments as assistant justices and declared the court would proceed with plain paper since it was impossible to get stamped. They did not allow Chief Justice Skinner's contrary opinion to be recorded.

Charlestown lived at a high pitch of excitement. It greeted repeal of the Act the following year with bonfires, bell ring-

ing, and illuminations—the mob declaring they would "insult" any house not illuminated. Christopher Gadsden announced "There ought to be no New England men, no New Yorker, etc., known on the continent, but all of us Americans." He was invited to address the mechanics, or blue collar workers, under the great oak tree in Mr. Mazyck's pasture, and join the celebration of the repeal. This tree became known as the Liberty Tree, and was the site of many patriotic meetings. Torchlight processions began at its foot, hundreds of "loyal, patriotic and constitutional toasts" were joyously drunk under its branches. It became such a symbol of rebellion that when the British occupied the town, they not only cut it down, but piled the branches round the stump and set fire to it.

The House ordered a marble statue of William Pitt, in gratitude for his role in influencing Parliament to repeal the act, ignoring the suggestion of William Wragg (who had been held by Blackbeard almost fifty years earlier), a staunch King's man, to replace Pitt's name with that of his Majesty George III!

The non-importation agreement gave rise to a heated controversy in the pages of the *Gazette*, and vehement protests by William Henry Drayton and William Wragg. Signees agreed not to buy or sell to nonsubscribers, whose names were published in handbills. Drayton wrote that no man of education would consult on public affairs with men whose only knowledge consisted in "how to cut up a beast in the market to the best advantage, cobble an old shoe in the neatest manner, or to build a necessary house." A reply from the mechanics pointedly reminded him that Drayton's fortune came from his wealthy wife.

The mechanics had a high time—they rejoiced when the Massachusetts Assembly voted 92 to 17 not to rescind an act opposing the Townshend Acts, and seized the cause of John Wilkes, imprisoned because issue No. 45 of his newspaper criticized the King—celebrating his release with toasts from 92 glasses under the Liberty Tree illuminated with 45 lanterns. Wilkes' release also triggered bell ringing, displaying of colors, and "abundant other Demonstrations of Satisfaction and Joy." In his paper, Timothy enumerated the forty-five toasts that the Club No. 45 drank at their "most elegant Entertainment" at Mr. Dillon's, and a group of forty-five met at the house of Capt. Benjamin Stone on James Island and fired forty-five cannon, served forty-five dishes at dinner, including a forty-five pound turtle, drank forty-five toasts, illuminated the house with forty-five candles, and the party dispersed at forty-five minutes after eleven!

A fine new exchange and customs house rose at the east end of Broad Street, on the site of the old court of guard fronting on the water. Josiah Quincy wrote "the new Exchange which pointed the place of my landing, made a most noble appearance." On December 3 a meeting was held in its Great Hall to protest the arrival of 257 chests of taxed tea, and this was commemorated in 1973 as the birth of the present South Carolina government. Charlestown had her tea party, too, but instead of dumping the tea in the harbor, the chests were stored in the basement of the Exchange and later sold to help finance the Revolution.

A black-bordered Extra announced the passage of the Boston Port Bill, which closed the harbor of that town as a result of the Boston Tea Party. Charlestown saw what the *Gazette* described as "a magnificent exhibition of effigies" in celebration of Guy Fawkes Day, including figures of the Pope; Lord North, the prime minister; Governor Hutchinson of Massachusetts, and the devil aiming a javelin at Lord North's head. They were on a rolling platform on Broad Street and the pope and the devil contained mechanisms so that they could be made to bow, and naturally the people they chose to bow to were Tories, a sight delightful to the mob. That evening, after being paraded through the main streets, the effigies were burned "in the presence of some thousands; who rejoiced to see the abbettors of American Taxation consumed."

There were several occasions of mob violence: "The Gunner of Fort Johnson (one Walker) had a decent tarring and feathering for some insolent speech he had made," and was conducted through town, stopping at various Tory houses to let them get an idea of what might be in store for them, too. Charlestown also passed furious resolutions, collected tons of rice "for the suffering poor of the blockaded port," and cash and produce sent from South Carolina to Boston exceeded those from any other colony, including Massachusetts herself.

Meantime, thirty Americans in London petitioned the House of Commons against the Boston Port Bill, and fifteen of them were from South Carolina; including two Izards, two Middletons, a Pinckney, two Fenwicks, a Motte, a Blake, a Heyward and a Laurens. On July 6 at a meeting in the Exchange Henry Middleton, John and Edward Rutledge, Thomas Lynch, and Christopher Gadsden were elected delegates to the First Continental Congress.

It was slightly over a week after a horseman had galloped down the King's Highway from Georgetown with the news of fighting in Massachusetts, that gun salutes announced the arrival of the man-of-war *Scorpion*, bringing Lord William Campbell, newly appointed Royal Governor, and his wife. There were no welcoming crowds, no parade, no loud acclaim when his commission was proclaimed from the portico of the Exchange—only ominous silence. It was a cold welcome for the young couple, even though Lord Campbell's wife Sally and Arthur Middleton's wife Polly were sisters. Until the house of her cousin Mrs. Daniel Blake, at 34 Meeting was ready for them, they were temporarily housed at Miles Brewton's, the brother-in-law of Mrs. Blake. Though friends called and the new arrivals were handsomely entertained, their being closely related to revolutionary leaders made for strained situations.

Lord William found his residence at 34 Meeting very convenient, since he could communicate by small boat from the rear of the house on Vanderhorst Creek with British ships in the harbor. This fact did not go unnoticed, however, and before he had been in Charlestown three months, he was charged with attempting to arouse the frontier settlements against the colonists. He was himself forced to escape by way of this backdoor route to the British sloop-of-war *Tamar*, taking with him the great seal of the province. So ended Royal Government in Carolina.

When Gadsden returned from Philadelphia with a copy of Thomas Paine's *Common Sense*, and declared himself in favor of the absolute independence of America, he horrified the Provincial Congress. John Rutledge said he would ride post by day and night to Philadelphia to prevent the disaster of separation from England. Armed forces were organized and Gadsden was chosen Colonel of the First Regiment, Moultrie of the Second, and William Thomson Lt. Colonel of the Third. Gadsden was needed in Charlestown to attend to his military duties, and fifty-eight-year-old Henry Middleton, newly married to his third wife, said "infirmities of age that were creeping on" kept him from serving as he had previously done, and requested that he not be re-appointed delegate to Congress.

The Provincial Congress re-elected John Rutledge, Thomas Lynch, and Edward Rutledge, and elected new delegates Thomas Heyward Jr. and Arthur Middleton, the latter "considered 'warm' even by New Englanders." When Gadsden refused leave for twenty-seven-year-old Thomas Lynch Jr. to attend his father, who suffered a stroke while in Philadelphia, Congress made young Lynch a sixth delegate, and he replaced his father.

On March 26, 1776, South Carolina seceded from Great Britain, setting up an independent government, and electing John Rutledge President. Addressing both houses of the legislature, Rutledge told them: "The eyes of Europe, nay of the whole world, are on America… the eyes of every other Colony are on this…a Colony, whose reputation for generosity and magnanimity is universally acknowledged. I trust, therefore, that there will be no civil discord here, and that the only strife amongst brethren will be, who shall do most to serve, and to save, an oppressed and injured country."

Moultrie combined the blue of his soldiers' uniforms with the silver crescents on their caps to design the first South Carolina flag. This flag was flying over little unfinished Fort Moultrie on June first, when fifty British ships under the command of Admiral Sir Peter Parker appeared off the bar. Only the front and one side of the fort were completed and the small open, square fort had walls of two rows of palmetto logs sixteen feet apart, with beach sand between, and boasted thirty-one cannon to oppose the fleet's two hundred seventy. Commanding General Charles Lee thought "it could not hold out half an hour, and that the platform was but a slaughtering stage," and suggested to Rutledge it be abandoned, but Rutledge indignantly refused, saying he would cut off his right hand before writing such an order.

Lee then had half the powder and a large number of the troops removed, since he considered the fort doomed, and Moultrie was ordered to spike his guns and retreat if his powder gave out. As a result of this action, Moultrie slowed down his fire so much during the battle that at one point the British thought the fort was out of commission. Captain Lempriere informed Moultrie: "Sir, when those ships (pointing to the men-of-war) come to lay alongside of your fort, they will knock it down in half an hour." Moultrie replied: "We will lay behind the ruins and prevent their men from landing." This in the face of the entire fleet—two of whose vessels carried twice as many guns between them as the fort numbered in all!

Sir Henry Clinton attempted to attack the fort from land by crossing Breach Inlet from Long Island (Isle of Palms) with some two to three thousand infantry. Detailed to stop them was Col. Thomson with 780 frontier sharpshooters. The accuracy of these riflemen coupled with a miscalculation in the depth of the water by the English prevented their crossing.

Three ships ran aground on the shoal on which Fort Sumter has since been built—one, the *Actaeon*, stuck fast. The fort concentrated on the flagship *Bristol*, and Lord William Campbell, who had accompanied the fleet, received a wound which was to prove fatal, and "Sir Peter Parker had the hindpart of his breeches shot away, which laid his posteriors bare."

Major Barnard Elliott wrote his wife: "The expression of a Sergeant McDaniel, after a cannon ball had taken off his shoulder and scouped out his stomach, is worth recording in the annals of America: 'Fight on, my brave boys; don't let liberty expire with me today!' Young, the barber, an old artillery man, who lately enlisted as Sergeant, has lost a leg… My old grenadier, Serg. Jasper, upon the shot carrying away the flag-staff, called out to Col. Moultrie: 'Col., don't let us fight without our flag.' 'What can you do?' replied the Col.; 'the staff is broke.' 'Then, sir,' said he, 'I'll fix it to a halbert, and place it on the merlon of the bastion, next to the enemy;' which he did, through the thickest fire."

The British shot sank harmlessly into the porous palmetto logs and sand, doing very slight damage and inflicting few fatalities. Thousands of civilians lined the Charlestown waterfront fearing that when the flag was shot down during the battle the fort had been lost. But dusk fell and the British navy retreated to its sea anchorage. General Charles Cotesworth Pinckney wrote his mother Eliza: "The Fort, though well peppered with shot, has received scarcely any damage, not a single breach being made in it, nor did the Palmetto logs, of which it is built, at all splinter."

Because the palmetto logs proved so effective the palmetto tree was added to the state flag, and later became the official state tree. The fort was named for Commanding General Moultrie, and the bridge that spans Breach Inlet today bears Colonel Thomson's name. For generations Charleston children learned the story of Carolina Day in the following verse:

The first of June the British fleet
Appeared off Charlestown harbor.
The twenty-eighth attacked the fort
And wounded Young the barber.
Sir Peter Parker, foolish man
To put his fleet in danger.
They shot the breeches off his back
And used him as a stranger.

Congressional President John Hancock sent Moultrie a message from the United States of America: "Posterity will be astonished, when they read that on the 28th June, an inexperienced handful of men under your command, repulsed with loss and disgrace a powerful fleet and army of veteran troops headed by officers of rank and distinction."

The last British ship sailed for New York on August 2, the same day that the four young Carolinians joined their fellow delegates in signing the Declaration of Independence. When the news arrived in Charlestown Henry Laurens wept, and later said he felt more pain at news of the Declaration than he did at the death of his son, for whom he was in mourning.

For the next several years the action shifted to the north, and except for a few encounters with British ships cruising offshore, Charlestown was fairly quiet. Major Benjamin Huger rode into town from his property on North Island near Georgetown, accompanied by two young foreigners, the Marquis de Lafayette and Baron de Kalb, who had been put ashore there because British ships were patrolling the Charlestown approaches. From here they rode to join General Washington. Twenty-two-year-old John Laurens returned home from his law studies at the Temple in London, to join Washington's staff, while his father Henry was serving as president of the Continental Congress.

Next year when another great fire broke out in Charlestown, and over two hundred fifty houses were burned in the Church Street area from Queen Street to Stoll's Alley, it was suspected that it had been set by Tories or men from a British man-of-war. Laurens sailed as commissioner to negotiate a loan and treaty with Holland. When his ship was intercepted by the British, he threw his bag of papers overboard weighted with shot, but the British hauled it up, and today some of the waterstained documents are in the files of the South Carolina Historical Society collection in the Fire-

24

The Marquis de Lafayette captured the hearts of Charlestonians upon his arrival with Major Benjamin Huger in 1777 when he came to assist in the American cause. This painting by Ary Scheffer hangs in the House Chamber in the National Capitol. Courtesy of Library of Congress.

106 Tradd, built by Col. John Stuart, His Majesty's Agent for Indian Affairs, has its original metal firemark over the first floor window. From a window in this house Francis Marion is said to have fallen and sprained his ankle. Courtesy of Historic Charleston Foundation

Center:
John Blake White has illustrated the possibly apocryphal story of a young British officer who was led blindfolded to Marion's camp in the Carolina swamp to negotiate an exchange of prisoners. Invited to share their dinner, which consisted solely of sweet potatoes, he was so impressed by the bravery and cheerful acceptance of hardships that he asked to be excused from fighting against the Americans, and declared, "You can't defeat men like that." Courtesy of Carolina Art Association

Henry Laurens, South Carolina delegate to the Continental Congress, was its President from 1777-78. En route to his post as minister to Holland he was captured by the British and imprisoned in the Tower of London for fifteen months until exchanged for Lord Cornwallis in 1781. This portrait, attributed to John Singleton Copley, was painted during his stay in the Tower. Courtesy of Library of Congress

proof Building in Charleston.

A sprained ankle was instrumental in preventing the British from consolidating their position in the Low Country. Just before the siege of Charlestown started, Francis Marion is said to have been a guest at a dinner party in the "house next to Roupell's," identified as present-day 106 Tradd Street. When the host locked the door so his guests couldn't leave until they'd partaken of his choice Madeira, Marion, who was a teetotaler, jumped out the window, so the story goes, and badly sprained his ankle. Ordered home to the High Hills of Santee to recuperate, he escaped capture in the fall of Charlestown. When he recovered he used guerilla Indian tactics to harass the British with his daring raids, eluding capture time and time again, and retreating to his swamp hideouts. It was Colonel Banastre Tarleton who gave him the name "Swamp Fox," when he said, "Come, my boys! Let us

Left:
In their unfinished sand and palmetto log fort, Col. William Moultrie and his inexperienced handful of men fight off the prestigious British fleet under Sir Peter Parker, June 28, 1776. Courtesy of The South Carolina Library, Columbia, South Carolina

Above:
Thomas Lynch Jr. is seated fourth from the left, and Arthur Middleton, fifth in a row of standing representatives, leans forward over Thomas Heyward, Jr. South Carolina's fourth delegate Edward Rutledge stands on the immediate right in this scene by John Trumbull of July 4, 1776 in Independence Hall, Philadelphia. Courtesy of Library of Congress

go back, and we will find the Gamecock (Thomas Sumter). But as for this damned old fox, the devil himself could not catch him."

In February of 1780 Sir Henry Clinton landed an army on John's Island, and they marched up James' Island to the mainland, while Admiral Arbuthnot and his fleet crossed the bar. St. Michael's steeple was painted black on the seaward side as camouflage, which the British said actually made it a better target against the sky. Peter Timothy was posted on the arcade level to watch the fleet movements and the army on James' Island, including about two thousand Hessian mercenaries.

Governor Rutledge and a few of his council left to preserve a nucleus of government when the city fell, and appointed Gadsden acting Lieutenant Governor. A month-long siege began with the bombardment on April 13. Three days later a shell hit Mr. Pitt's statue, and took off his right arm, the one holding the Magna Carta. During the siege Major John André slipped into town, disguised as a Virginia frontiersman, and was entertained in the home of Tory Edward Shrewsbury on East Bay.

When Charlestown capitulated, Miles Brewton's mansion was commandeered as headquarters for the occupying forces. Mrs. Motte, who inherited the property when her brother was drowned, was made to serve as unwilling hostess. According to family tradition she locked her two young daughters in the attic until the officers left. Owners of the houses taken over by occupying forces were often crowded into a room or two. Admiral Arbuthnot commandeered the John Edwards' home for his headquarters, and Hessians were quartered up the street in 32 Meeting.

When England received the news that Charlestown had fallen, the entire four thousand troops of the line were drawn up in Hyde Park and fired a feu de joie—the Foot Guards and Horse Guards celebrated, and Dublin was illuminated. In Charlestown the British established a dungeon, the Provost, in the basement of the Exchange, "a damp unwholesome place of sickness and death, where all were crowded into one common room, with no respect for age or sex," as Moultrie described it.

Armed soldiers arrested Charlestown citizens in their homes, among them thirty-three paroled prisoners, including Gadsden, Edward Rutledge, Richard Hutson, Thomas Heyward Jr., Peter Timothy, John Edwards, Thomas Savage, and David Ramsay, and imprisoned them in the Provost. They were later moved to the prison ship *Sandwich* moored near Fort Johnson. Later more joined them in exile, including Arthur Middleton, and they were subsequently taken to St. Augustine. Here Gadsden refused on principle to give the second parole required of him, and was shut up alone in a dungeon in the Castle.

Henry Laurens had been confined in the Tower of London after his capture at sea; two other Revolutionary leaders, Thomas Lynch Jr. and William Henry Drayton were dead, one drowned at sea, the other a victim of fever. Carolina and Charlestown were plundered—Tarleton restocked his cavalry from the famous Carolina stables, thousands of slaves were taken, and houses were looted of valuables. Henry Laurens wrote to his son John: "The British Parliament now employ their Men of War to steal those Negroes from the Americans to whom they had sold them, pretending to set the poor wretches free, but basely trepan and sell them into tenfold worse Slavery in the West Indies…what meannes."

Over two hundred citizens congratulated Sir Henry Clinton and Admiral Arbuthnot at the fall of the city—including John

26

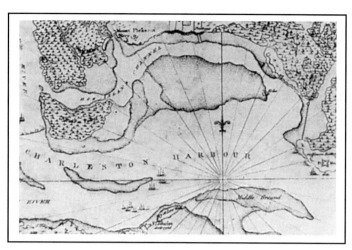

A sketch of Charlestown Harbour shows the disposition of Vice Admiral Mariot Arbuthnot's British fleet at the 1780 attack on Fort Moultrie. During the British occupation, the fort was renamed Fort Arbuthnot, and the Admiral commandeered the John Edwards House at 15 Meeting Street for his headquarters. Courtesy of South Carolina Historical Society

Wragg, Robert Wilson, Thomas Elfe, and Isaac Mazyck. Later an additional 163 swore allegiance; including former president Henry Middleton, Colonel Charles Pinckney, former president of the Provincial Congress, Gabriel Manigault, who had taken his fifteen-year-old grandson and helped defend the lines against General Prevost in 1778, Daniel Huger, Elias Horry, and Wade Hampton. However, the British role in inciting the Indians against the frontier settlers and the burning of meeting houses in the upcountry turned many against them who might otherwise have remained neutral. What incensed even more people, however, was the execution of Colonel Isaac Hayne.

Hayne, in order to remain with his dying wife, had given his parole, understanding that he would not be required to bear arms for the British. When he later was called on to do so, he considered himself released from parole, and he rejoined the American forces only to be recaptured. His sister-in-law brought Hayne's children and visited Lord Rawdon in the drawing room of 27 King Street, and pleaded for Hayne's life, to no avail. He was marched through crowded streets and hanged on a gibbet outside the city gates.

It was almost a year after Cornwallis' surrender at Yorktown that the last Redcoats marched through the town gates to Gadsden's wharf at the foot of Boundary (Calhoun) Street. With them went untold amounts of stolen goods—one historian says silver alone amounted to five hundred huge rice barrels full, and even St. Michael's bells were taken. It required four hours to embark, and as the British left, the Continentals moved in, and General Nathaniel Greene conducted Governor John Mathews and his Council to Broad Street. Moultrie wrote: "I can never forget the happy day when we marched into Charlestown with the American troops; it was a proud day to me, and I felt myself much elated at seeing the balconies, the doors, and windows crowded with patriotic fair, the aged citizens and others congratulating us on our return home, saying, 'God bless you gentlemen! You are welcome home, gentlemen!'"

Some Tories had their estates confiscated and were banished—others were fined a percentage of their property—and a few were lynched. Eventually confiscated property

On March 26, 1784, an Ordinance was passed authorizing the city to conduct lotteries. Private lotteries were forbidden in 1751, but the Episcopal and Presbyterian churches held them as late as 1814, and the Roman Catholics until 1828.

Above left:
The Charleston County Courthouse stands on the northwest corner of the laws. It was built in 1792 on the site of the first South Carolina State House that burned in 1788. Charles Fraser in his Reminiscences attributes the design to Judge William Drayton. Courtesy of Charleston Post-Courier

Left:
At Fort Motte the British built field works around the large mansion house of Mrs. Rebecca Motte. This painting by Charlestonian John Blake White shows Mrs. Motte giving Gen. Francis Marion and Col. Henry Lee a quiver of arrows with which they set fire to the shingle roof of her mansion, driving out the British. The fire extinguished, Mrs. Motte presided at a sumptuous dinner for officers of both sides. Courtesy of Library of Congress

was restored and the banished allowed to return, with the exception of a few of the worst offenders. The Reverend Mr. Cooper, rector of St. Michael's, refused to take the oath in support of the state Constitution, and the next Sunday his congregation found the doors of the church closed. Cooper and his family returned to England, as did Dr. Garden, leaving his son fighting as an officer in the American army. Louisa Susannah Wells describes leaving in the *Providence* with all the passengers banished except the Captain: "Captain Stevens sinking a ballast stone said 'When that rises, I return!' I really joined him from my heart." Nathaniel Russell, arriving from London, was not allowed to land, and for four months conducted his business from shipboard.

On August 13, 1783, the city was incorporated and Richard Hutson elected the first intendant (mayor), and it received its new and present name—Charleston.

Gradually life returned to normal. The College of Charleston was chartered, and the first classes were taught by Bishop Robert Smith in his rectory at 6 Glebe Street. He had been ordained in Christ Church, Philadelphia, as the first Episcopal Bishop of South Carolina and almost two hundred years later his descendants made it possible for the College to purchase and restore the rectory as the home of the future presidents of that institution.

André Michaux arrived from France to collect botanical specimens for the French Royal gardens, and established the French Botanical Gardens about ten miles up the Neck, where the Charleston Airport is today. He introduced camellias, the ginkgo tree, Chinese tallow tree, crepe myrtle, and chinaberry to this country. Scottish merchants organized the South Carolina Golf Club and played on Harleston's Green, and an act was ratified to move the capital to Columbia, nearer the center of population.

Charles Cotesworth Pinckney, his cousin Charles Pinckney, John Rutledge, and Pierce Butler represented South Carolina at the national Constitutional Convention. Butler was an ex-British army major, who married Colonel Thomas Middleton's daughter Mary, and resigned his British commission to serve in the American Army, and he and Ralph Izard became the first United States Senators from the state.

The most exciting event of the last decade of the century was George Washington's two-week visit in 1791. After breakfast at Snee Farm, Charles Pinckney's home in Christ Church Parish, Washington was met by Edward Rutledge and City Recorder John Bee Holmes at the Haddrell's Point (Mt. Pleasant), and was rowed across the Cooper River in a barge manned by thirteen ship's captains. Accompanied by a flotilla of crowded boats of all kinds and sizes, and two bands, he landed at Prioleau's Wharf at the foot of Queen Street. He recorded in his diary that "The lodgings provided for me in this place were very good, being the furnished house of a Gentleman at present in the Country; but occupied by a person placed there on purpose to accommodate me."

While in Charleston he breakfasted with Mrs. Rutledge, dined at McCrady's Tavern with members of the Cincinnati Society, attended services at both Episcopal churches, was entertained at a concert at the Exchange at which there were "at least 400 ladies, the number and appearance of which exceeded anything of the kind I had ever seen."

His journal has frequent references to the Charleston ladies he met. He remarked on a visit by "a great number of the most respectable ladies of Charleston, the first honour of the kind I had ever experienced, as flattering as singular,"

and had the good fortune to be seated at a state dinner with the wittiest lady in town, Miss Claudia Smith, on one side, and the most beautiful, Mrs. Richard Shubrick, opposite. He climbed to the arcade level of St. Michael's steeple "from whence the whole is seen in one view." He estimated sixteen thousand souls, about eight thousand of them white; described unpaved streets of sand and a number of very good houses of brick and wood but most of the latter. "The Inhabitants are wealthy, Gay and hospitable; appear happy and satisfied with the General Government."

In 1791 the Legislature rejected the petition of Thomas Cole, P. B. Mathews and Mathew Webb on behalf of free men of color, requesting their legal rights to testify in court and to trial by jury, of which the Negro Act of 1740 had deprived them. They argued that the Constitution considered them free citizens in the count for Congressional representation, but state law deprived them of their rights. The slave revolt on the island of Haiti in 1791 brought both black and white refugees to Charleston, as slaves and free blacks accompanied fleeing whites. Governor Pinckney could give no military support to the plea from the Colonial Assembly of San Domingo, as South Carolina was now a part of the United States and unable to wage war independently, but Charleston opened her doors to the refugees and provided temporary housing at the New Market.

The majority were well-educated, including doctors, businessmen, dancing masters, hairdressers, excellent cooks and bakers, artists and musicians, and they enriched the cultural life of the city. Reports of the murder of some two thousand whites and destruction of almost two hundred sugar plantations, nine hundred coffee, cotton and indigo properties, and cruel tortures which the refugees described, sent a chill of foreboding through the Low Country plantation owners.

Charlestonians were seized with enthusiasm for the French and their Revolution, and celebrated Bastille Day with a pageant, artillery salutes and peals from St. Michael's bells, returned to the steeple after their third sea voyage. French privateersmen paraded the streets in a fashion reminiscent of the pirates of a century before, but Charleston's ardor cooled when news of the widespread slaughter in France arrived. Young Francis Kinloch Huger, who sat on Lafayette's knee as a three-year-old when the great general came to Charlestown, tried to rescue him from a prison in Olmutz, but both men were recaptured before they could get out of Austria. Colonel Thomas Pinckney, then the United States minister to England, arranged for Huger's release.

In 1797 Charles Cotesworth Pinckney was sent to Paris by President Adams with John Marshall and Elbridge Guerry to confer with the French in what became known as the XYZ Affair. When the French demanded a bribe of a quarter million dollars before they would negotiate, Pinckney angrily replied, "No, not a sixpence." History books record his words more elegantly, as they were reported by Congressman Robert Goodloe Harper as "Millions for defense, not a cent for tribute!" On his return to Charleston Pinckney was received with a tumultous welcome, and when French attack seemed a possibility, a fort was built in the harbor and given the grand name of Castle Pinckney. The mechanics donated their labor to construct Fort Mechanic on East Battery, and public donations financed a locally built thirty-two gun frigate the *John Adams*. Fortunately all these warlike preparations proved unnecessary; the Franco-American issue was settled without bloodshed and the century ended peacefully.

Charles Cotesworth Pinckney (1746-1825), the son of Charles and Eliza Lucas Pinckney, was educated at Westminister School and Christ College, Oxford, and studied law at Middle Temple, London. A colonel in the Second South Carolina Regiment at the fall of Charlestown, he was paroled with General Moultrie to his cousin Charles' plantation house Snee Farm in Christ Church Parish. As U.S. minister to France, he participated in the XYZ Affair in 1796. Courtesy of South Carolina Historical Society

Left:
From 1790-1807, Charleston enjoyed a large and growing commercial prosperity. It was the depot for large amounts of European merchandise destined for the West Indies, and cargoes moving from those ports eastward. Fac-simile of bill of lading. Courtesy of South Carolina Historical Society

Above:
When war was threatened between France and the U.S., the mechanics (artisans and contractors) of Charleston donated their labor to build Fort Mechanic. Charles Fraser's watercolor shows the fort celebrating the 4th of July not long after its construction. Courtesy of Carolina Art Association

"Charleston is a pious place/and full of pious people/They built a church on Meeting Street/But could not raise the steeple." In 1838 this verse poked irreverent fun at the Circular Congregational Church which still lacked a steeple, though completed in 1806. Both the church and the South Carolina Institute Hall next door, where the Ordinance of Secession was signed, burned in the 1861 fire. Courtesy of South Carolina Historical Society

Chapter Four

"The Most Agreeable Society in America"

1800–1860
Ante-Bellum

For a brief period after the Revolutionary War, Charleston's economy was depressed. Many properties had been ruined, thousands of slaves had been carried off by the British, and waterfront warehouses had been demolished in preparation for the war.

Indigo production was no longer profitable with the loss of the English bounty. It was found, however, that cotton could be grown under the same conditions, and the recently invented cotton gin revolutionized the economic life of the state outside of the rice areas. Rice planters at the same time were making use of the force of the tides to push fresh water into irrigation canals and to drive mills. Cotton and this tidal method of rice cultivation brought a prosperity comparable to that of pre-Revolutionary days.

Charleston was the chief port of entry for the state as merchandise passed through her Custom house on East Bay. New Englanders, Scots and English began to replace the local merchant princes, who for the most part had become planters, and now looked down on those in "trade."

Retail stores filled the east end of Broad, Elliott and Tradd streets and they carried everything from plows to dry goods. On the bay were new warehouses and factors' counting houses. In the bows that are now a part of the Carolina Yacht Club, factors are said to have painted their furniture blue so the cotton and rice displayed there would look whiter by contrast. Cotton could now be shipped down the Santee Canal, completed in 1801 and linking the Santee and Cooper Rivers.

Governor John Drayton described the Carolinian of this period as independent and frank in language; traits that outsiders sometimes took for haughtiness and supercility. The typical Carolinian was polite and totally lacking in "that subtle cunning, which, between individuals, is in some countries constantly on the watch to delude or betray." Drayton also declared that politics never drew lines between friends. He considered the practice of duelling to be quite civilized; in fact, to him it caused respect and consideration for others.

Wealthier Charlestonians lived in the fashion of Europeans: "directed by many of their whims, and influenced by many of their follies," with costly carriages, many servants

and a renowned hospitality. One visitor stated "The small society of rice and cotton planters at Charleston, with their cultivated tastes and hospitable habits, delighted in whatever reminded them of European civilization.

"They were travelers, readers and scholars; the society of Charleston compared well in refinement with that of any city of its size in the world, and English visitors long thought it the most agreeable in America."

A few years later another visitor found "the men are of Idle disposition, fond of pleasures that lead them into a system of dissipation to which they are in a manner wedded…Their principal amusements in the City in the morning is Billiards…and in the Evening cards and Segars…

"For this purpose there are several Clubs every evening where they assemble…With respect to drinking the Carolinians may be compared with the Persians of old, for the more wine he can swallow the more accomplished he conceives himself.

"They are devoted to debauchery and probably carry it to a greater length than any other people…The fair Sex in Charleston, however, are quite of a different character…it may be said that the religious credit of the people of Charleston is vested in the Ladies…there cannot be a more Lovely and amiable female society any where."

Charleston offered a variety of amusements including regular plays and concerts in the winter, and a Vauxhall (pleasure garden) in the summer. Dancing was a favorite amusement at which Charleston ladies excelled.

Gentlemen's hunt clubs met regularly for deer hunting. Although Tarleton had taken some four hundred horses, many from the best stables, extensive studs were established after the Revolution and the pedigrees of race horses became as important as Charleston's blueblood lines. When the Washington Course was laid off in 1792, there began what John Irving, Club Secretary for twenty-five years, called "the golden age of racing" in South Carolina. Stores closed, courts adjourned, schools recessed and "the most venerable and distinguished dignitaries of the land, clergymen and judges, side by side on the course" joined with the hoi polloi for a carnival week, and Irving, who could never resist the opportunity for atrocious puns, declared the ladies' stand held a "galaxy of beauty." The Jockey Club opened its Wednesday night dinner with the president leading the singing of "The High-Mettled Racer" followed by much hammering of tables and rattling of glasses, and the ball on Friday was the grand climax of a week of celebration.

As tidal rice culture developed, the older abandoned fields became breeding places for mosquitoes, so that by the nineteenth century summer removal from the country had become a necessity. Although it was not realized that mosquitoes carried fever, it was apparent that a white person ran a fatal risk by spending a night on a plantation between May and November, so planters were frequently in town six months of the year. They often came at the end of January for the Dancing Assemblies, concerts, races, and St. Cecelia balls, as well as for settling accounts and conferring with their factors.

The factor was the planter's general agent—he bought all the supplies for the plantation, furnished money for the crop, handled its sale, and kept accounts. He looked after the planter's children when they arrived in town for school and was their "friend, advisor and confidant." The planter usually returned home in March to sow the rice, but by May the family left again—some to the "Salt" as the sea islands were called, or to the pinelands like Summerville or Summerton, named for the season they were occupied.

Wealthier families traveled abroad or to Newport, Rhode Island—known as the "Carolina Hospital"—though it was remarked that if one observed the tombstones in Trinity graveyard in Newport with the names of Carolinians, he might question its success as a hospital. A German visitor, Johann Schoepf, found Charleston "one of the finest of American Cities," but also quipped "Carolina is in the spring a paradise, in the summer a hell, and in the autumn a hospital." All Charlestonians who could avoided the "hell."

A supercilious English officer Francis Hall described it: "All the inhabitants who can afford it, then fly to a barren sand-bank in the harbour, called Sullivan's Island, containing one well, and a few palmettoes; here they dwell in miserable wooden tenements, trembling in every storm, lest, (as very frequently happens) their hiding places should be blown from over their heads, or deluged by an inundation of the sea." Charlestonians continue this practice today and fly to Sullivan's Island over the Cooper River Bridge, but the day of the "miserable wooden tenements" is long gone. Lieutenant Hall would never recognize the former barren sand-bank, which now boasts substantial year-round homes.

In 1800 Charleston's high land was frequently cut into by tidal creeks and marsh—where Murray Boulevard is today was then water. The Ashley River lapped at the edge of Isaac Parker's garden at 6 Gibbes Street, and water came up to the present Lenwood and Tradd Street. Salt water and marsh came as far as Beaufain Street, with fingers of land jutting out here and there. Colonel William Washington owned the fine frame house built by Thomas Savage at the corner of South Battery and Church streets, and a block to the west stood "that large, genteel and pleasant situated House on the South Bay, the property of Mr. John Ashe."

On the east, Fort Mechanic was the only structure south of Granville Bastion, and it wasn't until the sea wall was strengthened with cobblestones (after the great storm of 1804 swept away its logs and planks) that the first house was built by George Chisolm at 39 East Battery, constructed at an angle to afford a fine view of the harbor.

Not one of the street names remained in Christopher Gadsden's Middlesex—Virginia and Wilkes disappeared, and Pitt was absorbed by Laurens, and Massachusetts by Alexander, but his son Philip's brick house with marble quoins still stands tall at 329 East Bay.

Just to the north where Gadsden had met in Alexander Mazyck's pasture under the Liberty Tree, Mazyckborough was laid out. Wraggborough was divided among the heirs of Joseph Wragg, and the streets were given the names of the six Wragg children, five girls and a son John. This was a rural area when Wragg's grandson, Joseph Manigault built his large brick mansion (350 Meeting) designed by his brother Gabriel in the new Adamesque or Federal style. Lawyer and rice planter Gabriel brought architectural books with him on his return from London, and became Charleston's first amateur or "gentleman" architect.

Gabriel designed the First Bank of the United States, built on the site of the beef market that had burned in the 1796 fire. Today this is Charleston's City Hall and represents the northeast corner of the Four Corners of Law. Another of Manigault's works is the South Carolina Society Hall at 72 Meeting Street, designed for the schoolhouse of the former Two-Bitt Club. The Society still holds its meetings here, and

the hall on its second floor with a small musician's stand is a popular setting for debutante parties, wedding receptions and other social functions.

Nathaniel Russell built what is one of the finest Federal style mansions in the city at 51 Meeting Street, with a beautiful three-storied cantilevered stair. He became so wealthy that he was referred to as the "King of the Yankees," and in 1819 was named the first president of the newly organized New England Society.

William Blacklock from London was another merchant who made a fortune during the European war between France and England, and he built his handsome suburban villa in Harleston Village when this section was virtually open country, and he could look from his north piazza across the marshes of Coming's Creek.

In this notice published in 1807 is seen the Orphan House Chapel on Vanderhorst Street designed by Robert Mills.

Thomas Middleton painted this picture in 1827, describing on the back how "a number of gentlemen friends and Amateurs in musick, frequently met at each others houses during the sultryness of a Summer afternoon, to beguile away the time in listening to the soothing strains of their own music." Thomas is in the smock, his brother Henry sits in the left foreground, and their brother Arthur, the host, wears the hat. Courtesy of Carolina Art Association

This prosperity came to a temporary halt with the War of 1812. John C. Calhoun, Langdon Cheves, William Lowndes, and David R. Williams, all young South Carolina congressmen, were among the "War Hawks" who kept agitating for war with Great Britain. Calhoun wrote the bill declaring war, and one-sixth of the country's generals were from South Carolina. Major-General Thomas Pinckney was put in command of forces in the Southeast; David Williams was Major-Gen-

Charleston City Hall was designed by Gabriel Manigault for the first Bank of the United States. Before stucco was applied to cover earthquake damage, its Carolina grey brick provided a rich contrast with the marble trim. In the pediment is the seal of Charleston, and its motto, "Aedes, Mores, Juraque Curat;" she guards her buildings, customs and laws. Courtesy of Historic Charleston Foundation. Photo by Dick Burbage

In the drawing room of the Joseph Manigault House, c. 1803, hangs the portrait of Mrs. Peter Manigault, painted by Jeremiah Theus in 1757. The tea table is Charleston made. Property of the Charleston Museum, the Manigault house is one of the city's half dozen house museums that are open to the public year round. Courtesy of Charleston County PRT

eral of the Fourth Division; General George Izard served under Major-General Wade Hampton on the Canadian front; and Major Arthur P. Hayne fought under Jackson at the Battle of New Orleans. Governor Henry Middleton, Arthur's son, reported that the state's quota of five thousand troops had been made up chiefly of volunteers.

British vessels looted plantations, captured ships, and kept Charleston on the alert. For several years the British blockade made the port of Charleston inactive. Fort Mechanic was rebuilt, and cannon were placed along the waterfront, and lines of fortifications across the Neck have left their memory in the name of Line Street.

Following the war Charleston again was host to a president, when James Monroe, escorted by secretary of War John C. Calhoun and Major-General Thomas Pinckney, was rowed across the Cooper in an elegant barge manned by twenty-

one members of the Marine Society. Monroe was taken to the lines by a military escort and hundreds of citizens on horseback. After reviewing the troops, he proceeded to St. Andrew's Hall through streets of cheering onlookers. He visited forts, the theatre and had breakfast at the villa of Joel R. Poinsett, and the St. Cecelia Society gave a grand concert and ball in his honor.

In her delightful book *Charleston The Place and the People,* Mrs. St. Julien Ravenel tells us that Mr. Poinsett's breakfasts were social events. Poinsett, a distinguished diplomat, was as colorful as the Mexican Fire Plant, or Poinsettia, which he introduced into this country when he returned after serving as U.S. Minister to Mexico.

He had been a congressman, would become secretary of war under President Van Buren, and was widely traveled. A friend of Czar Alexander I, he turned down a position as

Nathaniel Russell's House at 51 Meeting Street represents one of Charleston's finest Federal style mansions. It is headquarters of the Historic Charleston Foundation, who open it to the public year round. Courtesy of Historic Charleston Foundation. Photo by Louis Schwartz

William Blacklock, wealthy merchant, built one of the most distinguished Federal houses in Charleston when the Harleston Village area was open country. Owned today by the College of Charleston, it serves as a faculty-alumni club. Courtesy of Historic Charleston Foundation. Photo by Louis Schwartz

colonel in the Russian army, traveled through the land of the Tartars with an escort of three hundred Cossacks and was presented to Napoleon. He helped frame Chile's constitution, led insurgent forces in Peru, and when he came back to Charleston, he became a leader of the Union party. Interested in botany, Poinsett was one of the founders of the National Institute for the Promotion of Science, forerunner of the Smithsonian. It is easy to believe that he must indeed have been "the most delightful of hosts and best of raconteurs."

General Lafayette returned to Charleston in 1825, forty-eight years after he had first arrived with Baron DeKalb, and the old French general received an enthusiastic welcome. This time he had come from laying the cornerstone of Robert Mills' monument to DeKalb, who had been killed in the battle of Camden in 1780. A guard of honor met Lafayette's coach on the Meeting Street Road, and members of the Washington Light Infantry and the Fusilier Francaise escorted him into the city.

Lafayette was accompanied by his son, George Washington Lafayette, Governor Manning and his old friend Francis Kinloch Huger, and they traveled through Charleston's streets with thousands of the townspeople throwing flowers, applauding and following behind the coach.

At George and Meeting streets Generals Thomas and Charles Pinckney joined the parade and the three men had an emotional reunion—with kisses on both cheeks in the French fashion. Lafayette stayed in St. Andrew's Hall and was entertained royally with public and private dinners as well as a fireworks display and a grand public ball at the Charleston Theatre at Broad and New streets.

In his *Statistics of South Carolina*, published in 1826, Robert Mills states: "A glorious destiny awaits South Carolina." He described Charleston as being higher and drier than formerly (debris raised the elevation). Several of its principal streets, (most of East Bay, all of Market, Elliott and the lower parts of Broad, Tradd and Queen streets), were paved with stone ballast, the footways paved with brick and shaded with Pride of India trees, locally known as Chinaberry. Rainwater ran off through brick drains under the streets, or was held for drinking and cooking in cisterns.

At the public marketplace he found the fresh fish and vegetables, venison, beef, and veal particularly fine, and sweet oranges could be bought for one dollar per hundred. To the south of East Bay a high stone wall had been built with the interior filled in and forming a promenade looking out over a harbor that had "vessels in full sail, entering and departing the harbor, the numerous sail boats, fishing canoes, and the rich planters' barges, handsomely painted and canvassed over." Sullivan's Island "appears like a city, floating upon the bosom of the wide waters, and glittering in the sun beams."

For twenty-five cents steam boats, sail boats or packets could be taken to the Island, which Mills declared "may

Salt water bathing could be found in two bath houses in Charleston. One was off the Battery, another at the foot of Laurens Street, and those who preferred warm baths could find them at 99 Church Street.

Maps of Charleston as early as 1841 show the location of a Bathing House extending into the Ashley River from South Battery. It was completely destroyed in the storm of 1885. Courtesy of South Carolina Historical Society

properly be considered as a part of Charleston, as its inhabitants (when the island is inhabited) are made up of our citizens, and the island served as "a summer retreat for pleasure and health."

He computed the population as seventeen thousand whites, twenty thousand slaves, and three thousand free-blacks, including in the figures the "suburbs" or Neck. Over half the houses were of brick, with tile or slate roofs, and the public buildings, churches and the Exchange (then the customhouse and post office) he described as showing how "faithfully public work was executed in 'the olden times.'"

The Charleston-born Mills was America's first native professional architect. He studied under James Hoban, who was in Charleston until he left in 1792 to work on the White House.

Mills worked in Washington as a draftsman under Hoban, used Jefferson's library as Monticello, and also learned engineering as assistant to Benjamin Latrobe. His public buildings are found up and down the eastern seaboard including the Washington Monument and Treasury Building in the capital city.

Among his Charleston structures are the Fireproof Building on Meeting Street, the old Marine Hospital on Franklin Street, and the First Baptist Church, which Mills immodestly called "the best specimen of correct taste in architecture of the modern buildings in this city."

Churches, the city government, and private individuals were putting money into buildings. Charleston selected Philadelphian William A. Strickland to design the central portion of the College of Charleston, and Thomas U. Walter, also a Philadelphian, was the architect for the Hibernian Society Hall on Meeting Street.

There were capable local architects also. When the wings and the large portico were added to the main College of Charleston building, it was Edward Brickell White who designed them, and the porter's lodge and ironwork fence as well. White was the son of John Blake White, an artist, dramatist and lawyer of Charleston. Young White was an engineering graduate of West Point, and one of the most prolific and eclectic architects to work in Charleston.

His designs include two Gothic style churches, the French Huguenot and Grace Protestant Episcopal, and Centenary Methodist modeled after a Doric temple. White designed the Market Hall like a small Roman temple and used Tuscan columns on St. Johannes Lutheran Church. St. Philip's distinctive spire also is one of White's contributions to Charleston architecture.

Another Charleston architect, Edward C. Jones, designed Westminster Presbyterian Church at 275 Meeting (now Trinity Methodist). He designed a house at 26 South Battery for a second Col. Ashe in Italianate style.

Francis D. Lee not only invented the spar torpedo which was attached to the semi-submersibles in the Civil War, and planned coastal fortifications, but left the city a Moorish style bank at 141 East Bay Street.

Residences built during this period were sometimes ostentatious, lacking the restrained taste and elegance of the pre-Revolutionary mansions, but giving Charleston fascinating additions to her architectural treasures. In the 1830s and '40s the Greek Revival style became popular with Charlestonians as well as the rest of the country.

This style was used in the buildings that replaced those destroyed in the great fire of 1838. A portico and massive columns appeared on the new Beth Elohim synagogue on Hasell Street.

Plantation barges rounding the bend of the Ashley River on the way to the Bay front wharves got an impressive view of William Roper's massive portico with its tremendous Ionic columns. It was built the same year that rice planter Col. William Alston bought the Edmonston House at 21 East Battery for his son Charles, who flaunted his coat of arms on the parapet.

In Harleston village Edisto Island cotton planter I. Jenkins Mikell built his town house in what was described as an American-version of an Italian villa, topping his columns with ram's head or "Jupiter" capitals.

The same year that Poinsett returned from Mexico, nineteen-year-old Edgar A. Perry was promoted to Sergeant-Major at Fort Moultrie. His real name was Edgar Allan Poe, and he was so fascinated with Sullivan's Island and its palmetto-covered sand dunes, dark swamps and marshes, that he used the island as setting for three of his stories: *The Oblong Box*, *The Balloon Hoax*, and *The Gold Bug*.

Edmund Ravenel, an American pioneer in the field of conchology had a summer home on the island, and is said to have been the model for the hero William Legrand in *The Gold Bug*. Dr. Ravenel published the first scientific catalog of sea shells of America, and his nephew, St. Julien, would later develop the phosphate deposits on his plantation in St. Andrew's Parish into fertilizer. Lewis R. Gibbes, a graduate of the recently founded Medical College of South Carolina, started his career as a distinguished botanist. John Bachman, pastor of St. John's Lutheran Church, worked with John James Audubon on his book *Birds of America*, and was co-author with him of the *Quadrupeds of America*. Two of Bachman's daughters married two of Audubon's sons.

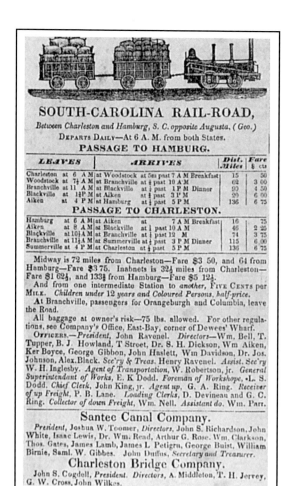

The South Carolina Canal and Railroad Company was chartered in 1827 to build a railroad in order to divert the trade of the upper Savannah River from the city of Savannah to Charleston. When the 136-mile South Carolina Railroad from Charleston to Hamburg was completed in October, 1833, it was the longest in the world. Courtesy of South Carolina Historical Society

On Christmas Day, 1830, the "Best Friend of Charleston" became the first steam locomotive to pull a train of cars in regular service on the American continent. A year later the Charleston Courier reported "on Saturday last, the first anniversary of the commencement of the railroad was celebrated. The first trip was performed with two pleasure cars attached, and a small carriage filled for the occasion, upon which was a detachment of U.S. troops and a field piece." Courtesy of South Carolina Historical Society

Arthur Middleton's youngest son, John Izard, returned briefly to Charleston, having lived most of his life in Italy and France, where he was a member of Mme. Recamier's salon. He was an excellent landscape artist, and wrote and illustrated the work *Grecian Remains in Italy,* published in 1812. He was described by Professor Charles Eliot Norton as "the first American classical archeologist." His older brother Henry, who was minister to Russia for ten years, returned to his estate at Middleton Place with portraits of the Czar Nicholas I and the Czarina.

While life on the surface seemed serene, there were disturbing signs that all was not well. Stories brought by refugees from the Santa Domingo slave uprising had shocked Charleston, and in 1822 there occurred what had always been dreaded in an area where slaves outnumbered whites—a slave rebellion.

The instigator was Denmark Vesey, a former slave who purchased his freedom with $600 of his $1500 winnings in the East Bay Street Lottery in 1800. He became a carpenter with such a good reputation that he was not arrested until several days after being charged, when the proof was too strong to doubt.

Vesey's former master had been a slave trader with whom Vesey had traveled, and he was familiar with the rebellions in both Santa Domingo and Haiti.

His co-conspirators were almost all trusted slaves of leading Charlestonians, generally of excellent character and in the confidence of their masters. They planned to seize the guard house opposite St. Michael's, the powder magazines, military stores, and arsenals. They even hired a white barber to make wigs and whiskers of white people's hair in order to disguise themselves when passing the guards.

Vesey did not trust house slaves, because being close to their masters they might remain loyal to them. In fact it was two slaves who were approached to join the conspiracy who did report it to their owners.

One hundred thirty-one conspirators were arrested. At the trial, a horrified community learned that the conspirators planned to murder all white males and any slaves who did not join with them, to ravish the women, and sail to Santo Domingo.

One witness stated that there were about nine thousand slaves involved from both country and city, but no actual count could be made. The barber testified against Vesey in a court composed of the most respected citizens. Vesey himself died without making a statement. Thirty-five of the conspirators were hanged, and the remainder were deported.

The result was tighter controls over slaves and free blacks. A state arsenal was built on Boundary Street, which later became the home of the military college of the South, the Citadel. The Guard was reorganized and patrolled every night after curfew, announced by the ringing of St. Michael's large bell at nine o'clock in winter, and ten in summer.

The Seamen's Acts were passed, by which free blacks on vessels arriving in port were put in jail until the ship left, and if the ship's master didn't pay their room and board they could be sold to take care of it. Free blacks were not allowed to enter the state, and if they left could not return. Sarah and Angelina Grimke were so horrified at the punishments that slaves received in the Work House, where they were whipped and made to walk tread-mills to grind corn, that they became abolitionists, and gave Theodore Weld sto-

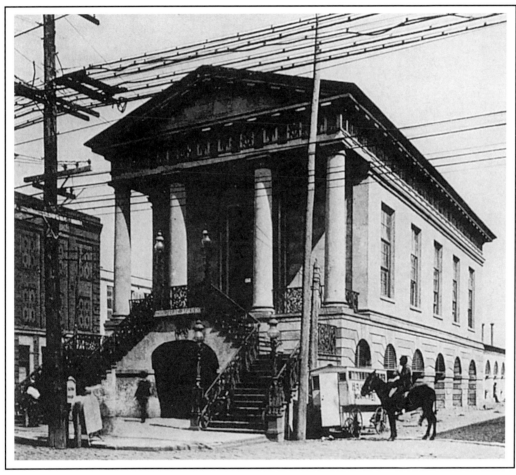

Edward Brickell White designed the Market Hall, built in 1841, as a Roman Temple with a freize of bucrania. This was most appropriate because the sheds to its rear included a beef market with some 112 stalls, as well as three sections for vegetables, a fish market and storerooms. Courtesy of South Carolina Historical Society

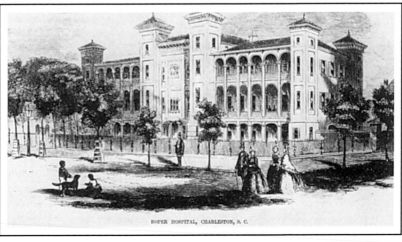

ROPER HOSPITAL, CHARLESTON, S. C.

Edward C. Jones designed the new Roper Hospital, completed in 1852, in Italianate style. Philanthropist Thomas Roper bequeathed $30,000 to the Medical Society of South Carolina for the establishment of a community hospital under their trusteeship. Damaged in the great earthquake of 1886, the wings were demolished in 1913, and the main part of the building became the Marlboro Apartments at 140 Queen Street. Courtesy of South Caroliniana Library

The Charleston Theatre on the west side of Meeting Street just south of Market, opened in 1837, and burned in the great fire of 1861. Courtesy of Charleston Library Society

Hours and rectors have changed since this photograph was made of St. Michael's churchyard gates, work of J.A.W. Iusti. Many illustrious Charlestonians are buried behind the brick wall, as the funeral urn motif in the gate design indicates. Courtesy of Historic Charleston Foundation

ries of the workhouse for inclusion in his book *American Slavery As It Is*. The sisters went to Philadelphia and became leaders in both abolition and women's suffrage, Angelina speaking against slavery and eventually becoming the wife of Weld.

The more vehemently abolitionists spoke out against slavery, the more Charlestonians, ever resentful of outside criticism, felt compelled to support it. Governor Thomas Bennett, in his message to the legislature, expressed the South's impossible position: "Slavery abstractly considered would perhaps lead every mind to the same conclusion; but the period has long since passed when a correction might have been applied. The treasures of learning, the gifts of ingenuity and the stores of experience have been exhausted, in the fruitless search for a practical remedy. The institution is established—the evil is entailed and we can do no more than steadily to pursue that course indicated by stern necessity and a not less imperious policy."

The Tariff Act of 1828 inflamed the state, which labeled it the "Tariff of Abominations," and a committee of Charleston City Council reported that because of the tariff, business and industry were moving away, that many stores had closed, houses were empty and grass was growing in formerly busy streets. William Gregg's pleas for diversification of agriculture and industrial growth fell on deaf ears, as settlers moved to the fertile lands in the Lower South and Southwest. With cotton rapidly becoming "King," and with planters and farmers opposing manufacturing for fear it would endanger slavery, South Carolina was on a shaky economic footing. Within a few years this one-crop economy and its attendant

Edward Brickell White added a massive portico and wings to William A. Strickland's simple College of Charleston. For over 150 years it has housed classrooms and administrative offices. Officially named Harrison Randolph Hall, it is affectionately called "Old Main." Courtesy of College of Charleston

Above:
26 South Battery was built in Italianate style for Col. John Algernon Sydney Ashe, son of the Col. Ashe who built 32 South Battery. It is a rare example of residential work by architect Edward C. Jones. Courtesy of Historic Charleston Foundation. Photo by Robert M. Smith Jr.

Left:
The Regency style house built in 1828 by Charles Edmondston at 21 East Battery was remodeled ten years later by wealthy planter Charles Alston who added a third story piazza and parapet with his family coat of arms. Courtesy of Charleston County PRT

evils were to put an end to the Southern way of life.

In 1830 when heated Congressional debates broke out over nullification, Senator Robert Y. Hayne of Charleston and Daniel Webster of Massachusetts led the opposing factions. Haynes argued that the several states had acted as sovereign nations in signing the Constitution and had the right to secede if they liked. He cited the Hartford Convention when New Englanders threatened to withdraw from the Union during the War of 1812. In Charleston, Calhoun, Hayne and their supporters conferred in the drawing room at 94 Church Street, to draft the Nullification Ordinance.

Unionist leaders included James L. Petigru, Joel Poinsett, Colonel William Drayton, William Gilmore Simms, David R. Williams, and Henry Middleton. Poinsett was issued arms and ammunition from Army stores at Castle Pinckney and he and his Unionist followers drilled secretly, while the Nullifiers, providing their own weapons, openly prepared for possible conflict. Mass meetings were held in the summer of 1830. The hall where the Nullifiers met opened on King Street, so they suggested that the Unionists use the Meeting Street exit of their building to avoid a confrontation. This so enraged the Unionists that they tore down fences to exit on King, and in the ensuing melee Drayton, Petigru and Poinsett were hit by brickbats.

The legislative election that followed saw voters bribed with wine, women and money, and promises of political patronage; others were bought and kept drunk until time to go to the polls.

The Nullifiers won by a fairly small majority. When the Ordinance of Nullification was passed by the General Assembly, declaring the Federal tariff laws of 1828 and 1832 null and void within the state, President Andrew Jackson issued a Force Bill and threatened to invade South Carolina with more than fifty thousand volunteer troops. He sent both armed forces and a fleet to stand by, anticipating the bill's enforcement on the first of January, 1833. The state guard at the arsenal was strengthened, and the Unionist convention in Columbia declared they would defend their rights with arms if necessary. Fortunately, Kentucky's senator Henry Clay proposed a compromise and South Carolina repealed the Ordinance, which settled the question for the time being and provided a brief respite.

When word spread that abolitionist tracts had arrived by mail, the Post Office was broken into and the tracts seized and burned in a public bonfire. Members of local Episcopal congregations cancelled subscriptions to the *Gospel Messenger* which circulated "Incendiary" and "infamous" publications sent by the Anti-Slavery Society of New York. The *Mercury* restored their faith in the local publication, however, when it reported that the offending *Gospel Messenger* in this case was a *Northern* publication.

During the Mexican War, funds had been provided by Charleston City Council for uniforms for the Charleston Company of the Palmetto Regiment—nicknamed the "Tigers" by General Winfield Scott—and the Palmetto flag had been the first to fly over the walls of Chapultepec when Santa Anna evacuated Mexico City. Charlestonians felt strongly that they had the right to take their slaves into the lands they had helped gain possession of, and when Pennsylvania congressman David Wilmot proposed an amendment excluding slavery in the Mexican Session, South Carolina considered this would mean the end of the Union.

Robert Barnwell Rhett, editor of the *Mercury*, agitated for

Shown is Rembrandt Peale's portrait of John C. Calhoun, States Rights Leader and advocate of Nullification. Calhoun served in Congress from 1811 to 1817, and was Secretary of War, Vice-President and Secretary of State at various times between his terms as Senator. He was so idolized in his native state that a popular joke declared that "when Calhoun took snuff, the whole of Carolina sneezed." Courtesy of Carolina Art Association

immediate secession, and open war if necessary. Rhett was one of the six Smith brothers who took the name of their pirate-fighting great-grandfather—Joseph Smith changed his name to Izard—and as one faithful retainer put it, "All the Smiths is rats and lizards now!"

Calhoun was dying of tuberculosis, and so ill that he sat in the Senate while Senator Mason of Virginia read his two-hour speech to congress for him. Calhoun predicted that "the agitation of the subject of slavery will, if not prevented by some timely and effective measure, end in disunion." If the stronger Northern states were not willing to settle the question fairly for the South, then "let the States we both represent agree to separate and part in peace. If you are unwilling that we should part in peace, tell us so, and we shall know what to do when you reduce the question to submission or resistance."

Calhoun died before Congress passed the Compromise of 1850, and though he was a native of Abbeville District, his family agreed to his burial in Charleston. At 8:00 a.m. April 25, a cannon announced the arrival of the steamer *Nina* with dignitaries and Congressional committees accompanying Calhoun's body. His remains were placed on a funeral car modeled after the funeral car of Napoleon—drawn by six horses with mourning trappings trailing the ground, and each attended by a groom in deep black. Accompanied by muffled drums, they slowly moved to the Citadel Square on Boundary Street where the body was formally surrendered to Governor Seabrook, and by him to Mayor Hutchison.

The funeral cortege was tremendous—ten divisions met at various points in the city and marched to the square—troops, fire companies, Masonic orders, societies, political officers, seamen, clergy, professors, students, citizens on foot and on horseback, and a two-hundred man Honor Guard, including Petigru, D.E. Huger, Jr.; Ralph, Thomas, and Henry A.

Henry Jackson's 1846 view of Charleston is from the site of Calhoun and Rutledge with Bennett's millpond in the foreground. The two large houses on the left still stand on Calhoun St., and near the center is the tower of St. Paul's Church, now the Episcopal Cathedral of St. Luke and St. Paul. The pond was filled in 1875, and for many years was the site of the Charleston Museum. Courtesy of Carolina Art Association

This 1842 map of the city shows the recently completed United States arsenal, the railroad station on Line Street, the terminal at Mary, and Gadsden's huge wharf, as well as many other buildings, and large ponds. Calhoun Street is still Boundary, Lenwood is Greenhill, and Rutledge still Pinckney. Courtesy of Carolina Art Association

Shown is States Rights and Union ticket broadside of 1832. The Union party was defeated and the Nullifiers got control of South Carolina. Courtesy of South Carolina Historical Society

Middleton; Rawlins Lowndes, John Rutledge, Edward McCrady, Henry Trescott, Charles Fraser, and Thomas R. Waring. Buildings were draped with mourning; on Meeting at Hayne large sable curtains closed the "mart and avenue of trade;" across Meeting hung banners reading "Tha Nation Mourns" and "South Carolina Mourns." Even St. Philip's steeple was hung with black. All business was closed, and with bells tolling, minute guns firing, muffled drums rolling, and a military band playing a dirge, the procession moved down King to Hasell, to Meeting, around White Point, up the Bay to Broad and to City Hall. It was the largest procession, it was said, ever seen in Charleston, taking two hours to pass any one spot.

At City Hall, the iron sarcophagus, in which the body came from Washington, was placed under a magnificent canopy surmounted by three white eagles holding black crepe in their beaks. The Honor Guard took turns standing watch as Calhoun lay in state until the next day. Thousands paid tribute, ascending the front steps under arches of palmettoes, women throwing flowers on the bier and covering it with bouquets. At dawn, bells of churches and public institutions began tolling, and continued until sunset, pausing only during the funeral services at St. Philip's. Bishop Christopher E. Gadsden, Calhoun's classmate at Yale, officiated.

Interment was in a temporary vault—a raised tomb lined with cedar in the western churchyard, and in 1880 the present massive sarcophagus was erected by the State Legislature.

It is ironic that Calhoun's great oratory and remarkable talents should have been devoted to a cause that was to destroy the South which held him in such honor. The controversy in which he had played so prominent a role, unfortunately remained very much alive.

With passage of the Kansas-Nebraska Act, South Carolina raised thousands of dollars and Carolinians rushed to sway the elections in "bloody" Kansas. Rhett's newspaper continued to urge secession. Petigru won $2,500 damages for a poor woodchopper who was beaten by members of St. Bartholomew Parish for simply being a Yankee, and a few Northern sympathizers were tarred and feathered. As the long hot summer dragged on, Charlestonians became more determined to secede should Lincoln win the national presidential election.

Historian David Duncan Wallace labels the period from 1832 to 1860 the bitter generation: "For South Carolina a generation in which her aristocracy reached its highest splendor and her poor a deep degradation, and the proudest society in America desperately staked its all on an obsolete economic order against the power of modern life constantly upbuilding a mighty North; a period of large illiteracy, of absolutely or relatively declining commerce, of a ceaseless drain of population and capital to the West, of wasting soil; a period in which the intellect of South Carolina had ceased to grow. Such were the results of South Carolina's binding herself to slavery and committing her mind to the support of impossible ideas."

In an editorial advocating secession, Rhett, referring to the Legislature which was on the verge of meeting wrote: "The eyes of the whole country, and most especially of the resistance party of the Southern States, is (sic) intently turned upon the conduct of this body." The statement was strangely reminiscent of Rutledge's speech of eighty-four years earlier—this time, however, the outcome would be far different.

Secession meeting takes place in front of the Mills House on Meeting Street. Opening in 1853, the Mills House was the first structure in Charleston in which both running water and steam heat were used on a large scale. At the opening banquet a poem to Otis Mills, the "Jacob Astor" of Charleston, was recited: "O 'tis Mills, 'tis Mills, 'tis Mills/In statue like a steeple/He's built a home in Meeting-Street/For all the Southern people/O 'tis Mills, 'tis Mills, 'tis Mills/He's acted well his part/With Yankee skill he's found his way/Right to the Southern heart." Courtesy of Citadel Archives

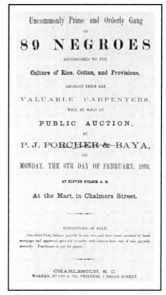

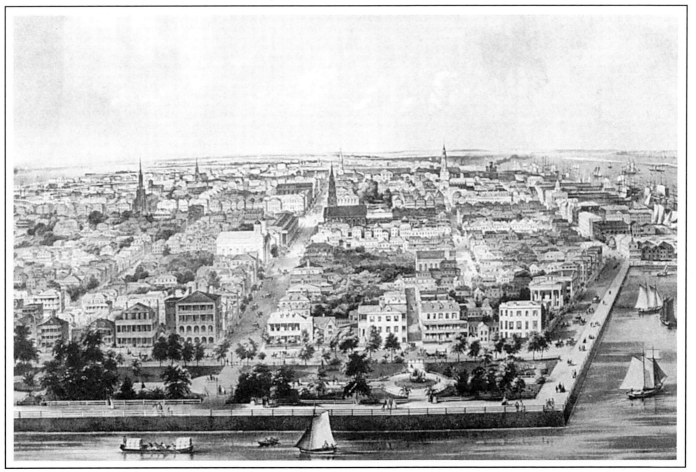

As harbor fortifications exchanged shots with Sumter April 12, 1861, "The anxiety was awful," Mrs. Ravenel tells us. "Those batteries were filled with the men of the town. Everyone from eighteen to sixty was there, and as the hours went on a silent, mute dread took possession. Not a woman looking on but had her heart on one of those islands. 'Have you any relative there?' asked a stranger of one young girl. 'My five brothers,' she answered." Courtesy of United States Department of the Interior National Park Service

Chapter Five

"Too small for a republic and too large for an insane asylum"

1860–1865
Civil War

The story goes that when a stranger to Columbia asked James L. Petigru where the insane asylum was located, Petigru pointed to the First Baptist Church where the Secession Convention was meeting. Whether he actually made the remark that "South Carolina is too small for a republic and too large for an insane asylum" is moot. However, when the bells proclaimed the passage of the Ordinance of Secession, Petigru heard them as firebells which "have this day set a blazing torch to the temple of constitutional liberty, and please God, we shall have no more peace forever."

From today's perspective it would seem that one must have been slightly mad to proclaim as Congressman George McDuffie did at the Nullification Convention: "We would infinitely prefer that the territory of the State should be the cemetery of freemen than the habitation of slaves," when he represented a state that already was over fifty percent slave. To the Carolinian of 1860, however, the black was a chattel, and for many until some hundred years later, was still Ralph Ellison's "invisible man."

When smallpox broke out in Columbia, the Convention moved to Charleston's St. Andrew's Society Hall, just next door to the former residence of John Rutledge, who had been elected president when South Carolina seceded from Britain in 1776.

On December 20, Broad Street was jammed with people when a shout arose that the Secession Act had passed. Like a shock wave the news traveled through Charleston and then by telegraph wires across the nation. "THE UNION IS DISSOLVED" read big black headlines in 6,000 extras that hit the street 15 minutes later and caused cheer after cheer from their readers. Rhett's pen flew: "Business was immediately suspended. The church bells rang out their joyous peals. The artillery salutes were soon heard thundering from the citadel. New flags were everywhere thrown to the breeze. The volunteers instinctively donned their uniforms, and were seen hurrying to and fro about the streets." At night there were bonfires and fireworks—houses and businesses were illuminated—lanterns hung on the "beautiful liberty pole at the head of Hayne street" and processions and bands and shouting people kept the town at a fever pitch until after midnight.

The members of the convention felt that this was so momentous a decision, that formal signing of the document should take place in a hall that could accommodate more witnesses than could St. Andrew's. That afternoon they met again, and solemnly proceeded down Broad Street and up Meeting to the South Carolina Institute Hall where they signed the document. When the fire of 1861 burned both of these buildings in a wide swath of destruction from the Cooper River to the marshes of the Ashley, the northern newspapers declared that the fire had been sent by the Lord in retribution for Charleston boasting of being the cradle of secession.

Excitement ran high as politicians harangued and military companies formed. Dr. John Cheves, who would construct the torpedo defenses used in the harbor during the war, created a "most lifelike and ferocious rattlesnake" which coiled round the palmetto that served as Christmas tree for his brother Langdon's family. Langdon was designer of a reconnaissance balloon used in the Seven Days campaign, and of Fort Wagner on Morris Island. His daughter Mamie wrote her cousin: "We are all very patriotically engaged in making flags. Papa is drawing a very ferocious alligator for mines," an alligator being a wooden device fastened on the prow of ships to detonate mines.

On December 26, Major Robert Anderson, commanding U.S. troops at Fort Moultrie, moved his men under cover of darkness into Fort Sumter, still unfinished on the Middle Ground, the same shoal that the British ship *Acteon* had grounded on during the battle of Carolina Day in 1776. Anderson's orders were to refrain from hostile actions, but to hold the fort unless its defense seemed hopeless.

Anderson was in a difficult position. His Kentucky background, his Georgian wife, and his many ties of friendship to the community of Charleston made his sympathies lie with the South; his duty was to the North and the Union.

The *Mercury* reported that Charleston was "thrown into a state of the wildest excitement," by the news that Anderson had transferred to Sumter. People climbed steeples and cupolas of public buildings, telescopes were brought out, but all that could be seen was dense smoke from Fort Moultrie and schooners unloading at Fort Sumter. A reporter was hastily dispatched to the former, but found a sentinel barring his way. He was told by islanders that the smoke was from burning gun carriages and that the guns had been tarred and spiked.

The next day Governor Pickens took over Castle Pinckney, Fort Moultrie and the arsenal with half a million dollars of munitions. Stowed away on the steamer taking the troops to assault Fort Moultrie, which proved, of course, to be empty, was John McCrady, professor of engineering and physics at the College of Charleston. Learning that his two brothers were with the forces, he had smuggled himself aboard. Volunteering his services, he was detailed to build a battery on Morris Island, and was not missed by the college until after the Christmas recess!

On January 9, the Federal ship *Star of the West* attempted to reinforce Sumter with some two hundred men and supplies. Major P.F. Stevens, Superintendent of the Citadel, commanded a detachment of forty cadets manning the battery called Fort Morris on Morris Island. This battery dominated the main channel, and as the supply ship moved within range, Cadet George E. Haynsworth of Sumter County pulled the lanyard of No. 1 gun, and the round shot splashed across the bow of the steamer. She ran up a huge garrison flag and continued on course, until she was hit three times by the cadets' fire, then Fort Moultrie fired, and with no sign from Sumter, the Federal ship turned and headed towards the bar.

President Jefferson Davis of the Confederate States appointed Brig. General Pierre G.T. Beauregard, army engineer and artillery expert of New Orleans, as commander of Confederate forces at Charleston. Beauregard set up headquarters at 39 Meeting Street. As Federal shelling reached further and further into the town, he was to move his offices accordingly further north until he occupied the Robinson-Aiken house at 48 Elizabeth Street.

By April Beauregard had Fort Sumter surrounded by a "ring of fire." When word came that Lincoln was sending reinforcements to Sumter, and Anderson refused Beauregard's demand to surrender, on April 12 at 3:30 a.m. a star shell rose over the harbor from Fort Johnson and exploded over the parade ground above the fort. At this signal the ring roared into action as Charlestonians crowded the Battery, and sat on rooftops on East and South Battery for a grandstand view of the beginning of what was to become the nation's bloodiest war.

The sound of cannonading carried to outlying areas and was reported heard at the Sinkler plantation Belvedere sixty miles from Charleston. Dorrie Walker, wife of H. Pinckney Walker, acting British consul at Charleston, wrote her sister Nellie in England: "Sophy and I stood the live long day seeing the bombardment from a beautiful Battery that runs the side of our harbor. The Shells like balls of Snow we saw fall into Fort Sumter and with a glass I could see the Cannon balls from Fort Sumter whizzing thro the air.

"I cannot describe the two days of awful anxiety we spent. Harry was serving a gun in the iron battery. Charlie was at a rifled cannon sent from England by a Charleston merchant as a present to his Native state…

"Strange to say that Cannon did the most efficient Service and it only arrived on Morris Island the night before the fight. When the first boat came up saying that up to that time nobody was killed no one dared believe the news as it seemed impossible.

"By that time we could discern the Ships of War off the Bar and of Course expected them to join in the fight every instant. But strange to say they never attempted to assist Anderson who sadly needed help. There they lay their steam up—plenty of surf boats—plenty of water on the Bar for them to have run the gauntlet of our Batteries but they never moved—

"They saw the flames roaring round the forts and finally their own flag shot away by our guns after Anderson had shown them signals of distress 3 times…Anderson only surrendered when the fire made it so hot that he and his men had to lie on their faces with wet handkerchiefs spread over them. Think how terribly he must have felt when he had to surrender to Beauregard who had been his pupil at West Point."

Anderson held out for thirty-four hours until the fort was in flames and the ammunition magazine had to be sealed off for fear of explosion. When he surrendered, it was discovered he had scarcely any food and provisions left. He and his men were permitted to embark on a Federal ship, taking with them the large garrison flag that had flown during the bombardment, bearing thirty-four stars. Secession of the Southern states had reduced the union by seven, and soon four more would leave. Four years later the garrison flag would once again be raised over the fort.

While Charleston was celebrating the fall of Sumter, news of the defeat of Union forces at First Manassas was received from Virginia. The first expressions of joy were followed by

sorrow as reports of casualties brought home the tragedy of war. Susan Middleton wrote her cousin Harriot, whose brother Henry was shortly to die of his wounds: "Today all is still—and like a very sad Sunday—the streets, however, full of soldiers, and the bells tolling. This afternoon the funeral of General Bee and Col. Johnson takes place…Oh, are not these dreadful days? Each hour seems to bring its own sad tale. And many say there are darker ones still in store for us, in spite of this great victory. The brilliancy seems very faint, amidst all this sorrow and suspence."

As in the Revolution families were again divided in their loyalties. Governor Henry Middleton's sons John Izard and Williams both signed the Ordinance of Secession and their plantations were destroyed by Northern forces, but his son Edward remained an Admiral in the United States Navy. Anna

The State of South Carolina.

At a Convention of the People of the State of South Carolina, begun and holden at Columbia, on the Seventeenth day of December, in the year of our Lord one thousand eight hundred and sixty, and thence continued by adjournment to Charleston, and there by divers adjournments to the Twentieth day of December in the same year—

An Ordinance To dissolve the Union between the State of South Carolina and other States united with her under the compact entitled "The Constitution of the United States of America"

We, the People of the State of South Carolina, in Convention assembled, do declare and ordain, and it is hereby declared and ordained, That the Ordinance adopted by us in Convention, on the twenty-third day of May, in the year of our Lord One thousand Seven hundred and eighty-eight, whereby the Constitution of the United States of America was ratified, and also all Acts and parts of Acts of the General Assembly of this State, ratifying amendments of the said Constitution, are hereby repealed; and that the union now subsisting between South Carolina and other States, under the name of "The United States of America," is hereby dissolved.

Done at Charleston, the twentieth day of December, in the year of our Lord one thousand eight hundred and Sixty.

D. F. Jamison Delegate from Barnwell and President of the Convention.

Thos. Chiles Perrine · Francis Hugh Wardlaw · Chesley D. Evans · R. W. Barnwell · D. W. Spratt
Edward Noble · R. G. M. Dunovant · Jno. M. Baxter · Jos. Daniel Pope · Williams Middleton
I. H. Wilson · James Parsons Carroll · A. W. Bethea · C. P. Brown · T. L. Phetnipton
Thos. Thomson · Wm. Gregg · E. W. Goodwin · John Ashmore · B. H. Rutledge
David Lewis Wardlaw · Andrew G. Magrath · William D. Johnson · Daniel DuPre · Edward McCrady
John Alfred Calhoun · James Tompkins · Alex McLeod · A. Mazyck · Francis I. Porcher
John Izard Middleton · James G. Smyley · John P. Kinard · Williams Cain · T. L. Gourdin
Benjamin C. Pressley · John Hugh Means · Robert Moorman · S. G. Snowden · Abel S. Palmer
I. A. Whitner · William Strother Lyles · Joseph Caldwell · Geo. W. Seabrook · John L. Nowell
James L. Orr · Henry Campbell Davis · Simeon Fair · John Jenkins · John S. O'Hear
I. P. Reed · Jno. Buchanan · Thomas Worth Glover · R. J. Davant · John G. Landrum
R. C. Simpson · James Furman · Laurence M. Keitt · E. M. Seabrook · B. B. Foster
Benjamin Franklin Mauldin · P. E. Duncan · Donald Rowe Barton · John A. Wannamaker · Benjamin H. Kilgore
Lewis Malone Ayers · W. H. Gray · Wm. Hunter · Elias B. Scott · Jas. H. Carlisle
W. Peronneau Finley · James Harrison · Maxcy Gregg · Jas. Jenkins · Simpson Bobo
I. I. Brabham · J. P. Kinard · Geo. A. Thompson · Langdon Cheves · Jno. Curtis
Benj. W. Lawton · T. J. Withers · Wilmot G. Gresham · George Rhodes · A. W. Green
Thomas W. Moore · James Chesnut · John Maxwell · A. P. Aldrich · Mathew Calvert
Richard Woods · Jno. W. Beaty · Jno. F. Hampton · Wm. Porcher Miles · Thomas Reese English Sr.
A. Q. Dunovant · Wm. S. Ellison · W. Ferguson Hutson · John Townsend · Chesley Daniel Evans
John A. Inglis · R. L. Crawford · W. F. de Saussure · Robert N. Gourdin · J. N. Whitner
Henry McIver · W. C. Cauthen · William Hopkins · J. Maner · J. Sims
Stephen Jackson · D. P. Robinson · James H. Adams · Theodore D. Wagner · Wm. H. Cai
W. Pinckney Shingler · H. E. Young · Maxcy Gregg · W. Gourdin Young · Langdon Cheves Jr.
Peter P. Bonneau · W. W. Harllington · John H. Kinsler · C. G. Memminger · Anthony W. Dozier
John P. Richardson · John D. Williams · Ephraim M. Clark · Gabriel Manigault · John G. Presley
John L. Manning · Wm. D. Watts · Alex H. Brown · John Julius Pringle Smith · R. C. Logan
John I. Ingram · Thos. W. Lee · E. S. P. Bellinger · Grace W. Hayne · Francis S. Parker
Edgar W. Charles · H. E. Coughman · Merrick E. Carn · H. Munroe · Benj. Faneuil Dunkin
Julius A. Dargan · John P. Geiger · E. R. Henderson · Rich'd De Treville · Sam'l Taylor Atkinson
Isaac D. Wilson · Paul Quattlebaum · Peter Stokes · Thos. M. Hanckel · Alex. M. Forster
John M. Timmons · W. B. Powell · Daniel Flud · A. W. Burnet · Wm. Blackburn Wilson
· · David C. Appleby · Thos. J. Ormond · Robert W. Alison
· · · Antonio J. Barry · Sam'l Rainey
· · · · A. Baxter Springs
· · · · A. I. Barron.

Attest, Benj. F. Arthur Clerk of the Convention.

Drayton wrote Alicia Middleton, "I believe I informed you in my last letter that Uncle Percy had resigned and he being still in the Navy…so write to undeceive you, as he changed his mind after I wrote you…I don't like to express any opinion for I rely too much on his judgment and sound principles to think he had done wrong but only think he is mistaken." Anna's father Brigadier General Thomas F. Drayton was commanding officer of Confederate forces at the battle of Port Royal, and his brother Commander Percival Drayton, U.S.N., commanded one of the attacking vessels.

With the fall of Port Royal, only sixty miles to the south, Federal forces controlled all of the Carolina coast from Winyah Bay to the Savannah River, with the exception of Charleston.

Before the year was over the worst of Charleston's great fires broke out. It began at 8:30 in the evening of December 11 at the foot of Hasell Street in the sash and blind factory of William P. Russell on the Cooper River waterfront. A group of slave refugees from an outlying plantation were keeping warm around a small fire on the ground near the factory. Suddenly the fire caught the wooden building. The winds rose to gale force and the blaze quickly spread across East Bay, down to Market Street, consuming the beautiful mansion built by Chief Justice Pinckney. Sparks flew through the air as the fire roared across town. The South Carolina Institute Hall, and the Circular Congregational Church next door were consumed by the blaze. The Mills House occupants hung wet blankets from the windows, and though the whole side was charred, the building was saved as the flames swept on toward the southwest. A sudden shift in the wind spared the Lutheran and Unitarian churches on Archdale Street, but the Cathedral of St. John and St. Finbar, where many had stored their valuables thinking it safe, burned furiously. The insurance on the cathedral had lapsed the week before, probably because the premium could not be gotten to the insurance company in the north because of the war.

The heat ignited the St. Andrew's Society Hall next door, and both sides of Broad Street caught on fire. Residents moved their furniture and possessions several times as each house they thought safe caught fire in turn. When there was nothing left to consume, the fire finally sputtered out in the marshes of the Ashley River, leaving 540 acres of scorched earth and blackened chimneys. Five hundred residences, 5 churches, and many public buildings were destroyed and estimated damages were between five to seven million dollars. It was the worst fire in the history of Charleston, and because it took place during the first year of the war, the scar remained across the city for years. Lt. Col. Freemantle of the Coldstream Guards said: "That portion of the city destroyed by the great fire presents the appearance of a vast wilderness in the very center of the town...this desert space looks like the Pompeians ruins."

A week later the harbor took on the appearance of a graveyard of ships with the arrival of the Stone Fleet; 16 old whaling ships from New England, loaded with granite, each with a 5-inch hole cut in the bottom and fitted with a pipe and valve so it could be easily flooded. These were towed into position, dismasted, and sunk so as to block the main channel off Morris Island. In January, a second group was brought in to block Maffitt's Channel—leaving only two entrances for Confederate blockade runners, and these were under guard by Federal blockading vessels. Northern papers exulted that a "rathole" had been stopped; England and France were horrified. The tide and currents soon began to destroy the hulks and the granite eventually sank into the mud.

As Charleston enjoyed a respite in the spring of '62, news came of Shiloh, the Seven Days battles near Richmond, Antietam, Fredericksburg, and casualty lists lengthened.

In May one of the most fascinating episodes of the war took place. The Confederate steamer *Planter* was tied up at her berth at Southern Wharf near the present Shrine Temple on East Bay. She had taken on board four guns from Cole's Island on the Stono River, to be transported to Fort Ripley, a raised battery built on the reef in the harbor. The order of Commanding General Pemberton that officers were to remain aboard at all times was not followed, and Captain C.J. Relyea had left the ship in charge of the African American crew headed by Robert Smalls.

Smalls had been trained as a sailmaker in his native Beaufort, and had become an expert pilot through his service aboard the *Planter*. The account Smalls gave to the Freedmen's

"It is known that the American Flag brought away from Fort Moultrie was raised at Sumpter precisely at noon on the 27th." Major Anderson assembled his entire force, including workmen, and knelt with the halyard in his hand as the chaplain made the invocation. As the band played "Hail Columbia," he hoisted the large garrison flag. Leslie's Illustrated News Jan. 26, 1861. Courtesy of U.S. Dept. of the Interior National Park Service

Society meeting in New York was reprinted in the *Mercury*: "The crew came on board one at a time so as not to create suspicion. Abraham, my friend, carried the trunk, as though he were taking it to his boat. The women and children were hid away in the engineroom of another boat.

"Abraham kept watch that night, and called me about twelve o'clock, the moon was shining right up and down. About three o'clock the fire was started and the wind blew the smoke over the city. I was scared. I feared the people would think there was a fire near the wharf, but nobody came.

"We moved out of our position, but had to return to take the women on board, and the boat moved so nicely up to her place we did not have to throw a plank or tie a rope. It was early, so we steamed slowly down to Fort Johnson. I didn't want to appear in front of the fort in the dark, for fear they might suspect me.

February 3, 1861, families of the Federal forces on Sumter sailed on the Marion for Fort Hamilton, New York. The troops cheered and the fort gave them a one gun salute as they passed. Courtesy of South Carolina Historical Society

Left:
Interior of Fort Moultrie is shown with the "hot shot" oven on the right where the balls were heated before firing so that they would set their targets afire. Just above it over the parapet can be seen Fort Sumter. Courtesy of South Carolina Historical Society

Below:
Seth Eastman's painting of Fort Sumter before the Civil War. Courtesy of Library of Congress

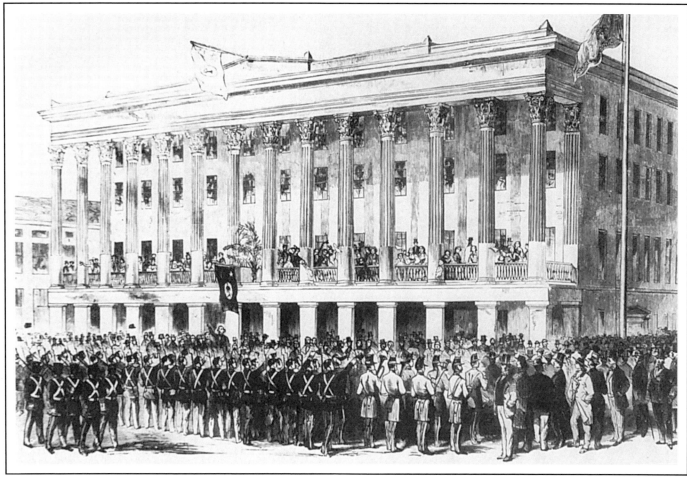

"At the right time I gave the signal—two long blows and a short one. I put on the Captain's straw hat, and stood so that the sentinel could not see my color. When beyond the range of the guns we put on plenty of steam. I hoisted a white sheet, taken from the bed, and reached the blockading vessels in safety, and we were received with cheers."

Smalls turned the steamer over to the Union commander and was taken to Port Royal, where he informed Admiral DuPont that Cole's Island had been evacuated. He and his crew were given prize money and commendations, and Smalls served during the war in both the Union Army and Navy, and eventually was made captain of the ship he had liberated.

Following the war, he was a delegate to the State Constitutional Convention of 1868, and was elected to the state legislature. He later became United States Congressman, and in Congress was given the nickname of the "Gullah Statesman," because of his thick Beaufort accent. After his retirement from politics Smalls was made Customs Collector of the port of Beaufort, where today a high school is named for him.

Charleston women were staunchly behind their men—the younger generation went to Fort Sumter to visit friends stationed there, and relieved their tedium with dances there and at Castle Pinckney. Days included walks on the Battery, tea with friends, visiting the Bee Store for goods that had run the blockade, "write to the boys regularly, and *think* as little as possible. (Oh! What fearful times! We know not what a day or hour may bring forth.)"

"Round dancing" scandalized Charleston mamas, and Alicia Middleton, after restraining herself for some time, wrote her older sister Harriott: "As it may perchance be less trying to your feelings to hear the fatal truth from my lips than from those of a stranger, know then that (in your eyes) I have disgraced my *name*, my *station*, my *sex*; I have done worse that *rouging*, or *flirting*, or *marrying a Brigadier General* (probably a reference to her cousin who had married Gen. Ripley), in short I have round danced!!!"

"...the band struck up an enchanting gallop...and...Satan in the guise of Willie Smith, flew up to me, put his arm round my waist and—The Serpent tempted and I did eat! The delightful band—the waxed floor, the lights, the man, proved too much for me, before I knew where I was, I found myself flying round in a heavenly manner."

In spite of being twenty-two years old, Alicia received a scathing letter from her mother and forewent any more of the "indecent" waltzes, Germans and polkas, which demanded too much body contact for proper Charlestonians. Later in the spring her cousin Anna Blake writes "I think it very unfeeling in all those young girls to be jigging about so soon after that dreadful battle in Virginia and Stonewall's death. They had much better be mourning his death than cutting capers with those apish creoles (old Pete's aides)." "Old Pete" was General Beauregard.

Alicia was in Flat Rock, North Carolina, and unable to be one of the bridesmaids when Adele, the lovely daughter of Governor R.F.W. Allston, married Confederate Major Arnoldus Vanderhorst in the Allston's beautiful Meeting Street mansion (the Nathaniel Russell House). One of the eight bridesmaids wrote her the details: "We all walked down stairs from her room, met the groomsmen at the foot of the stairs marched into the middle room, ladies filing to the right and gentleman to the left, and then the fair Bride leaning on the arm of the Major who was in uniform bran new, followed head bent, step firm and looking so lovely!

Left:
General McGowan addresses the 35th Abbeville volunteers in front of the Charleston Hotel. A number of them are accompanied by their armed servants, Leslie's Illustrated states, "as the barons of old were by their armed vassals. Their costume is most picturesque, being composed of the Garibaldi red flannel tunic, with crossbelt and black pants." The 35th was composed of over a hundred of the wealthiest citizens of Abbeville District. Courtesy of South Caroliniana Library

Above:
Confederate blockade runner Ella and Annie, owned by W.C. Bee and C.T. Mitchell of Charleston, was captured on a run from St. George's, Bermuda, to Wilmington, N.C. She had a cargo of 300 cases of Austrian rifles and a quality of saltpeter for manufacture of gunpowder. Her captain Frank Bonneau of Charleston was the only blockade-runner to be convicted of piracy, but the presiding judge set aside the verdict. Courtesy of U.S. Navy

Above:
Detachments of the Washington Light Infantry guard the state arsenal. This was the home of the Military College of the South (The Citadel) from 1843 to 1922. Courtesy of South Caroliniana Library, Columbia, SC

Left:
"At the bombardment of Fort Sumter, the Battery and every house, housetop and spire was crowded. On White Point Garden were encamped about fifty cadets, having in charge five, six and twelve pounders placed on the extreme of the eastern promenade." Courtesy of South Carolina Historical Society

Right:
The "Gullah Statesman" Robert Smalls was one of the most colorful figures in Republican politics during the post Reconstruction period. Born in Beaufort, South Carolina, his public career started when he successfully took the Confederate transport Planter *from a Charleston wharf and delivered it to the Federal fleet. Courtesy of South Carolina Historical Society*

Below:
William Aiken Walker's painting from a sketch made in 1864 gives a view from East Battery of the Federal siege of a badly . damaged Fort Sumter. From the left is seen Mt. Pleasant with Castel Pinckney in the foreground, Fort Moultrie firing from Sullivan's Island, Ft. Ripley just to Sumter's left, the Federal monitors in the distance, and on the right Batteries Simpkins and Wagner on Morris Island and Fort Johnson on James Island. Confederate gunboat Juno is to the left, and Confederate ironclads on the right. *Courtesy of Historic Charleston Foundation. Photo by Louis Schwartz*

Right:
The Confederate steamer Planter *was loaded with four guns from Cole's Island intended for the Middle Ground Battery (Fort Ripley). She was berthed at Southern Wharf the night of May 12, 1862, when her Negro crew under the command of Robert Smalls got up steam and headed for the nearest blockading vessel and delivered her to the Federal navy. Courtesy of South Carolina Historical Society*

"I was 3rd bridesmaid so of course stood very near, saw everything, heard their answers and then awaited the forthcoming of the ring—saw it placed on the finger...when all congratulations and shaking of hands was over we separated in pairs to different parts of the room and eat cake and drank to the health of the happy pair."

The *Courier* reported that the women of New Orleans had given the Confederacy a gunboat, and suggested that those of South Carolina do the same, with the result that a Miss Sue L. Gelzer sent a five dollar contribution, precipitating a rash of letters from women all over the state. They contributed anything that could be sold or raffled to a fair held at Hibernian Hall—jewelry, plate, works of art, china, lace, and even bales of cotton—and the *Mercury* announced they raised a total of $30,000. The Confederate Navy offered to accept their gifts for the ironclad under construction on the ways of Marsh

and Sons in Charleston, and the women were given the privilege of naming it. They decided on the *Palmetto State*.

A second gunboat, the *Chicora*, begun two months later at James M. Eason's shipyard behind the Post Office (Old Exchange building) on the Cooper River, was actually completed first. On October 11, 1862, spectators crowded roofs, windows and streets near Marsh's wharf for the christening of the *Palmetto State*. Col. Richard Yeadon, editor of the *Courier*, in full uniform of the Willington Rangers; Capt. D.N. Ingraham, naval commander at Charleston; General Beauregard and his staff; Brigadier General Gist, and other army and navy officers, and several ladies occupied honored positions on the upper deck. Miss Gelzer "broke over the head of the ironsheathed monster a bottle of choice old wine." Just as the ceremony was concluding, an appropriate touch was added by the *Chicora*, which came steaming up with colors

April 7, 1863, the ironclads attacked Fort Sumter. To the left is the Ironsides "looming up from the sea a formidable looking monster," behind her the double-turreted Keokuk, "most dreaded of the line." Fort Moultrie can be seen to the right of Sumter; Morris Island to the left, and in the distance the skyline of Charleston, Castle Pinckney with flag flying off to the right. Courtesy of U.S. Dept. of the Interior National Park Service

flying fore and aft and saluted the *Palmetto State*, accompanied by enthusiastic cheers from the crowd. The christening was followed in true Charleston tradition by "a bountiful collation" in Messrs. Marsh's workshops.

Arthur M. Wilcox, himself a naval reserve officer, points out in an article in the Centennial edition of the local papers that the Confederacy was so short of money and equipment that the gunboats "reflected the shortages and crude skills of the South" and were no match for the Northern monitors. They represented however, the indomitable spirit of Charlestonians and their fellow Southerners.

At two o'clock the following April 7, just as the officers on Sumter sat down to dinner, the first advance of a Federal ironclad fleet was announced to post commandant Col. Alfred Rhett. As it was some four miles off, they alerted Headquarters in Charleston by telegraph, then finished their meal. The "long roll" sounded at two-thirty, and men rushed to their guns "with shouting and yells of exultation."

The regimental band was ordered to the rampart, and the blue and white Palmetto state banner and elegant black and white colors of the First Regiment South Carolina Artillery were run up to join the garrison flag. After a thirteen-gun salute, the band struck up "Dixie." Seven monitors, "Hulls sunk down to water level and showing only a black line on the surface and a projecting turret and smoke stack each—the *Ironsides* looming up from the sea, a formidable looking monster, and the *Keokuk*, her hull more distinctly visible than the monitors, and with two turrets, the most dreaded of the nine," steamed towards the fort.

At three o'clock when the lead monitor was about fourteen hundred yards off, Fort Moultrie fired the first gun. At this the band hushed, musicians were dispatched to their posts and the order issued to open fire. Channel buoys gave the Confederates the correct range, and Sumter and batteries Bee and Beauregard on Sullivan's Island joined fire with Moultrie. As the *Keokuk* approached, Lt. Col. Yates sighted the Brooke gun and the first shot entered the open porthole of the foremost turret, and after a terrific concentration of fire, it managed to "crawl feebly off and escape." The *Passaic* suffered continuous bombardment for thirty minutes. On shore Langdon Cheves was attempting to detonate a large mine directly beneath the *New Ironsides*, but the cable was too long to be effective.

Charleston waterfront had a grandstand view of the battle, and late in the afternoon after two-and-a-half hours watchers saw the fleet withdraw, leaving behind the double-turreted *Keokuk*, which sank next morning off Morris Island in about eighteen feet of water, with the stack still visible. Her turrets, each containing a huge eleven-inch Dahlgren, were barely above the surface at low tide.

A work crew headed by Adolphus W. La Coste, civilian employee of the Confederate States Ordinance Department, his brother James, Edwin Watson a black man, and a few soldiers from Fort Sumter undertook to salvage the guns, sorely needed by the Confederates. They could work for only about two hours each night when the tide was low, practically under the noses of the blockading fleet. The sound of their chisels, hammers and crowbars traveled over the water as they cut through several thicknesses of iron plate, in waist deep water with the waves slapping their faces. After three weeks they succeeded in removing both guns. These were mounted at Battery Bee and Fort Sumter, and in 1898 the former was discovered buried in the sand, and was dug out by troops stationed at Fort Moultrie. Today it is mounted on the northeast corner of the Battery.

In July came news of the fall of Vicksburg, followed within twenty-four hours by word of the defeat of Lee at Gettysburg. Fort Sumter was strengthened with sandbags, cotton bales and rawhides. From Columbia Susan Middleton wrote: "We used to say that every *day* brought its own sad story, now, it seems to me, every *hour*, almost, comes laden with sorrowful tidings." She heard the firing to the south when Union forces landed on Morris Island and launched attacks on Battery Wagner after a terrific bombardment from land and naval batteries.

On July 18 General Gillmore with about six thousand men attacked Wagner in an assault that lasted approximately three hours, and resulted in some fifteen hundred Federal fatalities and 174 Confederate deaths. "Probably no battlefield in the country," wrote the editor of the *Charleston Daily Courier*, "has ever presented such an array of mangled bodies in a small compass as was to be seen on Sunday morning. The ground in front of the Battery was thickly strewn, but in the ditch around the Work the dead and wounded, white and black, were literally piled together. Blood, mud, water, brains and human hair matted together."

This remarkable picture was taken while the flying-sap was being pushed forward to the fifth and last parallel in the attack on Battery Wagner. Sharpshooters on the right kept a "quick and deadly fire on the enemy" as they advanced. Courtesy of South Carolina Historical Society

"The Grand Skedaddle" was the label given this sketch by prisoner Lt. Kirby of the 47th Massachusetts, showing Charlestonians evacuating in the face of Federal bombardment. Courtesy of South Caroliniana Library

The "Swamp Angel" or Marsh Battery was one of the most famous Civil War guns. Piles were driven into the twenty foot deep mud at a point 7,900 yards from St. Michael's steeple. A platform supported the 8", 200 lb. Parrott rifle that was skidded over the marsh and mounted behind the sandbag parapet. On the night of August 21, 1863, it fired sixteen shells filled with Greek fire into the heart of Charleston. Courtesy of South Carolina Historical Society

Fort Sumter and batteries Wagner and Gregg were bombarded by Union Batteries on Morris Island under command of General Gillmore, August, 1863. To the left is the Swamp Angel. Flags fly from Fort Johnson, Castle Pinckney, Fort Ripley, Sumter and the two Morris Island batteries. The New Ironsides is to the right, and the skyline of Charleston in the far left. Courtesy of The South Caroliniana Library, Columbia, SC.

Men were lying in all possible contortions from the 20-foot fall from the parapet: "pale, beseeching faces, looking out from among the ghastly corpses, with moans and cries for help and water, and dying gasps and death struggle—these are some of the details of the horrible picture which the night of Saturday had left to be revealed by the dawn of a peaceful Sabbath."

Burying the dead and removing the wounded continued far into Sunday night. Federal wounded were taken to the Yankee hospital in Queen Street, where, because of the close quarters at which fighting occurred, wounds were severe and there were many amputations. The body of Col. Robert Gould Shaw of Boston was buried in a pit with two of the dead black men of his 54th Massachusetts which had led the assault.

Fifty days of almost constant bombardment followed—the "noise disjoints one" a Charlestonian said. Because of this incessant pounding, the stench of decomposing bodies and the heat, the men in Wagner were relieved every three days, but always returned for more. On August 17 the Union fleet and their Morris Island batteries began the first of three great and eight lesser bombardments of Fort Sumter. In the first twenty-four hours almost a thousand shells were fired at the fort; seven guns were disabled and the walls were heavily damaged.

Sumter's last cannon sounded five days after the attack began, but she still held out. The men burrowed underground like moles, building shell-proof shelters beneath the rubble, where they stored their ammunition, worked and lived. The *Mercury* ran a notice: "SAND BAGS—we would again earnestly call the attention of all our citizens, not in the ranks, to the important movement now afoot to furnish sand bags for the protection of our harbor defenses. Messr. Williams Middleton and J. Bennett have taken charge of the matter." Charleston women stitched bags until their fingers were sore, and they were filled with earth and rowed over at night to replace the bricks knocked out by shells.

On the twenty-first of August, Gen. Gillmore demanded evacuation of Sumter and Morris Island, threatening to shell Charleston if this was not complied with. General Beauregard returned the message unanswered because it was not signed, and bombardment of Charleston began around one-thirty in the morning from an eight-inch Parrott rifle in the marsh off Morris Island. Called the Marsh Battery, the gun was named The Swamp Angel by Union soldiers. It shot mostly incendiary shells until, fortunately for the city, it burst on the thirty-sixth round. General Beauregard wrote Gillmore: "It would appear, sir, that despairing of reducing these works, you now resort to the novel measure of turning your guns against the old men, the women and children, and the hospitals of a sleeping city, an act of inexcusable barbarity."

As the shelling continued, the lower section of the city was evacuated, and those who could took refuge up-country. Many went to Columbia, where months before people and organizations had sent records and valuables, including the bells of St. Michael's. Eventually the lower part of the peninsula was deserted. Mrs. Ravenel wrote that going from the upper section of the city to the lower part of the town "was like going from life to death." Dorothy Walker wrote: "For the first time since my residence at the South I have beggars at my door, begging humbly for food and clothes—a thing unherd of at the South...Charleston is in the most pitiable condition without paint, without its usual inhabitants, the shops closed, the streets filthy, the pavements coated in dust...I only go out when I can't help it. I am, and all the children are, just as shabby as we can be. And everybody you meet is in the same fix, so we laugh at one another and turn upside down or inside out the old dresses and try to fancy they are new. All the gentlemen have adopted the fashion of having their coats turned."

The *Courier* printed letters from a mailbag that floated ashore on Sullivan's Island from the U.S. gunboat *Ottawa*. One, written the day the shelling of the town began, was from a Union serviceman to his mother: "The old fort looks quite bad now, and they have throwed a few shell over into Charleston City, to just stir them up a little by the way of a change, and so the British Consil does not appreciate it much and furthermore he does not seem to think it quite righ, but I don't see any way he can help himself, as they have been told to remove the women and children from the city—for we was going to shell the city, and so he can stay and take the contence or leave just as he chooses about it."

As Union forces captured Morris Island, batteries were established closer to town and the city was under almost continuous siege for a year and a half. First gunners sighted in on St. Michael's steeple, which was hit several times. On Sunday, November 19, the service was interrupted by firing from Morris Island, a shell exploding at the door as the congregation left. Sights were later shifted to St. Philip's spire, then eventually further north to the Second Presbyterian tower, which was about the extent of the range, although a few shells fell as far to the north as John Street. Episcopal congregations held services in St. Paul's on Coming Street, well out of danger of shell damage.

Charleston harbor, according to Wallace, was the site of the longest and heaviest naval operations of the war, and was also the chief center of Confederate blockade-running. Arms, ammunition, medicines, and civilian goods were sneaked past the Federal fleet.

It was also at Charleston that the submarine boat and the marine torpedo were introduced to naval warfare. Theodore D. Stoney, Dr. St. Julien Ravenel, and a young Confederate Army officer, Francis D. Lee; organized a company that built semi-submersible torpedo boats with a spar torpedo, designed by Lee, attached to a thirty-foot pole on the bow. This would be rammed against the hull of enemy ships at great danger to the attacking torpedo-boat.

The first was constructed at Stony Landing on the Cooper River near Moncks Corner by David Ebaugh, an engineer who operated a phosphate plant on Dr. Ravenel's plantation. It was named *David* in his honor. The *Davids* were wooden, cigar-shaped boats, and were frequently called "*Little Davids*" as they attacked the large ironclad Goliaths. On October 5, 1863, the *New Ironsides* was so badly damaged by a four man crew commanded by Lt. W.T. Glassell that she had to go North for repairs.

An even more dangerous weapon to operate was the *Hunley*. Made from an old steam boiler about twenty-five feet long and four feet wide, the *Hunley* was designed to dive under the enemy ship dragging a torpedo. When naval men saw it arrive from Mobile on a flat car, they called it a "veritable coffin," and so it proved to be. Some twenty-two volunteer crewmen, including inventor Horace L. Hunley, were to die either in practice runs or in attempting to attack the blockaders. The *Hunley* made the first successful submarine attack against a warship on February 17, 1864, when it

sank the *Housatonic* by exploding a torpedo attached to a spar under the hull. However, the resulting wave swamped the *Hunley*, and no trace of it or the crew have ever been found.

When Sherman burned Atlanta and began his terrible march through Georgia to Savannah, General Halleck wrote him: "Should you capture Charleston, I hope that by some accident the place may be destroyed; and if a little salt should be sown upon the site, it may prevent the growth of future crops of nullification and secession." Sherman replied that he didn't think salt would be needed, as the Fifteenth Corps would be in Charleston first and "they generally do their work up pretty well. The truth is," he added, "the whole army is burning with insatiable desire to wreak vengeance upon South Carolina. I almost tremble at her fate."

Acting consul Walker wrote his sister: "Divers threatenings of how we are to be used, how our dwellings are to be demolished, their sites to be ploughed up, and salt to be sown, from time to time reach us. I can only say that if such is the plan, the operators must bring their salt with them, or the harvest will never repay the sower, for that simple article has been selling here for ten pounds per bushel."

When the wind blew from the southeast, the cannonading could be heard all the way to Columbia, one hundred miles inland, and the refugees knew their beloved home was under bombardment. Sherman, however, was racing to engage the Confederate army of General Joseph E. Johnston at Durham, North Carolina, and therefore he took the most direct route by way of the high sand ridges and the railroad, so that it was Columbia, and not Charleston, that lay in his path.

Turkey buzzards and rats occupy the interior of the Bank of the State of South Carolina after shelling by Federal forces. The building, at One Broad Street, was occupied in 1980 by Bankers Trust. Courtesy of South Caroliniana Library

On February 17, he entered Columbia and his troops razed 84 out of 124 city blocks, burning and looting Charleston valuables and even St. Michael's bells were melted in the heat. The same night, Confederate forces were evacuating Columbia's sister city Charleston. As the Confederate rear guard retreated to the northwest, the Twenty-First United States Colored Troops landed at the wharves on the lower peninsula, and marched up Meeting Street led by a black soldier riding a mule and carrying a banner marked "Liberty." Behind came the 55th Massachusetts singing "John Brown's Body." An old black woman ran out, and unable to reach the rider, hugged the mule and cried: "Thank God! Thank God!"

"Some say the thing looks like a log on the water, others that it is like a gigantic metallic coffin—but all say it is wonderful, only the sanguine believe it will work wonders," wrote Susan Middleton of the Confederate submarine Hunley, made from a converted boiler. Etching by C.W. Chapman. Courtesy of South Carolina Historical Society

Federal forces enter Charleston, the Massachusetts regiment singing "John Brown's Body." Courtesy of South Carolina Historical Society

Steamers, including General Gillmore's flagship "Diamond," dock at Fort Sumter with their colors flying as crowds estimated at 3,000 gather April 14, 1865 for flag-raising ceremonies. Precisely at noon General Robert Anderson raised the garrison flag, which he had lowered on his evacuation of Sumter four years earlier, on the tall white pole to the right of the speakers' platform, and the Rev. Henry Ward Beecher expressed the hope that "As long as the sun endures, or the stars, may it wave over a nation neither enslaved nor enslaving." Courtesy of Library of Congress.

Chapter Six
"A New Era"
1865–1900
Post Bellum

Occupying forces found a sadly changed Charleston, with the waterfront deserted, blackened walls and chimneys standing sentinel over water-filled cellars gaping like open graves—"a place of widowed women and rotting wharves, of buzzards perched in melancholy rows upon the roofs of deserted warehouses, of weed-grown gardens and miles of grass-grown streets."

Confederates had set fire to cotton piled in the public squares, and small boys playing with gunpowder caused the Northwestern Railroad Depot to explode, killing 150. Fragments from burning gunboats ignited nearby wharves, the bridge across the Ashley River was afire, and once again Charleston was burning from river to river.

The Citadel was taken over as headquarters by Lt. Col. A.G. Bennett, Commander of the 21st U.S. Colored Troops, who, with the 127th New York Volunteers, were made the permanent city garrison. Miles Brewton's mansion at 27 King Street was again used as headquarters by the occupying forces. On the nineteenth of August the colored soldiers went on a tour of looting, and Harriott Middleton wrote her cousin Susan from Columbia, "We never think of Charleston. All our friends there describe it as so dreadful."

Williams Middleton informed his sister Eliza, wife of J. Francis Fisher of Philadelphia: "No one in the country in which you live has the slightest conception of the real condition of affairs here—of the utter topsy-turveying of all of our institutions, rules, regulations, habits and opinions and indeed everything which can possibly be reached or affected by the control or action of the yankee authorities. Property is only safe when concealed, if at all tempting and as far as comfort in life of anykind it is not to be thought of…I am tired to death of the constant repetition of disgusting occurrences of every day."

His "superintendent" A.C. Anderson ("the word overseer being unmentionable to the ears of Freedmen") informed him that "On Middleton Place every single building is burned…our country is in a terrible state of disorder—there are about Twenty-five thousand Negros in the different Islands on our coast and they are constantly making Raids in the Main, Murdering the whites, and committing all sorts of depredations in consequence of which, all of the plantations *at all*

adjacent to the coast have been abandoned by the whites—there is no white person living in any of the plantations in St. Andrews parish at all."

Yankee officers tried to bribe Jack, one of Williams' former slaves, to steal Williams' "valuables for their benefit and receive therefor a bribe; all of which to their great astonishment he refused to do; and the result was that they broke into the house one night and helped themselves to about $1200 worth of silver."

On March 3 an unusual ceremony took place on the parade ground in front of the Citadel, with Col. Bennett and Brigadier General Milton S. Littlefield, later to be called the "Prince of Bummers" (bummers were disreputable, wandering, foraging wartime rogues) major participants. An honor guard of black soldiers in blue and scarlet uniforms stood at attention as a huge crowd of black men, women and children and a few whites watched thirteen black women, elaborately costumed to represent the thirteen original states approach the general. One presented him with a flag, another a bouquet, and a third a fan of white swan feathers for Mrs. Lincoln.

The fan was never to be delivered, for less than two weeks later President Lincoln attended Ford's Theatre and was assassinated by John Wilkes Booth. In Charleston on the morning of that same day, April 14, another celebration was taking place at Fort Sumter.

"The day, the occasion, and the event marks a new era for South Carolina," the *Courier* pontificated. On February 21 the paper had been taken over by the military authorities, who announced it would be turned over to Messrs. George Whittemore and George W. Johnson, "who are hereby authorized to issue a loyal Union newspaper" by order of General Gillmore. The occasion marked the return of Robert Anderson, now a Major General, who had come back by Presidential order exactly four years after his evacuation of the fort to raise the 1861 garrison flag over the ruins.

By ten o'clock crowds were thronging the wharves and streets of Charleston. All the vessels in the harbor were decorated, and each had fired a 21-gun salute as its flags were raised. While bands played and crowds cheered, nine steamers, their flags flying, cast off their moorings and steamed down river. The *Canonicus* carried visiting officers and civilian guests, and the post band of the 127th New York volunteers, who greeted General Hatch and his staff with "Hail Columbia" as they came aboard. Robert Smalls captained the *Planter*, and among the blacks crowding her deck stood the son of Denmark Vesey and the outstanding Major Martin Delany, "Father of Black Power."

William Lloyd Garrison, publisher of "The Liberator" and well-known abolitionist the Reverend Henry Ward Beecher, were honored guests. At noon, as General Anderson raised the flag, all on the stage joined in holding the halyards, and hats and handkerchiefs waved for five minutes, bands played, and Fort Moultrie sounded a hundred-gun salute.

In his address the Reverend Mr. Beecher quoted Christopher Gadsden, "When the passage of the Stamp Act in 1765 aroused the colonies," he said, "it was Gadsden of South Carolina that cried with…enthusiasm: 'There ought to be no New England man, no New Yorker known on this continent, but all of us American.' That was the voice of South Carolina; that shall be the voice of South Carolina," continued Beecher.

"Faint is the echo, but it is coming. We now hear it sighing sadly through the pines, but it shall yet break upon the shore. No North, no West no South." He laid the burden of the war on "the polished, cultured, exceedingly capable and wholly unprincipled ruling aristocracy who wanted to keep power...the ambitious, educated, plotting, political leaders of the South." He urged that blacks be educated. "It is better for industry, religion, political integrity, for money, to educate the black man and by education, make him a citizen!" He predicted "a good day coming for the South."

As the day's festivities ended with a supper, a ball and fireworks, within the locked gates of the tall garden walls and behind the closed shutters of Charleston's pre-Revolutionary homes there was bitterness and anger. The Reverend Alexander W. Marshall, rector of St. John's Episcopal Church, was banished by Federal authorities for omitting the Episcopal prayer for the President of the United States in the service. His congregation was warned officially that they were "marked persons and any act done, or word uttered in justification of his disloyalty" would cause them to meet the same fate. The Rev. Charles Cotesworth Pinckney of Grace Episcopal Church, when ordered to include the prayer for the President, is said to have replied he would gladly obey the order, for he knew of no one who needed praying for more than the President of the United States!

The thousands of freedmen pouring into Charleston threatened famine in the city, and desolation to the country, as "Fieldmen, who have been all their lives raising corn and rice are flying from their homes on the farms to enjoy their new freedom by idleness in the city." Col. William Gurney announced in the *Courier*: "Freedmen the Union brought you the right to be free, but not to be idle," and asked how they expected to be fed in Charleston where nothing was grown, and told them to return to the farm and send rice and corn and vegetables to town. Gurney ordered that the Ward Committees report all able bodied idlers to the Provost Marshall who would put them to work on the public streets, and reminded them also that planters were anxious to hire workers.

The *Courier* reported that "No one unless having visited the hovels of the suffering poor in this city, can form an idea of the abject want and misery that prevails in our midst," and continued, "It must not be supposed that the colored are the only people who claim our sympathy in this respect. If the committee will take the trouble they will find in their respective wards numbers of white families who know not where to obtain their next meal."

Louisa McCord Smythe (niece of Captain Langdon Cheves) watched from her window at 18 Meeting Street as the crowds surged towards the Battery, which had always been off limits to blacks, and therefore was now their favorite promenade. "As a general thing," she reminisced for her children, "the crowd would be good-natured in a riotous, savage, undisciplined way, but just let anything happen to excite them! One day we saw this crowd turn round the Battery in pursuit of some white boys and rush up King Street, through Smith's Lane (Lamboll Street) back to Meeting Street, where they stoned one of the boys to death!"

"Little explosions of the kind were not infrequent, though not near as frequent as might have been expected considering the constant urgings on to deviltry that the negroes were receiving from politicians, and school ma'arms who came from 'down-east' like grasshoppers, and also strange negroes from the surrounding plantations who had come to town with the conviction that everything was to be 'shared out' to them."

"Here," wrote Northern journalist Sidney Andrews, "enough of woe and want and ruin and ravage to satisfy the most insatiate heart...One marks how few young men there are, and how generally the young women are dressed in black." Of the state's arms-bearing population, which numbered 55,046, some forty-four thousand volunteered and ultimately some seventy-one thousand (both elderly and the very young) entered the service, according to Simkins and Woody in their book *South Carolina During Reconstruction*. They cite 12,922 as killed or dying of wounds—twenty-three percent of the arms-bearing population, more than any other state, in comparison to the ten percent average loss of all Confederate armies and five percent average loss of all Union armies.

They point out that this loss occurred at a time when baffling economic and social problems needed to be faced, compounding the tragedy, and suggest that the lack of distinctive achievements by South Carolinians since the Civil War may

The Clubhouse at the Washington Race Course stands forlorn in 1865, having been used as housing for Federal prisoners during the war. The stand was designed so that ladies might alight from their carriages and make their way up the protected stairs to a "Handsome saloon" with large windows, celing to floor, and a wide balcony with a full view of the course. It held several hundred people with retiring and refreshment rooms on either side of the saloon. Courtesy of Citadel Archives

be due to this loss of a whole generation. The currency and Confederate securities representing lifetimes of toil were worthless scraps of paper with the collapse of financial resources.

During the war men of first families had endured the difficult camp life and women had managed plantations and suffered privation: now with defeat the old qualities of self-reliance and independence reappeared. Both sexes worked

"Yesterday it was the finest place I ever saw, now all destroyed," wrote Dr. Henry O. Marcy, medical director on Sherman's staff, in his diary February 24, 1865, describing Middleton Place. This stereoptic view shows the main house and north flanker after burning by Federal forces on February 22/23, 1865. Courtesy of Middleton Place Foundation

"Even the valley of desolation made by a great fire in 1861, through the very heart of the city, remained unbuilt. There, after the lapse of seven years, stood the blackened ruins of streets and houses waiting for the coming of a better day."

Ruins of the Circular Church and the walls of Institute Hall are in the foreground. Courtesy of Citadel Archives

Below:
*The crowd gets "food tickets"
and supplies at no. 5 Hayne
Street. "There is nothing that
will mix a crowd so thoroughly
as hunger. In Mr. Crane's
Charleston sketch we see the
memorable sable pastor next to
the somewhat seedy southern
belles," wrote the correspondent
of Leslie's Illustrated News.
Courtesy of The South
Caroliniana Library, Columbia,
SC*

Right:
*Laborers wash phosphate rock.
Phosphate rock beds included
both river and land deposits,
with those bordering the Ashley
River being the best on land.
Their discovery contributed
significantly to the revival of the
ruined fortunes of the state.
Courtesy of South Carolina
Historical Society*

at whatever employment they could find. Lt. General Richard H. Anderson was a railroad yardworker; Williams Middleton rented rooms in his house at one Meeting Street; Henry Manigault and his wife were Steward and Matron of the Alms House; James Heyward's family took in sewing; Governor Allston's widow ran a boarding school; ex-Confederate officers drove street cars. Nathaniel Russell Middleton advertised that "a number of Southern Ladies impoverished by the war" would supply rice by the tierce or half-tierce to public institutions, as well as fill orders for individual groups for rice, conserves, fine needlework and knitting, and would deliver to New York City. The end of slavery brought a total change in lifestyles.

One of the most urgent problems was the need of a new state constitution to permit South Carolina's readmission into the Union. President Andrew Johnson appointed Benjamin F.

Perry of Greenville provisional governor and instructed him to call a convention. When the convention met in Columbia, it was composed of men who had been state leaders before the war.

One hundred and three blacks in Charleston signed a petition asking that the constitution include no clause placing a color bar on the rights and privileges of citizens. The petition read: "Prosperity can only be secured by reconciling the seeming antagonism between the white and colored classes of the community...We know the deplorable ignorance of the majority of our people, we are also sensible of the deficiencies of those among us who have acquired some degree of education, and we ask not at this time that the ignorant shall be admitted to the exercises of a privilege which they might use to the injury of the state.

"But we do ask that if the ignorant white man is allowed to vote, that the ignorant colored man shall be allowed to vote also. We would be unmanly and uncandid did we not express our sorrow that freedom to us and our race is accomplished by the ruin of thousands of those for whom, notwithstanding the bitterness of the past and the present, we cherish feelings of respect and affection...we try to believe that the people of South Carolina are capable of rising superior to the prejudices of habit and education."

In his address to the Convention Governor Perry said that it was the earnest desire of all the members that the right of black suffrage "may be ignored *in toto* during the session." He mentioned this petition and trusted "for the future safety and welfare of the State that the document will not be placed on the records of the proceedings." It was not read either at

this convention, nor at the legislature, to which it was later sent, and the most significant legislation of 1865 was enactment of a Black Code, an effort to restrict the blacks as much as possible within his new status as freedman.

The "Colored People's Convention" met in Zion Church in Charleston, marking the beginning of concerted political action by state African Americans such as Robert C. DeLarge, A.J. Ransier, J.J. Wright, Beverly Nash, Francis L. Cardozo, Martin R. Delany, and Richard H. Cain, who would take leading roles in state politics. They appealed to Congress to abolish the Black Code and permit equal suffrage. The *Chicago Tribune* editorialized: "If ever a people have deserved extermination and banishment, it is the unprincipled, obstinate, ignorant and treacherous ruling class in South Carolina...To permit the state to come back into the Union...would be a mockery of freedom and perfidy to the honor of the Government." When Congress refused to seat the South Carolina delegates on the basis of the State Constitution of 1865, there began the period of "Congressional Reconstruction," a vindictive program of revenge.

On January 1, 1866, General Daniel E. Sickles, military commander of the District of North and South Carolina, declared the Black Code void, and overriding President Johnson's veto, Congress enacted the first in a series of Civil Rights Acts. With the state's rejection of the Fourteenth Amendment (making blacks citizens and preventing former government officials who had joined the Confederates from holding office until pardoned by Congress) the First Reconstruction Act was passed, leading to control of the state by blacks, carpetbaggers and scalawags. Carpetbaggers were Northern speculators who came South to profit by existing conditions,

Above:
Rice and salt in Charleston were turned over to city authorities after evacuation by Confederate forces. Separate days were appointed for whites and blacks to receive their allotment each week at the West Point Rice Mill on the Ashley River. Leslie's Illustrated News states they were mostly old men, women and children, wives and families of Confederate soldiers. Courtesy of South Carolina Historical Society

Top:
"A gallant sight it is to see/The buzzards in their glory,/Fall out about an old beef knee/And fight 'til they are gory." Known as "Charleston Eagles," the buzzards served a useful purpose as scavengers until the Health Department put an end to the practice of throwing refuse in the streets. Courtesy of South Carolina Historical Society

many bringing all they possessed in their carpetbags, forerunners of the modern suitcase.

Scalawags were Southern whites who also took advantage of the situation, and more especially, took advantage of the uneducated blacks. Carpetbaggers came also to determine that blacks be enfranchised, for before the war slaves were counted as three-fifths of their actual number for purposes of representation, and unless African Americans were now allowed to vote, the conquered whites would have more representation in Congress and the Electoral College than they had before the War.

Writing some years later on what he called "The Frightful Experiment," Massachusetts carpetbagger Daniel Chamberlain, who was counted with the corruptionists when he became South Carolina governor in 1874, said this Congressional

Reconstruction of the South was the result of a determination by the Republican party to control the South and the nation by the black vote, and the reconstruction acts would never have been passed had the black vote been Democratic.

A new constitutional convention met in Charleston January 14, 1868, with over half the delegates black and all but four, Republicans, over two-thirds of the electorate who selected them being black. Robert K. Scott, carpetbagger from Ohio, became governor, and there ensued what Northern newspaperman James S. Pike termed "a mess of rottenness." Little wonder that "Republican" remained a dirty word in South Carolina for almost a hundred years.

The Constitution enacted was drawn from contemporary Northern models, especially New York and Ohio, and was retained for twenty-seven years. It marked an advance in democracy, and provided for a public school system, with non-segregated and free elementary schools, which were set up on paper, but no attempt at implementation was made until 1877.

Scott, saying South Carolina whites were fit only to be ruled by Winchester rifles, armed the black militia and state police, and reinforced them with New York toughs. Whites responded with defensive measures, and in some counties joined the Ku Klux Klan, organized in 1866 in Tennessee, and active in the South Carolina upcountry where white economic competition with the black man was a factor.

In Charleston Rifle Companies were formed. Louisa Smythe remembers: "They were on guard day and night—a squad always on duty. Everything was systemized even to feeding them when on duty but everything was done with the most absolute quiet. I only remember that a note would come to me occasionally requesting me to have so many sandwiches and so much coffee ready at such an hour. It was ready packed in buckets and handed to the man who came for it.

"That was all I knew. The riots in the streets were frequent, and the alarms more so. Some terrible things happened. Young men of our acquaintance were beaten to death in the streets by negroes. At the slightest alarm, apparently without a word, the streets would be filled by 'our men' each with his gun in his hand and we never knew when the whole city would be bathed in blood. It was only by the greatest coolness that the most awful scenes were prevented…I think as I look back that the forebearance of our men was wonderful but it was right.

"There were many among the negroes that would have suffered with the guilty. Poor things, they were in a pitiful position between two fires. They knew that their interest and their affections lay with the white people, and yet they were so afraid of the turbulent element among their own people that they were obliged often to pretend to what they didn't feel.

"One evening during one of these riots your father was riding home on Gipsey, tired out. Just as he came near the corner of Legare and Tradd streets, a negro rushed from a dark doorway to his horse's head. He was just about to make Gipsey try her usual defense of rearing, when the negro whispered to him as he hung on to the rein, 'Go back sir, go round for God's sake—they're ready for you at the corner.'

"Then he ran back and disappeared, and your father was left there in a pleasing state of doubt as to what he ought to do. It was quite possible that it might be a trick to get him in some trouble at the other end. But as he had to risk it somewhere, he took the man's advice and went back, coming home by the Battery and Legare Street without any trouble.

"I wonder that our generation of women have any nerves

Above:
Avery Institute was founded in 1865 following a gift by the Rev. Charles Avery of Pittsburgh to the American Missionary Association. Operated as a private school through 1946, from 1947-54 Avery was a public city school. Many leading members of Charleston's black community received their education here, in what was considered comparable to Charleston's best public schools. Courtesy of Citadel Archives

Top:
Shown here is engraving of citizens of Charleston taking the Oath of Allegiance. "There can be no neutrality, no evasion. The government recognizes but two parties in the issue now before the country—Union men and rebels—and it is for the inhabitants of Charleston to say to which side they belong." Courtesy of South Carolina Historical Society

left at all. The amount of watching and waiting that we have done seems almost incredible as I look back, and it is so provokingly impossible to give an idea of it to others."

In 1872 Scott was succeeded by scalawag Franklin J. Moses, Jr., "the Robber Governor." In *The Prostrate State* Pike declared "A white community…lies prostrate in the dust, ruled over by this strange conglomerate, gathered from the ranks of its own servile population. It is the spectacle of a society suddenly turned bottomside up."

Perry commented on the election of 1872 that "The State Government has, confessedly, fallen into the hands of rogues, swindlers and corrupt men, who have openly plundered the public treasury, robbed the people, forged State bonds, increased the indebtedness of the State $27,000,000 in four years, levied and collected intolerable taxes, and enriched themselves by the most bare-faced bribery and corruption, as well as by arrant roguery and plunder."

Young Daniel J. Jenkins, Baptist minister, opened the Jenkins Orphanage in 1892. The Orphanage owned a farm where the children learned trades to make most of them self-supporting. Their band was a familiar sight on Charleston streets, and they even made a tour of England in 1895. Courtesy of South Carolina Historical Society

Right:
As late as 1897, the "Blue Line" horse-drawn street cars operated on Broad Street, with the "Red Line" on Rutledge Avenue, and "Yellow Line" on Meeting. A gentleman rose when a lady entered, doffed his hat, gave her his seat, took her fare and dropped her nickel in the box. Often the conductor would wait while a passenger made purchases in a nearby store. Courtesy of South Carolina Historical Society

Right:
Last trip of the Sullivan's Island mule car was taken July, 1898, by E.H. Schultz Engineer Corps, U.S.A. Courtesy of Collection of the Charleston Museum, Charleston, SC

Below:
East Battery promenade as it appeared in 1880. Notice the ubiquitous buzzards. Courtesy of South Caroliniana Library, Columbia, SC

The legislature ran a free bar in the capitol for themselves and guests, and payment for passage of bills and for state offices was often made with state funds.

Wallace points out that many of the black leaders were superior morally to the average scalawag or carpetbagger and some were of outstanding ability. Francis Louis Cardozo, whose mother was half Indian and half black, was reputed to be the son of J.N.Cardozo, economist and editor of an anti-nullification newspaper of the 1830s. He was a graduate of the University of Glasgow, studied theology in Edinburgh and London and came to Charleston from New Haven to serve as principal of Avery Institute, a free school for blacks that was established and financed by Quakers. Cardozo was Secretary of State in South Carolina for four years, and was Secretary-Treasurer from 1872–1876.

Thomas Ezekiel Miller, educated in Charleston before the Civil War in a school operated by free blacks, became the first president of the South Carolina State College at Orangeburg. In 1882, he served as state chairman of the Republican party, was a member of the legislature, and of Congress.

Two of the most admirable black leaders were Richard Harvey Cain and Martin R. Delany. Cain was born free in Virginia and came as a missionary to Charleston, where he edited the *Missionary Record*. He served as state senator and for two years as United States Congressman. Cain had no use for the carpetbaggers who exploited his race. He founded Lincolnville in Charleston County, as a completely black municipality.

Delany, who was a candidate for Lieutenant Governor in 1874, was a full-blooded Virginia born black of a free mother and a slave father who later bought his freedom and moved to Pennsylvania. Delany had an extraordinary career. He and Frederick Douglass were co-editors of *The North Star*, a leading anti-slavery paper of western New York. He studied at Harvard Medical School and practiced as a physician and surgeon in Canada, and explored Africa. Delany, a major in the U.S. Army, was in command of the sea islands and a portion of the mainland at Hilton Head and was sub-assistant commissioner of the Freedman's Bureau, in which capacity he arbitrated between planters and their field hands.

He resigned as aide-de-camp to Governor Scott because of corruption and frauds. In 1874 Delany addressed the Independent Republican Convention. "The time has come," he said, "when the black men must stand up side by side with the intelligent and honest white men of the state" and end the corruption taught them by "the Sixth ward New York politicians." He declared that social equality must regulate itself, and that no one, black or white, should be forced to sit at table with the other. He is considered the originator of the "black is beautiful" concept and, like Cain, was bitterly opposed to white carpetbaggers who misled the blacks.

The election resulted in a large voter turnout, but Major Delany and Judge John T. Green were defeated by Chamberlain, who had come to South Carolina to settle a friend's estate, having served as a lieutenant of black cavalry in 1864. Although he was closely associated with corruption while serving as attorney general from 1868 to 1872, when he assumed the position of governor in 1874 it was as a reformer. When the Legislature elected Moses and corrupt black man W.J. Whipper judges, Chamberlain refused to commission them, and in an interview with the *Courier* said, "I look upon their election as a horrible disaster—a disaster equally great to the State, to the Republican party, and, greatest of all, to

Three of the first black national Congressmen were from South Carolina. Robert C. DeLarge was a former Charleston tailor, Joseph H. Rainey had been a barber in the Mills House before the war, and Robert B. Elliott, a Bostonian and Eton graduate, had come to Charleston as a soldier in a Negro regiment and stayed on after the war. *Courtesy of Carolina Art Association*

those communities which shall be doomed to feel the full effects of the presence of Moses and Whipper upon the bench." He foresaw the reorganization of the Democratic party to combat a "terrible crevasse of misgovernment and public debauchery," and in answer to an invitation of the New England Society to their annual banquet, wrote, "if there ever was an hour when the spirit of the Puritans, the spirit of undying, unconquerable enmity and defiance to wrong ought to animate their sons, it is this hour, here, in South Carolina. The civilization of the Puritan and the Cavalier, of the Roundhead and the Huguenot, is in peril."

It was at this nadir in the history of South Carolina that the one man appeared who could check the influence of the radicals and through his own personality, his wisdom, moderation and integrity gain the trust of and control the people of the state. This man was General Wade Hampton. The Columbia *Daily Register* quoted an ex-Radical black as saying he didn't "believe the Almighty made Hampton like He made other men, He just dropped Hampton down from Heaven!"

He won the election of 1876 with the support of nearly every white South Carolinian and some fifteen thousand Blacks, so that even a Republican count gave him a majority. In 1867 Hampton had advocated a restricted ballot with property or educational qualifications applied to all alike, which was rejected at the time. In his campaign for governor he pledged to defend the rights of blacks equally with those of whites, countering the propaganda of the Radicals who convinced many blacks that the Democrats would once more enslave them should they regain office. Hampton insisted on power without force, and white Democratic rifle clubs used a show of strength to prevent violence, and their Red flannel shirts became the symbol of Hampton's campaign. U.S. Senator Morton had waved a crimsoned shirt which he said was stained with blood of a Louisiana Black. Democrats claimed this was a fake, and "Waving the bloody shirt" became political slang for arousing sectional prejudice. It was in derision of this, Williams explains in his book *Hampton and His Red Shirts*, that Hampton supporters adopted the red shirt as their uniform. According to Williams it first appeared at a parade in Charleston on August 25, 1876, which included 500 mounted whites and 500 black Democrats, guarded closely by the whites from attack by Republicans, for it was against black Democrats that their own race directed their greatest animosity.

When a riot broke out in Charleston on September 6, 1876, Williams gives a first person account of being called out as a member of the Carolina Rifle Battalion and standing restively in double rank before Hibernian Hall facing City Hall Park for an hour and a half while distant shots and shouts could be heard from King Street. Criticized at the time, it was not until later that he realized that their restraint was necessary. "That was the soul-testing choice the white people of South Carolina were forced to make many times in the months from August 1876 to April 1877—choice between what looked like meek and craven submission to insult and outrage, or use of superiority in arms and organization which would vent temper and wreak vengeance at the moment and bring years of oppression, ruin and misery." The riot was instigated by the Hunkidories and Live Oaks, black Radical Republican secret organizations, who attacked a meeting of the "Colored Democratic Clubs" of Ward 4. After desperate fighting at Citadel Green the white men present managed to get the black Democrats to the safety of the U.S. soldiers quartered in the Arsenal, after which the mob pursued and beat every white man they encountered, smashed windows and threatened to exterminate the white population. Williams points out that the account of the riot "spiked the best guns of the...Radical extremists who were trying to persuade Northern people that the Negroes of South Carolina were innocent, pathetic, helpless victims of white ruffians intent on regaining power and starting a new Secession movement," and that from then on Charleston, aroused to its danger, was under virtual martial law from dusk to daylight as rifle clubs and mounted patrols guarded black Democratic meetings and the homes of leading black Democrats in addition to patroling the town.

When Chamberlain contested the election and Federal troops took control of the State House, it was Hampton who prevented what might have become another civil war. The New York Herald correspondent in his eyewitness account wrote: "There has never been a more critical and dangerous conjunction in the history of American politics...The credit of preserving the peace at Columbia yesterday is due to General Wade Hampton, Democratic candidate for Governor. He had only to lift his finger, he had only to signify the slightest assent and the State House would have been rescued from the Federal soldiers and his supporters could have controlled the organization of the Legislature."

After four months of Chamberlain meeting in the capitol and Hampton and his legislature, formally recognized by the state Supreme Court as the lawful legislative body, in Carolina Hall, President Hayes requested a conference with the two leaders. As a result Hayes ordered Federal troops withdrawn on April 10, and Chamberlain, denouncing this decision, turned the keys of the governor's office over to Hampton.

Hampton's policy of reconciliation and inclusion of the blacks in politics was opposed by the extremists led by General Martin W. Gary. When Hampton immediately after his re-election in 1878 simultaneously suffered a hunting accident which cost him a leg and took him out of politics for six months, and was elected United States senator, removing

68

Above:
The old foreman and hands appear in front of a Negro house at the summer home of Mrs. W.J. Lucas on South Isle in June 1893. The large mortar and pestle were used for husking rice. Photo by Maham de Lisle Haig. Courtesy of South Carolina Historical Society

Top:
"The elements are fast doing their work upon the ruins at M(iddleton) P(lace) and the walls are falling pretty rapidly," Williams Middleton wrote to his sister Eliza Fisher, May 10, 1874. Courtesy of Middleton Place Foundation

One of two South Carolinians commemorated in Statuary Hall in the U.S. Capitol, General Wade Hampton "embodied the best tradition of Southern friendship for the Negro." Generally remembered as leader of the Red-Shirts, his announced policy was to appoint men to office who were best qualified without reference to race. His vision encompassed the rights and needs of black and white, but he was defeated by extremists of both North and South. Courtesy of Library of Congress

Above:
In 1867 Mrs. Mary Amarinthia Snowden and her sister mortaged their Church Street home to finance their purchase of this property at 62 Broad Street and organized the Home for Mothers, Widows and Daughters of Confederate Soldiers. In this picture of their school, Mrs. Snowden stands on the piazza at the right with her hands folded on the railing. One mother wrote: "Can not pay in advance, if you take her and wait until spring when my cotton comes in, I can pay then." Tuition of $100 a year was paid "if possible."

Right:
In 1889, Dr. Charles U. Shepard established an experimental tea farm in Summerville. Unable to pay high labor prices, he ran a school for black children, and the older ones were trained to pick tea for which they were paid by the pound. Courtesy of South Carolina Historical Society

him from the state, there was no one of his stature who could capture the confidence and trust of the blacks as he had. Unable to split the Black vote as he had done, South Carolina whites were faced with the unacceptable return to black supremacy, or some method of limiting the black majority. In 1881–2 the legislature enacted the "Eight-Box-Law," which prescribed certain conditions of voter registration and separate ballots for state officers which effectively eliminated ignorant illiterate voters. The solid Democratic Party gained strength, and by 1890 when Ben Tillman was elected governor, white supremacy was uppermost in politics and a Tillman-controlled constitutional convention of 1895 openly set out to deprive the Blacks of as many rights as was legally possible within Federal law.

They were denied the right of a voting membership within

o'clock, waves beat down the seawall, driving the Norwegian ship *Medbor* ashore, and hurling waterspouts against houses. At high tide the water in the harbor was level with the High Battery walk, and was just a few inches lower inside on East Battery, and was up to six feet in some of the houses. A half hour later the large gilt ball and weathervane on St. Michael's spire fell 186 feet to the sidewalk and made a dent in the pavement.

Both sides of the peninsula suffered and as the eye of the hurricane passed and winds blew from the west, several hundred feet of causeway approaches to a new bridge being built across the river to St. Andrew's Parish were swept away. After the storm East Battery seawall was strengthened with huge flagstones four inches thick that have withstood all storms since, and iron railings supported by neatly carved cedar

the Democratic party primary that was not to be challenged until 1947. In that year Federal Judge J. Waties Waring of Charleston ruled that since the primary was the real elective force in the state, it must be open to all registered voters regardless of "race, color, creed or national origin."

Tillman capitalized on his humble origins by adopting the nickname "Pitchfork Ben," and became governor following an almost unbroken line of leaders from the low country planter aristocracy. It was not until 1938 with the election of Mayor Burnet Rhett Maybank that a Charlestonian again occupied the governor's mansion.

Before Charleston had recovered from the war, a series of natural disasters once more occurred. On August 25, 1885 the wind began blowing, increasing steadily during the night as lightning flashed and church bells set off by the storm boomed incessantly. As the storm reached its peak near eight

posts were placed along its top. By August 30, 1886, the ball was back atop St. Michael's, the steeple repaired and repainted and the scaffolding removed.

That night soon after the bells chimed the third quarter after nine under a cloudless sky, came a long rolling, rumbling roar from the earth, as buildings shook, floors heaved and collapsed, and walls swayed and crumbled. Gas lights and jets flickered through a pall of dust, and St. Michael's clock stopped three minutes later at 9:54.

Firemen and police worked steadily to control the city, as almost twenty fires broke out and terrified Charlestonians rushed outside. Four more quakes occurred before midnight. Twenty-seven persons were killed outright, and another 83 died from injuries, shock or exposure. All telegraph lines were down and until the following day there was no communication with the outside world, where rumor spread

Many buildings such as the old Exchange seen here were propped up after the earthquake; then metal stabilizing rods were run through to strengthen them. Charlestonians call these "earthquake bolts," and the large washers at their ends are in various shapes, those on the Exchange being lions' heads. Courtesy of Collection of the Charleston Museum, Charleston, SC

By 1907 High Battery wall has been repaired, a new railing and cannon are in place, Bernard O'Neill has redecorated One East Battery with balustrade and cast iron balconies, and a boarding house, the Shamrock Terrace, is operating at the far end of the walk. Courtesy of Author's collection

The Hibernian Society Hall, designed by Thomas U. Walter of Philadelphia in 1840, lost its entire portico in the earthquake of 1886. Courtesy of South Carolina Historical Society

Opposite page:
Washington Park beside City Hall was one of many "tent cities" that sprang up in open areas after the earthquake as tremors continued to threaten further danger from falling buildings. Courtesy of Collection of the Charleston Museum, Charleston, SC

Prominent King Street merchant and banker Samuel Wilson was one of the few Charlestonians who could afford to build in 1890. His Queen Anne style house is on a granite foundation, with leaded stained glass windows, bent siding, mahogany window frames, medieval type chimneys, corner turrets and piazzas. Owned by the College of Charleston, it is now a women's residence hall. Courtesy of College of Charleston

that Charleston had been swept away by a tidal wave.

To the one-and-a-half million dollars' damage of the previous year, the earthquake added five million dollars more. Letters and telegrams of sympathy, including a cablegram from Queen Victoria, poured in from all over the world. A concert was given in Paris for the benefit "des catastrophes de Charleston États-Unis," and the Lord Mayor of London appealed for aid in the *Times*.

The old century held one more catastrophe. In 1893 a storm so severe that for many years it was called the "Great Hurricane" covered the lower city from Tradd Street south with water up to five feet deep, as a thirteen foot tide swept up the harbor. Storm signals hoisted August 25 were not lowered until the thirtieth, and the area was swept with such high winds that for four days no birds were seen in the city.

A *News and Courier* reporter found the entire western section of town under six to ten feet of water, houses isolated like islands, and he swam from the corner of Rutledge Avenue and Bull Street to a house where a group of eight women, children and a man were huddled by the light of a candle. Again the wires were down and the city isolated. Three hundred excursionists from Savannah arrived during the hurricane and "all that they saw of the city was what flew past their hotel windows in chunks!"

Sullivan's island residents took refuge in Fort Moultrie, although it was "a dark and dreary place to seek shelter." In Mt. Pleasant the newspaper reported that the tide came up to the council chamber on Pitt Street on the east end, but that there was slight damage away from the waterfront. It was on the sea islands to the south, however, that there was the "most terrible visitation which the inhabitants have ever had," as

whole settlements were swept away on St. Helena, not a soul left on Coosaw Island, and hundreds dead on Ladies Island. At Port Royal rescuers came upon dozens of bodies at a time. Red Cross workers came to the area and Clara Barton took charge of sea island relief efforts. In June she came to Charleston exhausted from overwork, and established headquarters in a warehouse on East Bay, where she and her staff slept in tents on the second floor.

By the following year High Battery's inner walk had been widened and rebuilt and four double flights of stone steps were in place. Sidewalks of concrete were replacing the dirt and board walks of earlier days and a "modern roadway" of cinders was placed on St. Philip Street. A coat of stucco covered the earthquake cracks on City Hall, and by 1896 a new Federal post office replaced the Guard House destroyed by the quake, making the fourth "corner of the law," and adding Federal to State, Municipal and Church structures. At the time it was called a "handsome specimen of modern architecture," but some referred to it as "pork-barrel Rennaissance" in style!

Murat Halstead wrote in the Brooklyn New York *Standard-Union* that: "Charleston is a plucky old town. She has had more history within the last forty years than any other spot in the World. It was there the war began, and Charleston was besieged and bombarded by the year. She suffered next from a devastating fire, and then from a series of earthquakes. Lastly, she has been the objective point of two cyclones. Cut off from the world by warfare, earthquakes and cyclones, and swept by a whirlwind of fire, she emerges to say she is doing business at the old stand. It is high time for her turn of good fortune. In politics she is not agreeable, but she manages always to be interesting."

In July of 1898, 7000 soldiers arrived by railroad for embarkation to Cuba, and individual parents as well as the mayors of Oil City, Pennsylvania, and Eau Clare, Wisconsin, wrote thanks to the city for the welcome and kind treatment provided in Charleston. "If anyone asks you what you think of Charleston, just tell them it is the best place outside of home," wrote Leo Howell of the 16th Pennsylvania to his father from transport #21. Courtesy of South Carolina Historical Society

A buggy with Confederate flags flying pulls up to Thomson Auditorium, decorated for the United Confederate Veterans' Reunion May 10, 1899. The site was formerly Bennett's Mill Pond, and the auditorium was constructed in hopes of attracting conventions. From 1907 to 1980 it served as the Charleston Museum. Courtesy of South Carolina Historical Society

The Cotton Palace is seen at night when the Exposition grounds became an unbelievable fantasyland. Courtesy of Carolina Art Association

Chapter Seven

"There is a good day coming"

1900–1975
Recovery

T he new century found Charleston making efforts to attract industry and recreate her position as a leading port. Ground was broken for the South Carolina Interstate and West Indian Exposition, a mini World's Fair on a state level.

Opening day came "with a blaze of sunshine, a flashing of banners, a booming of guns" and such a parade as was "never witnessed in Charleston before. Flags decorated the whole city and hung from the rigging of all the vessels in the harbor."

"It was a day on which to believe and hope—a day on which to prophesy—a day on which to dream dreams and to see visions!"

The First Artillery Band opened religious ceremonies on Sunday, December 1, 1901, with the "Priests' March" from *Athalia*, as Jewish rabbis, Roman Catholic priests and Protestant ministers participated. The secular opening next day saw a tremendous parade of some twenty-two thousand, including sculptors, architects, carpenters and all who had worked on the gigantic task of readying the "Ivory City."

There were fourteen main buildings, ivory-colored with red tile roofs. States and cities sponsored buildings and exhibits, and handiwork was exhibited in the "Women's Building," still standing at the foot of St. Margaret Street. Booker T. Washington of Tuskegee Institute organized the black department of the Exposition, with Dr. W.D. Crum, Charleston physician, and Thomas Ezekiel Miller as vice-presidents. Dr. Crum was later appointed Collector of the Port by President Theodore Roosevelt, and President Taft appointed him as Minister to Liberia.

On the twenty-two acre midway were Eskimos, East Indian tigers, West Indian dancers, a panorama of the Battle of Manassas, golden chariots and an "educated horse."

There was a Venetian canal complete with gondoliers and an artificial moon. A former bandstand now stands forlorn in Hampton Park.

The Women's Building was "The Grove," former residence of William Lowndes, and at the time of the Exposition the property of Captain F.W. Wagener, president of the Exposition Company. Wagener also owned the Pine Forest Inn in Summerville, where he entertained President Theodore Roosevelt during his visit to the Exposition.

On Saturday, May 31, 1902 taps sounded at midnight, and the lights of the Exposition went out. It had attracted more visitors to Charleston in six months than had come in the preceding six years. It had brought Charleston national publicity, as well.

Financially, however, the Exposition was a failure, ending in receivership. Concrete results were the American Cigar Company factory, the development of a oyster canning industry, and the start of banana imports by the United Fruit Company.

An even more important event of 1901, however, was the transfer of the United States Naval Station from Port Royal to Charleston. The Station had been established at Port Royal during the Civil War when that area had been occupied by Union forces, and the move gave a tremendous boost to Charleston's economy.

Admiral F.W. Dickens arrived on the flagship *Texas*, heading the Coast Squadron of the United States Fleet. He cited the Charleston Naval Yard as being nearer to the West Indies bases than any other yard on the mainland—with a port deep enough for any battleship and roomy enough to accommodate sixty-five ships, a thousand feet apart.

The admiral praised the city's hospitality, saying that Charleston was "famous in this respect throughout the civilized world." The slogan, "Charleston must look to the sea" was soon adopted by the city.

That same year a group of immigrants from Belgium, Holland and Austria arrived on the steamship *Wittekind*. They were greeted by several Charleston residents who had come from Bremen nearly fifty years earlier. This was the first successful immigration from Europe to a South Atlantic port in approximately fifty years. Many of the new arrivals went to work in the textile mills of the Piedmont areas, but some two hundred settled in Charleston, finding here a congenial group of German ancestry.

By 1910, the Jubilee Edition of the *News and Courier* reported that Charleston was doing over 94 million dollars in business—that despite fire, war, storms and earthquake, population and trade were expanding.

There were some twenty companies engaged in mining, manufacturing or handling fertilizers. Sixteen companies were involved in manufacturing and woodworking industries.

There were two railroads—the Southern and the Atlantic Coast Line—and shipping had increased almost five times in the last twenty-five years. Banking, the Post Office and the Custom House all showed increased receipts. Charleston County was the second largest truck growing district in the country, and the lumber industry showed steady development.

The construction of a seawall was completed from King Street to Chisholm's Mill at the west end of Tradd Street, and a mix of mud and sand was pumped from the bottom of the Ashley River as fill. Large amounts of cobblestones, Belgian blocks and oyster shells were dumped on the outside. Forty-seven acres of mud flats at the west end of the peninsula were filled and a total of 191 lots created, with ninety-five of these owned by the city and the rest by private individuals.

Construction of jetties improved the harbor, which had been nearly sealed off by a crescent-shaped bar ten miles long that extended from Sullivan's Island to Morris Island. The jetties are a legacy of Charleston's former enemy, Union General Q.A. Gillmore, who designed them, but died before the jetties were constructed.

New buildings went up all over the peninsula city. Thomson

75

A panoramic view of the sunken gardens looking from the Cotton Palace north towards the bandstand. The grounds were designed by architect Bradford Lee Gilbert to radiate from the bandstand, which was the architectural center of the Exposition grounds. Today the sunken gardens form the focal point of Hampton Park. Courtesy of Carolina Art Association

Auditorium opened as a convention center, in hopes of attracting visitors; Mitchell School was built, and police headquarters moved to a new station at St. Philip and Vanderhorst Streets.

The South Carolina Military Academy (The Citadel) expanded into the old police facilities on Marion Square to accommodate a 25 percent increase in enrollment.

In 1911 Charleston received a severe setback. A great hurricane hit the coast and delivered the death blow to the rice industry. It not only destroyed that year's crop, but washed out so many dikes that the storm, coupled with increasing midwestern competition, virtually ended commercial rice growing in the state.

At almost the same time, the arrival of the boll weevil in local cotton fields completely ruined the profitable long staple cotton industry in the Sea Islands.

World War I provided a temporary boost to Charleston's economy, as the city became a major port of embarkation for soldiers and material. Additional wharves were constructed as soldiers, equipment, ammunition, mules and horses left for France. Remount Road is a reminder of these days, being the road used to ride horses from the railroad to the piers, after they were taken from the railroad cars and "remounted."

Many rural people moved into the city at this time as jobs became available in the defense program. Streets were laid off in North Charleston as that area began to grow. Reynolds Avenue running from Meeting Street Road to the main gate of the Naval Station became one of the first sections of concrete paved highway in the state.

After the war, city officials moved to counteract an economic slump by establishing the Port Utilities Commission, which took over the wartime docks and railway spur lines and began to actively promote trade. This was a predecessor of the South Carolina State Ports Authority established ten years later. A huge coal tipple was built on the Cooper River that could lift entire railway cars of coal, tip them over and dump the coal into a chute fed directly into a ship, and Charleston became a leading coaling port for steamers as well as a center for coal export.

John P. Grace, elected mayor in 1911, considered his election to be revolutionary, because the "Bourbons," the aristocratic segment of the population, had fought him for years. He represented a new type of Charleston leader—of Irish immigrant stock, a Roman Catholic and not an S.O.B. (South-of-Broad resident!). He declared that it was prejudice that held Charleston back—the ancient curse of Charleston being "not what's what, but who's who."

He stated that the spirit of Charleston had never surrendered to the idea of equality of all men under the law that was the true meaning of the peace at Appomatox, and that the American flag was still a foreign flag to Charlestonians, who flew the flag of "privilege, bigotry, intolerance and proscription."

In October 1915, *Evening Post* reporter Sidney J. Cohen was killed and four persons were wounded in a fusillade of pistol shots in the committee room at the southwest corner of King and George streets. A meeting of the city Democratic executive committee was about to declare the nominee of the primary election and the militia marched to the scene with fixed bayonets. Major Tristam T. Hyde won the nomination over the incumbent Grace, but four years later Grace became mayor once again after a bitter election campaign.

Again, the militia stood by as women voted for the first time in a city election: "our own wives and mothers casting their ballots with bayonets at their breasts and under the muzzle of machine guns," moaned Grace.

Grace was succeeded in 1923 by Thomas Porcher Stoney, from an old established Charleston family, who said: "Charleston needs more perspiration and less talk about inspiration of ancestors." He said that the city could move ahead if her citizens adopted the right "mental attitude and community spirit," and urged selling Charleston to Charlestonians before trying to sell it to outsiders.

He called for civic unity from "the Battery to the Boundary," and for assumption of the obligations of citizenship. The city had a debt of over $350,000 when he assumed office, and Stoney's survey of the city government resulted in a reduction of its work force from an unwieldy fifty to eight

departments. This put the city's financial affairs on a sound and businesslike basis, and for the first time funds for publicity became an item of the city budget.

Gas lamps were replaced with electricity, Andrew Buist Murray gave funds to pave the boulevard and to run a roadway around Hampton Park, and construction began on the Ashley River Memorial Bridge to the west. By legislative action Charleston was now "The State Port," and Stoney encouraged cooperation and no more "calamity howlers." Union Pier at the foot of Market Street began operation, the National Foreign Trade Convention held its first meeting on the South Atlantic coast here, and by 1926 Charleston was becoming known as a convention city.

With the formal opening of the Ashley River bridge that year subdivisions across the Ashley began to grow. In 1929 the municipal airport moved to its present location, its terminal building standing on the approximate site of André Michaux's eighteenth century French Botanical Gardens. Also in 1929 a three-day celebration of parades, races and fireworks marked the opening of the John P. Grace Memorial Bridge over the Cooper River.

It was, however, World War II that provided the real impetus for Charleston's economic recovery. As the War approached, Naval Base construction increased and airport facilities were enlarged. The census of 1940 showed an urban population of 71,275, but the Charleston Yearbook listed over one hundred thousand people—including industrial war workers, defense activities at the Navy Yard, Charleston Shipyard and Drydock, other related industries and the military personnel on duty in the area.

Low cost housing projects were undertaken and the Charleston Housing Authority was established to build sixteen rental projects financed by bond sale, with slum clearance occurring as a by-product.

Charleston observed the coastal dimout regulations, and hundreds of people were trained as air raid wardens, auxillary firemen and policemen. Spotters watched for planes from the top of the Fort Sumter Hotel and other strategic locations. Wounded arrived from the European war zones for treatment at the Charleston Naval Hospital and Stark General Hospital, now the site of Stark Industrial Park.

Charleston became a vital defense center as men and supplies moved through the Army Port of Embarkation and bomber groups and Army Air Transport personnel were trained at the Army Air Field. The Sixth Naval District set up headquarters in the Fort Sumter Hotel.

Hardly had the city recovered from the news of President Roosevelt's sudden death on April 12, 1945, when it went wild with joy at news of Germany's surrender. Three months later the City Council recessed to listen to President Harry S. Truman announce Japan's surrender on August 14.

With the end of the war, Charleston now had a skilled labor supply and housing to accommodate it. The Charleston Development Board was established by the business community to interest other industries in the area and work began on paving, draining and sewer projects that had been set aside for the duration of the war.

Slum clearance and public housing projects continued, and land was reclaimed on both sides of the peninsula, and in the 1950s Charleston's return to prosperity began to accelerate.

Top:
What would these well-covered bathing beauties of 1908 think of the bikini-clad beachgoers of 1980! In shoes, black cotton stockings, dresses and caps, *Harriott Cheves and Caroline Williams bathe in the Ashley River off the sea wall at the rear of 39 South Battery. Courtesy of Author's collection*

Above right:
Excursion steamers were always crowded with tourists every spring when they took visitors to the Ashley River Gardens. Here in 1907 are the General French and E.H. Jackson at the landing at Magnolia-on-the-Ashley, *whose gardens John Galsworthy described as "a kind of Paradise...a miraculously enchanted wilderness." Courtesy of Magnolia Plantation and Gardens*

Above left:
A joggling board provided extra seating and gentle exercise on many Charleston piazzas. Entitled in a scrapbook "The Millionaires," this idyllic scene was taken at Sullivan's Island in *1905. Charlestonians have long enjoyed pleasures of the seashore, surf-bathing, fishing and sailing that elsewhere are reserved for the wealthy. Courtesy of Author's collection*

Opposite page:
The hurricane of 1911 had winds of 105 m.p.h., and left seven dead the morning of August 28. Charleston has been the focal *point of some 88 hurricanes between 1686 and 1980. Courtesy of South Carolina Historical Society*

78

Charleston harbor became known as the "Golden Port of the South Atlantic," and for the first time in her history, Charleston trade reached across the Ohio Valley and the Midwest to Minnesota. As the nation's textile industry continued to move south centering in the state's Piedmont area, ships docked at Charleston with long staple cotton from Egypt and Peru, wool from Australia, New Zealand, Africa and South America, and meat, also brought on the wool ships, became an important cargo.

Interstate Highway 26 connected Charleston with Cleveland, Ohio just as the use of containerized shipping was making tremendous changes in ocean freight handling.

Business and local government combined to establish the Bushy Park project. This huge tract of land on the Cooper River provided several thousand acres for industrial development, with an abundant supply of fresh water for industry on one side and a salt stream on the other for disposal of treated wastes.

Marl tunnels connected the project to the City of Charleston's Goose Creek Reservoir, giving the city a back-up source of fresh water. Another eight and a half foot in diameter marl tunnel runs under the Cooper River, conducting fresh water from the Bushy Park reservoir to a multimillion dollar plant of Amoco Chemical Corporation.

Today important industries at Bushy Park include Du Pont, South Carolina Electric and Gas, General Dynamics, and A.G. Bayer of Germany.

As Charleston developed a diversified industrial base, military installations expanded also. Santee-Cooper Hydroelectric Project built the first of a series of huge steam generating plants, and private utility construction jumped as electricity became the number one industrial need.

As competition from foreign textile industries and development of synthetics made production of cotton less profitable, farmers began planting their fields in pine trees for harvest as timber or pulpwood, and growing soybeans. The state soon became a leading producer of this versatile Asiatic bean.

The General Assembly approved a 21 million dollar construction program that included towering grain elevators at North Charleston, giving the state's farmers a nearby ocean outlet for their crops. Charleston in the 1960s became the major East Coast assembly base for Polaris missiles and home port for nuclear-powered submarines, as Sputnik provoked the United States into building up its military.

Higher education expanded locally as the Citadel, under the direction of its president, General Mark W. Clark, hero of World War II and former Army Chief of Staff, added barracks and classroom buildings and set its maximum enrollment at two thousand. Baptist College at Charleston opened off I-26 north of the city, and in 1970 the College of Charleston became a state supported institution and began an expansion program that increased enrollment from five hundred to five thousand within less than ten years. This resulted in a building program of some twenty acres in extent in the inner city, centering around the original one block square campus, and winning for the College in 1975 an award from the National Trust for Historic Preservation for its outstanding work.

The Medical College of South Carolina received university status in 1969 and by 1980 was educating some 2,300 students in its Colleges of Medicine, Nursing, Dental Medicine, Allied Health Sciences, Graduate Studies, and Pharmacy, in addition to providing practical training in its teaching hospital and eye institute.

Charleston Technical Education Center opened, member of a statewide system of thirteen technical education centers that trained skilled technicians and craftsmen, and recruited and trained workers at state expense for specific jobs in new plants.

In 1960 the first city expansion in a hundred years brought an estimated nine hundred new residents into Charleston with the annexation of a portion of St. Andrew's Parish. When the Silas Pearman bridge opened in 1966 the development of the East Cooper area began to increase.

Startling changes on the political front accompanied new patterns in industry and agriculture. For the first time in history a United States senator was elected by a write-in vote when a political whirlwind swept former governor J. Strom Thurmond to the U.S. Senate.

This came about because of the death of the incumbent senator, Burnet R. Maybank. The Democratic State Committee instead of holding a primary, giving lack of time before the election as their reason.

The Charleston *News and Courier* organized a protest and initiated the write-in-movement for the Thurmond candidacy. For two months newspapers editorialized on the write-in campaign citing people's rights to choose their own representatives. Thurmond not only won, but ten years later, bolted the Democratic party and became South Carolina's first Republican senator since 1878.

As 1970 drew to a close, the nation joined Charleston in mourning the death of Senator L. Mendel Rivers, the chairman of the House Armed Services Committee and the man who represented the First District of South Carolina for thirty years. His political career had begun in 1933 when he was elected to the General Assembly from Charleston, and he was largely responsible for locating military installations and related industry in the Charleston area.

In the mid-twentieth century preservation became a leading concern to Charlestonians. The easy money nationwide of the 1920s posed an unexpected threat to Charleston. Out-of-state buyers bought woodwork from entire drawing rooms and iron balconies became collectors' items. The drawing room woodwork of the Mansion House on Broad Street is at Winterthur Museum, the cypress panelling from the dining and drawing rooms of Col. John Stuart's house on Tradd Street was sold to the Minneapolis Museum of Fine Arts. Gradually the city was disappearing bit by bit.

The 1920s had seen an increasing migration of African Americans from rural areas into the city, giving rise to the black sections of modern Charleston. Until the end of the 1930s, however, former slave quarters in the city still housed descendants of slave families. It wasn't until later decades that the quarters and carriage houses were converted into apartments.

Slums ran through parts of today's most fashionable sections, and the southeastern area of the city below Broad was crisscrossed by alleys and depressed blocks of housing. It was said in 1906 that "no one would care to live in Elliott Street today, nor would any lady be seen there."

Later Elliott Street would be shown on the candlelight tours of Historic Charleston Foundation, but until World Wart II most Charlestonians were "too poor to paint and too proud to whitewash," as the saying goes. Northern visitors found the lack of paint depressing. Very few could afford to replace their eighteenth century houses with the then popular Victorian styles, or even to add fashionable mansard roofs, so that their poverty preserved Charleston's eighteenth century treasures.

When the depression of 1929 spread over the country, a local businessman bitterly remarked that Charleston was already so near the bottom that she never felt it! Because of widespread unemployment a civic committee was appointed to raise emergency relief funds through public conscription. Ladies raised additional thousands with penny-a-meal jars and the city issued script when it ran out of money to pay its employees.

The Society for the Preservation of Old Dwellings, forerunner of the Preservation Society of 1980, was organized with less than the proverbial shoestring; its immediate purpose was to prevent the destruction of the Joseph Manigault House at 350 Meeting Street. They achieved their objective, but the house, described by architect John Meade Howells as the "finest masonry town-house of the so-called Adam style in America," was later sold for taxes. It was the generosity of the wealthy Princess Pignatelli, herself of Charleston extraction, that resulted in its present ownership by the Charleston Museum.

In 1931 preservation received a tremendous boost with the passage of a zoning ordinance, providing for use, height and area districts, and establishment of a section designated as "Old and Historic." This was the first historic area zoning in the country, and attracted national attention, being termed "One of the most forward advances in city planning work and architectural control that we have ever yet had in the country." Robert D. Kohn of New York, president of the AIA, hailed it as "the most progressive ordinance ever adopted in America."

In 1933 the city established a Historical Commission, and maps and historic folders were printed for distribution to local hotels. W.P.A. workers put up historic markers in the city's first attempt to publicize its historic treasures, and in 1941

Today's Rainbow Row is hardly recognizable in this picture taken when the large drawing rooms of some of these houses were partitioned with scrap lumber frames covered with newspapers into as many as six smaller rooms. In 1931 when Judge and Mrs. Lionel K. Legge restored Othniel Beale's house, just beyond the telephone pole, a cleanup of the neighborhood was sparked. Courtesy of Historical Charleston Foundation. Photo by W. Jordan

Left:
Not war, earthquake, nor fire, but "progress" in the form of a parking lot and department store demolished the Orphan House Chapel designed by Robert Mills. He described it as "a remarkably neat building, erected back of the orphan house, and presents a front ornamented with a projecting pediment, supported by columns rising to the roof," and states that it was attended not only by the orphans but neighborhood residents as well. Courtesy of Historical Charleston Foundation

Below:
This crowd is apparently drawn by the opening of the 5 & 10¢ store at 289 King Street, first listed in the Directory for 1902. At 285 were James Allan and Company jewlers at the Sign of the Drum Clock, and across the street the Charleston Teapot advertised hams at 12½¢ a pound, breakfast bacon at 13¢ a pound, and New Orleans molasses at 10¢ a can! Courtesy of South Carolina Historical Society

the first historic sites survey was completed, and published by the Carolina Art Association as *This is Charleston* three years later.

In 1947 the Historic Charleston Foundation was organized, operating under a new concept, a non-profit organization working with a revolving fund for area preservation. In 1959 the Foundation started the Ansonborough Rehabilitation program, and today includes a three phase thrust: area rehabilitation financed in part by proceeds from spring tours of historic private homes and two museum houses open all year round. Further ordinances and amendments have enlarged the protected areas and extended zoning regulations, and in cooperation with the State Department of Archives and History the city conducted an inventory of historic architecture.

In 1966 the City Council tripled the size of the Old and Historic Area to include the entire city as far north as Calhoun Street and later amendments set up the Old City District including the other areas south of Line Street. Today, preservation and its significance to the total configuration of the city is very much in the public eye.

The twentieth century, too, was not without natural disasters. Charlestonians were accustomed to hurricanes, but on the 29th of September, 1938 they suffered a new and terrifying experience.

That day dawned warm and rainy. About 7:50 in the morning, with a noise like a rushing freight train that grew louder and louder, a deadly tornado swooped down on Gadsden Green, cutting houses in half, sucking up furniture, twisting playground equipment in nearby Harmon Field and leveling Calvary Baptist Church.

Across town the second of five tornadoes swept from the Ashley River with a roar of death and destruction. It tore a huge hole in St. Michael's roof, moments after communicants had rushed home from the 7:30 service of St. Michael's and All Angel's Day. It then hit City Hall across Broad Street, ramming a several-hundred-pound desk through doors that were one-and-a-half inches thick.

The desk ended up fifteen feet away in City Council Chambers, its letters and papers scattered more than a mile off. One of the most ironic tragedies occurred at 45 State Street where six people, who had moved to that address the day before, were killed in seconds when their house became a pile of splinters and brick.

Eight more people died in the Charleston Paper Company and eight died in the collapse of the eastern end of City Market sheds. The death toll there would have been higher had not most of the vegetable vendors stayed home on the islands because of the rain.

Hundreds of dead and injured from the city and surrounding areas crowded the hospitals. Roper Hospital gave emergency treatment to over three hundred people in the first five hours. Telephone, telegraph and power lines were down, and gas and water mains broken.

The military and police patrolled the city. Washington Park by City Hall held soup kitchens to feed the Eighth Infantry from Fort Moultrie, who were quartered in the Court House. Not one case of theft or vandalism was reported.

Hurricanes slammed into the coast, but improved prediction and warning systems lessened their impact. Hurricane Able howled onto land just south of Charleston on Labor Day weekend of 1952, and two years later Hazel passed offshore. She sent ten foot tides over Myrtle Beach with 110-mile an hour winds that threatened to wipe that resort area off the map.

Top:
Seventeenth and Twentieth Centuries meet in Charleston harbor as a modern day sub and the "Adventure," reproduction of an early trading ketch pass one another. Courtesy of SC Dept. of Parks, Recreation & Tourism

Above:
Vice-President John N. Garner, Gov. Olin D. Johnston, and Senator James F. Byrnes are shown with Mayor Burnet R. Maybank in the Azalea Festival Parade of 1938. Courtesy of Collection of the Charleston Museum, Charleston, SC

On September 19, 1959, Hurricane Gracie crashed ashore on 125 mile an hour winds and the next year Donna spawned a tornado that dealt a glancing blow to downtown Charleston as well as devastating a West Ashley shopping center and doing tremendous damage to coastal beaches.

It was not until 1979 that Charleston again faced a hurricane. Folly Beach, Sullivan's Island, the Isle of Palms, as well as other low-lying areas were evacuated as Hurricane David threatened to hit at high tide, something local residents had long feared. Fortunately for the inhabitants, David moved inland near Savannah, Georgia, so winds were not as strong as anticipated, and damage was confined chiefly to downed utility poles, uprooted trees and beach erosion from the extremely high tides.

The big stories of the middle and latter half of the twentieth Century, however, were the changes that took place in Charleston because of the Civil Rights Movement, the Tricentennial Celebration of the founding of South Carolina, and the coming of Spoleto, USA.

In December of 1950, with the support of the NAACP, forty Clarendon County parents filed suit asking the Federal courts to declare school segregation unconstitutional. When a Federal court decision in Charleston upheld racial segregation

Above:
When construction of a $15.5 million drydock to accommodate cruisers, destroyers and Polaris submarines at the Charleston Naval Base threatened destruction of Marshlands Plantation House in 1962, Navy,

Municipal and preservation organizations cooperated. The 1801 mansion, balanced on two barges, was floated down the Cooper River and across the harbor to its present site at Fort Johnson. Courtesy of Author's collection

in public schools, the case was appealed to the Supreme Court. South Carolina argued that a multi-million dollar school program then underway to give black and white schools equal facilities fulfilled the 14th Amendment, but in a history-making decision the court ruled that separate but equal schools were unconstitutional.

In 1950 the Supreme Court wiped out state and local bus segregation laws, and the *News and Courier* saw mixing races as "courting trouble, violence and sometimes murder." The legislature banned members of the NAACP from state and local government jobs. Mrs. Septima Poinsette Clark, who began a forty year teaching career in 1916 at the age of eighteen, was dismissed from her position at Rhett Elementary School for holding office in the NAACP.

Demonstrations and agitation over civil rights continued in the 1960s, with lunch counter "sit-ins" and parades by blacks, protesting segregation practices in Charleston. A demonstration of Columbus Street aimed at the publishing plant of Charleston's two local papers resulted in injury to six city policemen. In 1969 National Guard road blocks and patrols were stationed throughout the city as Charleston endured a three month curfew as organized labor and civil rights supporters joined forces to engineer a strike of black

The street crier's contest was one of the most popular Azalea Festival events, and Wilson, with his colorful yellow, blue and red cart sang, "Pop-eye mullet and greasy rice/Makes the po'man loss he wife/Lem a deddy de boun/Raw swimp," and was regularly met by all the cast on Legare Street for a shrimp

handout. Gone, alas,, is the day when you could "literally hear shrimp, or flowers, or vegetables coming down the street and recognize a coming huskster as you would a Wagnerian hero, by the characteristic motif of his call." Courtesy of Carolina Art Association. Photo by Charles Paul

hospital workers at the Medical University of South Carolina Hospital, which spread to the Charleston County Hospital, until a compromise settlement sent workers back to their jobs.

With passage of the Civil Rights Act of 1964, widespread school integration began, but it wasn't until the fall of 1970 that Charleston County schools opened on a fully integrated basis, with a resulting decrease of 778 students, mostly white, in the first thirty-day period in the Charleston County School District.

The largest loss occurred in the peninsula city, District 20, where the decrease in students of both races reflected also the population loss in the old city because of the growth of suburbs. In 1970 when schools opened, black pupils made up 95 percent of the school population of 10,087, with 505 white pupils to 9,582 blacks.

Dr. Martin Luther King, Jr. addressed a rally at County Hall on a hot July afternoon of 1967. He declared that racism, poverty and war were America's greatest problems, and stated: "Instead of 'Burn, Baby, Burn' I'm going to say 'Build, Baby, Build.'" Under the auspices of the Southern Christian Leadership Conference, the 1964 Nobel Peace Prize winner told Charlestonians, "We have made the world a neighborhood, but failed to make it a brotherhood."

Even President Kennedy became involved in 1961 over the fact that blacks on visiting centennial delegations from the North could not get accommodations at Charleston's segregated hotels.

The New Jersey Civil War Centennial Commission prepared to open the second Battle of Fort Sumter by threatening to boycott the national observance of the first attack, until a truce was achieved by housing the delegation at the integrated Charleston Naval Base.

Charleston-born Ashley Halsey, a magazine editor living in the New Jersey area, fired a salvo declaring segregation was widely practiced in New Jersey, which therefore had no right to criticize South Carolina. The fracas led elder statesman James F. Byrnes to remark wryly that obviously the passage of a hundred years was not enough to end the bitterness of the Civil War.

With little fanfare or disturbance, however, Charlestonians proceeded to make history in their own way. St. Julian F. Devine, interviewed by a reporter after a five-to-one vote assured him of a seat as the only black in the sixteen member Charleston City Council, informed him, "Well, I grew up with most of them, over there on Mary Street. I just was talking to Johnny Jessen, the building inspector. We lived in an integrated neighborhood. Raised pigeons together." In January, 1975, alderman Devine became the first of his race to serve as mayor pro tem.

In 1970, for the first time in the history of Charleston County, a black won in the Democratic primary. Three out of four blacks in the race won on the first count and James E. Clyburn and Herbert U. Fielding were two of the leading vote-getters in the Democratic party primary on June 10th. At the same time Lonnie Hamilton III became the first African American candidate nominated for Charleston County Council.

History was made again when Charleston natives Fielding and Hamilton both won seats in the general election on November third. Fielding, a life member in the NAACP, was vice-president of the Charleston Fielding Home for Funerals, founded by his parents in 1912. His brother Bernard was admitted to the South Carolina bar in 1958 and sworn in as probate judge in 1976.

Above:
The highlight of Charleston's Tricentennial year was the Charleston Symphony Orchestra's production of "Porgy and Bess" with a cast of over a hundred local blacks. Here the cast rehearses before the set designed *by Emmett Robinson for the first local performance of the folk opera written by Charleston author DeBose Heyward, with musical score by George Gershwin. Courtesy of McKenzie Fine Arts*

Top:
"We went to the door and face such a scene of wreckage. Every house we faced roofless, piazzaless and windowless and the street a chaos of wreckage. It *was unbelievable. What five minutes before had been so orderly." The white picket fence of the writer's house can be seen to the left "scattered hither and yon."*

Right:
General Mark Clark makes a dashing Confederate officer as he participates in Centennial celebrations of the Firing on the Federal supply ship Star of the West January 9, 1961. Clark, who commanded allied invasion forces in World War II, became president of the Citadel in Charleston after retirement from the United States Army. **Courtesy of The Citadel**

Charleston piazzas were usually built to the south or west to catch the prevailing summer breeze. This row on South Battery illustrates the individuality which actress Fanny Kemble admired in 1838 "as every house seems built to the owner's particular taste. This variety is extremely pleasing to the eye." On the horizon is seen the aircraft carrier "Yorktown," nucleus of Patriot Point's Maritime Museum at Mt. Pleasant. Courtesy of Charleston County PRT

Above:
From the top of Bond Hall, central administration building of The Citadel, an eagle eye is kept on the parade ground. From left to right are Mark Clark Hall, Summerall Chapel and The Citadel Library. Courtesy of The Citadel PRO

Left:
This aerial view shows the modern Four Corners of the Law; clockwise are St. Michael's Church, Federal Post Office, County Court House and City Hall. The long building to the right is the Confederate Home at 62 Broad Street, with Washington Park to its left and the Fireproof Building behind City Hall. It was taken prior to 1964 for the old Timrod Inn appears behind the Court House with the St. John Hotel two doors beyond. Courtesy of St Michael's Church

Richard E. Fields, graduate of Avery Institute and Howard University School of Law, became the first African American in modern times to be named as Judge of the Municipal Court of Charleston. In March of 1980 he became the second black circuit judge when the General Assembly appointed him to the Ninth Circuit Court.

In 1974 James B. Edwards of Mt. Pleasant became South Carolina's first Republican governor since Reconstruction, and Charlestonian Nancy Stevenson, after serving two terms in the state legislature, became the first female lieutenant governor of the state in 1979.

The performance of *Porgy and Bess* was the climax of a successful year of Tricentennial events, including a series of six lectures on three hundred years of state history that drew packed houses. Other highlights included a pageant, parade and the dedication of Charles Towne Landing with astronaut Charles Conrad sharing the speaker's platform with Governor Robert McNair, Charleston Mayor J. Palmer Gaillard, and Bishop John E. Hines, Presiding Bishop of the Protestant Episcopal Church of America. By the first of January the next year, 336,405 visitors had entered the gates at the Landing, where a modern pavillion combined up-to-the-minute techniques of display with Indian artifacts and colonial treasures. Here trails wind through an animal forest housing indigenous animals such as bobcats, alligators and panthers in their native habitat, and a settlers' area depicts life as the early Charlestonians lived it in the 1670s.

The London Philharmonic Orchestra presented a concert, with their chairman the Tenth Earl of Shaftesbury on hand for the event.

Some three thousand Episcopalians participated in a mass communication at the Citadel Armory celebrating the three hundredth anniversary of St. Philip's parish and the 180th annual convention of the Episcopal Diocese of South Carolina. The gathering heard an address by the Lord Bishop of London, who described Charleston as a "Crossroads of history," where the past and present meet.

Before the glow from the Tricentennial had faded, Charleston was the scene of Spoleto U.S.A., a companion to the arts festival held for twenty years in Spoleto, Italy.

In the late 1920s Charleston had experienced the beginning of a cultural revival. The Poetry Society was organized with early members including W. Hervey Allen, author of *Anthony Adverse*, John Bennett, whose best known work is probably *Master Skylark*, and Dubose Heyward, author of *Porgy*.

Definitive works on Charleston silver and furniture have been written by E. Milby Burton, Director of the Charleston Museum; on Charleston architecture by Beatrice St. Julien Ravenel; and on Low Country plantations by Samuel Gaillard Stoney.

Charleston artists include Alice R. Huger Smith, best remembered for her hauntingly beautiful Low Country swamp and marsh landscapes and her rice culture series, and Elizabeth O'Neill Verner, internationally known both for her scenes of Charleston and for her delightful books.

Interest in the arts received a tremendous boost with the coming of Spoleto as national and international performers converged on Charleston, and for twelve days in May and early June of 1977 Charlestonians enjoyed what has been considered the "world's most comprehensive arts festival."

If, as many said, Charleston was "America's best kept secret," then Spoleto let the secret out of the bag.

Mrs. Septima Poinsette Clark accepts congratulations after receiving an honorary degree from the College of Charleston, March 11, 1978. Courtesy of College of Charleston

Charleston native Lonnie Hamilton III was not only the first black member of Charleston County Council, but the first black chairman of Council and first chairman elected after an advisory referendum. Hamilton was choir director of Calvary Episcopal Church, director for 20 years of Bonds-Wilson High School band and in 1977, director of Adult Education for the Charleston County School Board. Courtesy of Charleston Post-Courier. Photo by Bill Murton

Governor James Edwards, left, and General Lyman Lemnitzer, right, watch as Gen. Mark Clark presents HRH Prince Charles of England with a photograph album in his 1977 visit to Charleston. Prince Charles reminded Clark that it was at his great uncle Lord Mountbatten's suggestion that the periscope and items from the British sub Seraph, before which they are standing, were presented to the Citadel. This was the sub that briefly became American to rescue French Gen. Giraud from German capture in WW II, and which took Clark on a secret intelligence mission into North Africa just before allied landings there. Courtesy of The Citadel

Above:
Is there a family likeness? The Tenth Earl of Shaftsbury stands beside the portrait of his ancestor Anthony Ashley Cooper, first Earl of Shaftesbury, who was the most influential of the Lords Proprietors of Carolina. The tenth Earl and his wife visited Charleston in January of 1967, marking the official start of Tricentennial publicity. Courtesy of Carolina Art Association

Left:
Shown here is Spoleto Festival U.S.A. 1979. One of the Intermezzi, a series of informal afternoon concerts, is presented in St. Mary's Church before a painting of the Crucifixion by John S. Cogdell, dating to 1814. St. Mary's is the mother church of Catholicism in the Carolinas and Georgia, and the painting survived the fire of 1838 which destroyed an earlier church on this site. Courtesy of Work/Play: W. Patrick Hinely

Chapter Eight

"Where Past and Present Meet"

In 1950 Mayor R. Goodwyn Rhett, speaking for the native Charlestonian, said: "It is almost impossible for anyone in whose life a place of residence...is but an incident to appreciate the feelings which the great majority of the people of Charleston have for their city.

"It is no incident to them—it is a part and parcel of their lives; it is their home and the home of their forefathers. Its welfare is ever present in their thoughts and in their prayers. Its glories and misfortunes have been theirs and their forebears for generations and they love and cherish the name of Charleston."

In her exquisite book *Mellowed by Time*, Charleston artist Elizabeth O'Neill Verner quotes Rebecca in the Gullah dialect that is rapidly disappearing: "Chas'n don't change none and it keep all odder place on earth from seem natchel."

Since Rebecca made that remark, however, Charleston *has* changed and *is* changing—intangibly and tangibly. Her houses are in better condition—their paint shines—her people look prosperous—her streets are crowded. While her peninsula shape protects the old city from expanding defense installations, and the growing industrial complex to the north, she feels the impact in traffic congestion, crime statistics, a rapidly rising demand for real estate and a concurrent jump in real estate values.

An increased volume of tourist trade continues to further aggravate her traffic situation and threatens the tranquility of long-time residents.

Mayor Joseph P. Riley Jr., recognized Charleston's twentieth century problems in his report to City Council in January, 1978, when he termed Charleston:

"A City that sees urban problems, opportunities and challenges. A city that has the same commitment to excellence that its forbears had some two hundred years ago. A City that is at the cutting edge of solving urban problems and of seeking new initiatives to brighten the lives of its citizens." Today Charleston has evolved into an attactive and dynamic cosmopolitan center, poised to meets the challenges of the twenty-first century.

The following section of color photographs is a document of a vital Charleston against the backdrop of three hundred years of history and the inescapable influence of the men and women who made it their home.

George Copley's portrait of Mary Rutledge Smith and the magnificent "free-flying" stair at the Nathaniel Russell House complement one another. Mrs. Smith, sister of John and Edward Rutledge, was a contemporary of Mr. Russell. Removed for safekeeping during the Civil War to the State College at Columbia, the portrait received a bayonet thrust through the neck.

Generations of youngsters have enjoyed climbin on this 7-inch Brooke Rifle, unearthed at Fort Johnson and mounted on the Battery in 1900. Beneath the barrel is a capstan from the Battleship Maine, and the second cannon on the left was salvaged from the Keokuk, the ironclad that sank off Morris Island in 1863.

Across the gas-lighted cobblestones of Chalmers Street stand the German Volunteer Fire Company Hall and the Old Slave Mart Museum. Thomas Ryan and his partner James Marsh acquired the site of the latter in 1853 and built the present structure, originally called Ryan's Auction Mart. Here Ryan, one of some thirty auctioneers of his day in Charleston, auctioned everything from steamboats to slaves.

The shine on Charleston brass is
the result of years of applied
elbow grease and brass polish,
not a secret formula as visitors
often think.

Top:
President George Washington's
portrait by John Trumbull is
flanked on the left by Gen.
Zachary Taylor and on the right
by Gen. P.G.T. deBeauregard.
The twelve members of
Charleston City Council meet
here twice a month, and this
Council Chamber in City Hall is a
favorite stop on sightseeing tours
of Charleston.

Above:
The Flea Market, once beef,
vegetable, and fish stalls, was
built on filled-in creek and
marsh lands donated by the
Pinckney family to the city.

Joseph P. Riley, Jr., Park in the foreground, The Citadel in the background. The military college moved from Marion Square to the banks of the Ashley River in the northwestern section of the city in 1922. Courtesy of the Post and Courier

Charleston is known for its fine
antique shops, some of which
offer reproductions of
18th-century furniture, made
in Charleston.

St. Michael's chancel window,
installed in 1893 by Tiffany Glass
Company, is a copy of Raphael's
"St. Michael Slaying the
Dragon," which hangs in the
Louvre. Photograph by
Peggy McKenzie

*Licensed guides offer leisurely
carriage tours of the Historic
District.*

A few of the old plantation slave streets survive with their rows of cabins. Doors and windows were frequently painted blue to repel "plat-eye," an evil spirit. Photograph by Andrew Simons, Jr.

Otranto on Goose Creek, former property of botanist Dr. Alexander Garden for whom the gardenia was named, is the setting for luncheon on a low-country plantation tour.

Originally the site was named Yeshoe and belonged to Arthur Middleton, former merchant of London and Barbados. Photograph by Andrew Simons, Jr.

In 1738 John Drayton bought land just south of his father's plantation, Magnolia, and began Drayton Hall, one of America's architectural treasures. Today owned by the National Trust, it is

the sole survivor of the great plantation houses that once bordered the Ashley River. Photograph by Andrew Simons, Jr.

The South Carolina Aquarium.
Photograph by Michael Levkoff
and Barbara Baker

Charleston sculptor Willard
Hirsch's dignified Cassique of
Kiawah stands before the
pavilion at Charles Towne
Landing, the embodiment of
physical beauty, integrity, and
humanity.

Left:
Sergeant Jasper points through
the oaks on the Battery towards
Fort Moultrie, and a freighter
looms in the Cooper River. In
the foreground is a monument
to William Gilmore Simms, 19th-
century Charleston author,
journalist, and historian whose
best-known book was "The
Yemassee."

Opposite top:
At low tide wading birds stalk
fiddler crabs and small fish, and
oysters and clams are free for the
harvesting. Photograph by
Andrew Simons, Jr.

"Still Life with Open Book"
(1991) by Linda Fantuzzo.

"Charleston Charm" (2000) by
John Carroll Doyle. Private
collection

Cleo Parker Robinson Dancers
at Gaillard Auditorium performs
for 2002 MOJA Arts Festival,
produced by the City of
Charleston's Office of Cultural
Affairs. Photo courtesy of the
City of Charleston

Charleston Ballet Theatre's Opus One *production at Piccolo Spoleto. Photograph by Mary Ellen Millhouse, Courtesy of City of Charleston Cultural Affairs*

Spoleto Brass Quartet performing. Courtesy of City of Charleston Cultural Affairs. Photograph by Mary Ellen Millhouse

*The Charleston County Library,
Calhoun Street. Photograph by
Michael Levkoff and Barbara
Baker*

*The City Market. Market Hall,
in the foreground, was built
from 1840 to 1841. Local
tradition holds that the building
was a recruiting center for
Confederate soldiers.
Photograph by Michael
Levkoff and Barbara Baker*

The aftermath of Hurricane Hugo:
Fishing boats came to rest next to
Silver Hill Plantation near
McClellanville after the hurricane's
tidal surge. Courtesy of the Post and
Courier

Above: Manning Williams's painting for "Larger than Life," featured at Piccolo Spoleto. Photo courtesy of artist

Charleston art galleries on Broad Street and Church Street. Photographs by Michael Levkoff and Barbara Baker

Opposite page: Middle left: Fountain at Waterfront Park.
Bottom left: The Hollings Judicial Annex (1987) to the Federal Courthouse.
Bottom right: The Wagner-Ohlandt building (1880), now rehabilitated and the site of a popular restaurant. Photographs by Michael Levkoff and Barbara Baker

Mayor Joseph P. Riley (center) and members of City Council in the early twenty-first century. They are seated in the mayor's elegant office in City Hall, which was originally constructed from 1800 to 1804 and remodeled throughout the nineteenth century. Photograph by Bill Murton

Chapter Nine
"The Age of Riley"
1975–2003

O n December 15, 1975, Joseph P. Riley, Jr., was sworn in as mayor of Charleston. At age 33, he was the youngest mayor in the city's history. But Joe Riley was an experienced politician. He had been born and raised in downtown Charleston. He was the son of prominent parents and a politically active and successful father. He had graduated from The Citadel and served in the South Carolina House of Representatives for six years. A Democrat and a protégé of Senator Ernest F. ("Fritz") Hollings, Riley was deeply concerned about the city's African American citizens. He was also committed to the city's business establishment, which had confidence in Riley's integrity and sympathy for its concerns.

It was clear after the 1971 mayoral election that Charleston politics had changed. As a result of the Federal Voting Rights Act, more black voters were able to vote, and they were eager to participate in the electoral process. Despite Mayor Gaillard's strides in integrating city council and appointing the first black judge in the state since Reconstruction (Richard Fields as municipal judge), the black community was dissatisfied with his administration. Challenged by William Ackerman, a prominent attorney and businessman in the primary, and by Arthur Ravenel, an affable developer, in the general election, Gaillard survived to serve his last term. But it was clear that politics would never be the same. Many of Riley's black supporters, such as Marjorie Amos, came from the Ackerman camp, but many of Gaillard's supporters also lined up behind Riley. In the 1975 election, the Republicans, resurgent in the city since the Goldwater and Nixon presidential campaigns of 1964 and 1968, ran a serious candidate for mayor, Nancy Hawk. Energetic and articulate, Mrs. Hawk championed the conservative point of view but was handily defeated by Riley and his broad-based coalition.

In his inaugural address, the boyish mayor acknowledged "long standing urban problems in a period of economic recession," but promised civility and economic progress for "all of our citizens." Riley promised Charlestonians that there would be "more blacks and more women in positions of authority," that his administration would fight crime, seek to expand the city by annexations, preserve the historic district, and rejuvenate King Street. He called on his fellow Charlestonians to "join with me and with city council, in a new age of tolerance, harmony, and creativity." Thus began the Age of Riley, a golden age of progress, not only in material and physical improvements to the city, but also in improved race relations and a cultural renaissance in the arts and literature.

Mayor Riley's first term was a whirlwind of activity. The city embarked on numerous development projects, the boldest of which was Charleston Place, which originated in the previous administration when city planners determined that a major hotel or convention center on the site would revitalize the King Street retail district. Charleston Place and the Omni Hotel (bounded by King, Beaufain, Meeting, and Hasell) were financed through a combination of public and private funding, and were designed to bring conventions to Charleston, rejuvenate the central business district, and focus tourism in the Market area. The project was extremely controversial throughout the 1980s when some preservationists fought the original developer and plan (then called "Charleston Center") in the courts, in government, and in the political arena. Riley prevailed in building Charleston Place after the Historic Charleston Foundation, other preservation groups, and the city ultimately negotiated a compromise plan for the development. The modern King Street-Market Street retail district is a product of this controversy in the late 1970s and 1980s.

The city council had been reorganized and elected by single-member districts as a result of a federal lawsuit. There were now six black and six white, male and female council members. The Gaillard administration had settled the lawsuit, assuming that the city council would consist of seven whites and five blacks, accurately reflecting the city's demography. But Charlestonians are hard to predict. In one majority white district, Arthur Christopher, a black moderate,

Marjorie Amos, a union organizer and political leader, was a key member of the Riley political organization in 1975. Courtesy of Marjorie Amos

defeated a white liberal candidate supported by blacks. When asked by the mayor how the council turned out six to six (black and white) instead of seven to five, corporation counsel Morris D. Rosen, replied, "How could we know that the whites would vote for the black candidate and the blacks for the white candidate?"

Riley was seen by both black and white Charlestonians as eager to bring African Americans fully into city government, to provide equal municipal services to black neighborhoods, to recognize black history and culture, and to appoint blacks to responsible governmental positions, many of which they had not historically held. Arthur McFarland became chief judge of the municipal court in December 1977. James Etheredge became director of city finance in December 1979. Riley appointed Veronica Small as the first black female municipal court judge. Vanessa Turner-Maybank was hired as tourism director in March 1984. By January 1995 she was the clerk of city council and chief tourism official. Riley was determined to put an end to discrimination in the public arena and, in 1978, he and a group of Democrats in tuxedos escorted Arthur Clement, Jr., a retired black businessman, to the formerly all-white St. Patrick's Day dinner at the Hibernian Society.

Riley targeted parks and playgrounds in black neighborhoods for improvement. A portrait of Denmark Vesey, the leader of the famous (or infamous, depending on one's point of view) slave rebellion in 1822, was placed in the Gaillard Auditorium. "This is," the mayor told 250 black and white citizens assembled at the dedication, "part of the effort . . . of the administration to see that parts of history heretofore forgotten are remembered." Bishop Frank M. Reid, Jr. of the

A.M.E. Church described Vesey as "a liberator whom God had sent to set the people free from oppression."

Thus, it came to be that a free black man, who was tried and executed by city officials for leading a slave insurrection conspiracy, was honored by city officials one hundred and fifty years later. Riley's efforts at reconciling black aspirations and white anxieties were generally successful. He had the support of the business community, the newspapers, and most community leaders. Some whites, however, reacted angrily calling the mayor "LBJ" for "Little Black Joe" and sneering at the Vesey portrait as offensive to many white people and akin to honoring Hitler.

One of Riley's earliest and best-known achievements was the Spoleto Festival USA. Twentieth-century-Charlestonians had long sought to establish a festival to publicize the city and attract tourists. The Azalea Festival, for example, began in 1934 and featured horse shows, golf tournaments, balls, parades, beauty contests, and even a street crier's contest. That festival fell apart about 1953. During the period that followed, civic leaders debated various proposals.

In the mid-1970s, Gian Carlo Menotti, the founder of the Italian Spoleto Festival of Two Worlds, came to Charleston at the instigation of an Italian transplant to the Low Country, Countess Alicia Paolozzi. Menotti had founded the Italian festival in 1957 and wanted to bring it to America. Menotti looked at many cities. After numerous preliminary meetings and conferences with civic leaders, it appeared that the curtain would not rise on the first festival. The two original leaders of the coordinating committee resigned. Mayor Riley asked Theodore S. Stern, the former president of the College of Charleston who had successfully presided over the great

Piccolo Spoleto Children's Festival at Marion Square Park, produced by City of Charleston Office of Cultural Affairs. Courtesy of the City of Charleston.

expansion of that school in the 1970s, to head up the effort to establish the festival. Stern capped his astonishing career, Keith West wrote in *Charleston* magazine, "by guiding the infant Spoleto Festival USA through its birth pangs."

The result was the first Spoleto Festival, USA, held in 1977.

Spoleto brought to Charleston the best in the arts from around the world: the Eliot Feld Ballet, the Westminster Choir, The Queen of Spades, The Consul, plays, jazz, films, and lectures. In 1978 it brought Zulu dancers, Ballet's Felix Blaska, Il Furioso, Vanessa, a Tennessee Williams play, and more jazz, chamber music, dance, music, crafts, lectures, film, and street theater. "This bill of fare," *Newsweek* said of the 1977 festival, "is like nothing else on the international scene, and Charleston is proud of it." The festival got rave reviews in the national media. It had, by the 1980s, become a Charleston institution, and celebrated its 25th anniversary in 2001.

Accompanying the Spoleto Festival beginning in 1979 was Piccolo Spoleto, a community arts festival featuring local artists and free or modestly priced offerings. Hundreds of events—ranging from film, classical concerts, dance, theater, and late night events, to the Festival of Churches, Jazz After Hours, and the Children's Festival—were presented by the city's Office of Cultural Affairs, under the direction of Ellen Dressler Moryl, and a community advisory committee with both public and private funding.

Riley sought to raise the city's national profile by bringing the Miss USA beauty pageant to Charleston in 1977, but this experiment fizzled. Charlestonians, it appeared, had greater aspirations than being a Southern version of Atlantic City, New Jersey. In 1978 the first Cooper River Bridge Run was held. Its "origins held no clue," the *Post and Courier* observed in 2002, that such a race, one of the longest road races in the United States, "would flower."

Charleston continued to make amends for its racist past. In 1978 the Crosstown highway was named in honor of the distinguished civil rights leader Septima P. Clark. In 1982 a bronze sculpture of Judge Waites Waring, the federal judge who had courageously ruled in favor of blacks' civil rights in several landmark cases (and had subsequently left Charleston for New York), was placed in the corner of city council chambers overlooking the Federal Courthouse. "It's time to bring him home," the mayor said privately. In 1985 a portrait of the Reverend Daniel J. Jenkins, founder of an orphanage for black children, was also hung in city council chambers.

Joe Riley was reelected without opposition in 1979 and 1983. He asked Septima Clark to administer his second oath of office in 1979. "The thing I'm proudest of," Riley said in his second inaugural, "is bringing together the black and white communities of Charleston."

In 1981 the city's respected police chief, John F. Conroy, committed suicide. Conroy, who had served under Gaillard, had kept a steady hand on the potentially violent hospital strike in 1969 and had earned the nickname "Mr. Cool." Popular with all Charlestonians (at least the law-abiding ones), he "was the right man at the right time," the *Evening Post* said. Conroy was a tough act to follow, but Riley did. He conducted a national search and appointed the city's first black police chief, Reuben Greenberg, in April 1982. Greenberg, who was also Jewish and the holder of two master's degrees from the University of California at Berkeley, attracted national media attention throughout his long career as an innovative and sometimes controversial crime fighter.

A youthful Joseph P. Riley announcing the appointment of Charleston's first black police chief, an equally youthful Reuben Greenberg, in 1982. Photograph by Bill Murton

In May 1982 construction began on Charleston Place. It became one of the city's biggest taxpayers and largest employers and put Charleston on the map as a convention destination. Empty and dilapidated buildings now fetched hitherto unimaginable prices. Riley fought with business and property owners who could not visualize a rejuvenated King Street to create parking lots and upgrade the infrastructure. Gradually the real estate adjacent to the keystone project began to come back to life. The old Riviera Theater was renovated as a conference center. Richard Widman established the first of several bed and breakfast historic hotels, the King's Courtyard Inn in 1983. A handsome new office building sprang up where the old Charleston Hotel had once stood on Meeting Street. Downtown property values soared.

Riley was determined to expand the city's boundaries. The city first expanded west of the Ashley River and on James Island, annexing white, middle-class suburban areas and also expanded north, taking in black neighborhoods on the Neck between Charleston and North Charleston. When Riley was elected in 1975, the city consisted of 16.7 square miles and a population of 70,132. By 1988 the city was 41.63 square miles large and had a population of 80,879.

Charleston's percentage of blacks in the population declined with the annexations. In 1970 the city's white population was 36,576 and its black population 30,251. By 2000 there were 60,964 whites and 32,864 blacks. Because Riley was a Democrat, these annexations strengthened his political opponents but the mayor's vision of the city took priority over his politics.

Low-cost public housing has also been a focus of the Riley administration. "Scattered site" or "in fill" housing meant fewer units in one location and less isolation for residents. One such program received the Presidential Award for Design Excellence for one hundred and thirteen units "exemplary in their social, architectural, and urbanistic goals" and designed to resemble the traditional Charleston single house complete with piazzas.

Charleston Place, King Street. The construction of an impressive hotel and convention center in 1986 led to a building boom in the downtown area. Photograph by Michael Levkoff and Barbara Baker

Innovative public housing, based on traditional Charleston architecture, was a hallmark of the Riley administration, as exemplified by the Freedom House on South Street. Note the modern version of "piazzas." Courtesy of The Housing Authority

The world premiere of Pat Conroy's The Lords of Discipline *at the Ultra-Vision theater created the first of many late-twentieth century controversies about Conroy's alma mater, The Citadel. Courtesy of the* Post and Courier

In 1985 ABC filmed its historic television miniseries, *North and South*, in Charleston. Hollywood had discovered the Holy City, and old Charleston was now stepping onto the silver screen. Based on the North and South trilogy by the renowned storyteller John Jakes, the twelve-hour miniseries starred Patrick Swayze, Leslie Anne Down, Elizabeth Taylor, Kirstie Alley, and Hal Holbrooke. Set in the years preceding the Civil War, the story follows two families, one Northern and one Southern, as their lives are nearly destroyed by the civil war. A sequel, *North and South, Book II*, appeared a year later. Earlier in the decade, The Citadel had refused permission for Pat Conroy's novel, *The Lords of Discipline* (which was highly critical of the military college especially in racial matters), to be filmed on the campus, igniting an ongoing debate about the film industry and the city. A few years later, an actual incident of alleged hazing of a black cadet at The Citadel created a national sensation and had Charlestonians wondering whether life imitated art or vice versa. *The Lords of Discipline* was shot in Charleston and the movie premiered at Charleston's Ultravision Theatre.

Governor Dick Riley created a state film office in the early 1980s, and, as a result, numerous films were shot in whole or in part in and around Charleston, including *Swamp Thing* (1981), *A House Divided: Denmark Vesey's Rebellion* (PBS, 1982), Turner Network Television's *The C.S.S. Hunley* (1999) filmed in North Charleston, *The Patriot* (2000), and *Cold Mountain* (2002). Kiawah was the backdrop of Robert Redford's *The Legend of Bagger Vance* (1999).

For several years in the 1990s, Charleston was home to the World-Fest-Charleston International Film Festival. In 1991 Sidney Poitier came to Charleston to portray Thurgood Marshall in an ABC miniseries *Separate But Equal*, the story of the famous South Carolina desegregation case, Briggs vs. Elliott which became a part of the landmark decision, Brown v. Board of Education, which ended segregation in the public schools. (Judge Waring argued in his dissent in Briggs that segregation was unconstitutional.) The real-life hearings

were conducted at the federal courthouse on Broad Street where the movie was filmed. *Paradise*, starring Melanie Griffith and Don Johnson, was shot in the area in 1991; *Queen*, a television movie in 1992. Josephine Humphreys's *Rich in Love* was made into a movie starring Albert Finney and Jill Clayburgh and was filmed in Mt. Pleasant in 1993.

The filming of *The Patriot*, starring Mel Gibson, was exciting for most downtown residents, but some Charlestonians had their noses out of joint. "While some residents sat on their steps, sipped wine, and enjoyed the show," the *Post and Courier* reported, "others lost sleep and got snarled in traffic." The president of the Charlestowne Neighborhood Association said there was substantial opposition to any filmmaking south of Broad Street. City council enacted more rules regulating filmmaking in the city. *The Patriot* told an important story: The incredible bravery and sacrifice of South Carolinians in helping to win the War for Independence. The British press, however, was incensed with *The Patriot's* brutal portrayal of their soldiers.

The Riley administration continued its efforts at revitalizing the historic district. In September 1986 when Charleston Place opened, thirty historic buildings in the immediate area were restored or on the drawing boards. The project created seventy-five new or restored storefronts and fourteen hundred new jobs. The number of shops on King Street increased by forty to fifty by the end of 1988.

Private citizens, preservationists, organizations, and the state also contributed to revitalization. In 1981 one of the city's most important landmarks, the Exchange Building, had been restored to its 1771 appearance. Saved from destruction by the Daughters of the American Revolution earlier in the twentieth century, the building was restored by the state to its original grandeur. In 1988 the South Carolina General Assembly met at the Old Exchange in celebration of the bicentennial of the ratification of the United States Constitution. Playing *Battle Hymn of the Republic* the Fife and Drum Corps of the United States Army Band, resplendent in colonial uniforms, accompanied the governor and state representatives and senators down Broad Street to the Old Exchange. A great deal had changed since 1861.

Charleston's revitalization and affluence was accompanied by a literary and artistic renaissance. Although not a Charlestonian, Pat Conroy had been a Citadel cadet, as he made millions of readers painfully aware, and wrote extensively about Charleston and the Carolina Low Country. His novels and the movies based on some of them included *The Boo* (his first novel about his life at The Citadel); *The Water is Wide* (about his days as a teacher near Beaufort) and the movie based on it, *Conrack* starring Jon Voight; *The Great Santini* (a movie about Conroy's father, starring Robert Duvall); *The Lords of Discipline* (more about The Citadel); *The Prince of Tides* (with Barbra Streisand); *My Losing Season* (about Conroy as a Citadel basketball player), all of which described and projected the city, The Citadel, and the Low Country to a national, and indeed, an international audience.

Josephine Humphreys, a Charlestonian who grew up in the historic district and attended Ashley Hall School, began publishing novels set in the Charleston area in 1984. By the early 1990s, she was recognized as "one of the South's most elegant and engaging literary voices" (San Francisco Chronicle). In *Dreams of Sleep* (1984), *Rich in Love* (1987), and *The Fireman's Fair* (1991), Humphreys described and analyzed Charlestonians and Low Country South Carolinians. And like many Charleston authors of the past, both Humphreys's and Conroy's works are sensitive to issues of race, and sympathetic to the aspirations of African Americans. Like Faulkner's novels, they were also attuned to the idiosyncracies of Southern life.

While the most prominent of Charleston's creative literary community, Conroy and Humphreys were not alone. Robert Jordan, a Charleston native (born James Oliver Rigney, Jr.) and a nuclear engineer, wrote fantasy fiction including the *Conan* series (beginning with *Conan the Destroyer* (1980) and the *Wheel of Time* series (beginning with *The Eye of the World*). Padgett Powell's first novel, *Edisto*, read, according to *Newsweek*, as "Holden Caulfield come to the South Carolina swamps." Charleston became home to the nationally syndicated columnist James J. Kilpatrick and the acclaimed Civil War historian, Gordon C. Rhea. In 1993 William Baldwin of McClellanville published *The Hard to Catch Mercy*, a comic novel about the early twentieth century Low Country. Harlan Greene described Charleston in a Southern Gothic mystery, *Why We Never Danced the Charleston* (1984). The old city was the setting of Sandra Brown's *The Alibi* (1999). Anne Rivers Siddons, author of *Colony, Low Country,* and *Outer Banks*, moved to Charleston. Native son Edward Ball won the National Book Award with his *Slaves in the Family*, the story of his ancestors and literally the slaves in his own family. Native daughter Dorothea Benton Frank wrote lovingly and wittily about her hometown in *Sullivan's Island: A Lowcountry Tale* (2000) and *Plantation: A Lowcountry Tale* (2001), both of which earned a place on the *New York Times* best-seller list. Sue Kidd Monk of Mt. Pleasant published *The Secret Life of Bees* to rave reviews in 2002.

The flame of literary romantic frivolity was kept alive by Charleston native Alexandra Ripley who wrote *Charleston* (1981) and a sequel, *On Leaving Charleston* (1984), a *New York Times* best-seller. She later wrote *Scarlett*, the (authorized) sequel to *Gone With The Wind* (1991), in which Scarlett

Pat Conroy with Simba, 1976. Photograph by Dottie Ashley.

Dorothea Benton Frank, born and raised on Sullivan's Island, describes her life in the Low Country in her novels—all of which landed on the New York Times *best-seller list. Photograph by Joe Gaffney. Courtesy of The Penguin Group US*

pursues Rhett after his move to Charleston. Scarlett, it must be said, did not like all those Yankees in Charleston after the Civil War. Rhett's local reputation was still terrible and then there was the boating accident in the inevitable (you guessed it) Ashley River. "'It's the Ashley River,' Rhett pronounced the name with exaggerated distinctiveness," Ms. Ripley wrote. Scathingly reviewed by the critics ("At this point," the *New York Times* noted, "one more negative review of 'Scarlett' . . . constitutes what is known in football as 'piling on'"), the novel nonetheless sold millions. Hundreds of Charlestonians stood in line at Ashley Hall School, Ms. Ripley's alma mater, to have her autograph their copy.

Fascinated by the "often bloody history of the region," John Jakes, a resident of Hilton Head for twenty-five years, published a best-selling novel, *Charleston*, in 2002. The multi-generational saga of the fictional Bell family, the novel describes almost one hundred years of Charleston's history. Thus, Charleston's history continued to captivate the nation—from Ripley's romance novel, *Charleston* (1981) to Jake's serious historical fiction, *Charleston* (2002).

Charleston's cultural renaissance in the late twentieth century also included a blossoming in paintings and the visual arts. Painters and art galleries, long a mainstay of old Charleston, began to dot the landscape. By 1999 there were Art Walks involving thirty-three galleries. While artists of the early twentieth century, such as Alice Huger Smith, Alfred Hutty and Elizabeth O'Neill Verner, recorded and interpreted Charleston's defeated, decadent decline, artists of the late twentieth century celebrated Charleston's affluent, aesthetic ascent. John Doyle painted, among many other things, Charleston's landscapes, wildlife, marshes, and people. West Fraser portrayed the city in his unique American plein air impressionist way. Manning Williams, a pillar of the Charleston artistic establishment, attracted national attention. Linda Fantuzzo also earned a national reputation in impressionistic classical and landscape paintings. Margaret Petterson and Betty Anglin Smith, among others, portrayed the natural beauty of the Low Country. Sculptor Jon Michel enriched the city's public space with his statue of George Washington in Washington Park, and his bust of Gedney M. Howe, Jr., at Courthouse Square. Accomplished photographers such as Jack Alterman and William Struhs recorded Charleston's lifestyle.

The Charleston metropolitan area expanded dramatically in the last quarter of the twentieth century. The population of the metropolitan area rose from 278,961 in 1960 to 430,462 in 1980 to 549,033 in 2000. In 1975 the City of Charleston itself consisted of the peninsula and a few sections of West Ashley. By 2001 it consisted of those areas plus much of James Island, the Neck, Daniel Island and Cainhoy for a total of almost 90 square miles.

The city of North Charleston was incorporated in 1972 after many years of political warfare. John Bourne, Jr., and Jim Gonzales spearheaded the effort to create a new city, which quickly became the fourth largest in South Carolina. Bourne served for nineteen years and created a vibrant new city government complete with a city hall. Bourne was defeated in 1991 by Bobby Kinard who served until 1993. In 1995 Keith Summey became mayor. By 2000 North Charleston was the third largest city in South Carolina.

Numerous suburbs were built as a result of the construction of Interstates 26 and 526. The Silas Pearman Bridge had been built in the 1960s and a third Cooper River bridge, the Don Holt Bridge, opened as a section of Interstate 526. Three

Josephine Humphreys. Photograph by the Post and Courier

John Bourne, Jr., first mayor of North Charleston. Photograph by the Post and Courier

The present mayor of North Charleston, Keith Summey. Courtesy of the City of North Charleston

huge shopping malls—Northwoods (North Charleston), Citadel (West Ashley) and Towne Centre (Mt. Pleasant)—joined the original suburban shopping centers West of the Ashley, South Windermere and St. Andrews. Urban development (or, to its critics, urban sprawl) engulfed massive land areas in Mt. Pleasant, James Island, and North Charleston leading to explosive growth in other communities in the metropolitan area including Goose Creek, Ladson, Hanahan, and Summerville. The latter, in Dorchester County, had become an affluent bedroom community of Charleston by the 1980s. Dorchester County had a population of 58,761 in 1980. By 2000 it was 96,413.

Next came the islands north and south of Charleston. Influenced by the brilliant achievements of the visionary Charles E. Fraser at Hilton Head, Kuwaiti investors developed Kiawah Island beginning in the 1970s. Formerly a family plantation, the island became an internationally famous resort and residential community, and the site of the international Ryder Cup Golf tournament in 1991. Neighboring Seabrook Island was developed beginning in the 1970s. To the north of Charleston, the development of Wild Dunes on the Isle of Palms began in 1972. Even Dewees Island, north of the Isle of Palms, with no bridge between it and the mainland, was developed as a residential community. The Isle of Palms, Folly Beach, and Sullivan's Island, formerly beach resorts with chiefly summer residents from the city and other parts of South Carolina, now became affluent year-round suburbs of Charleston.

The affluence and expansion of the period affected public education. Major demographic changes occurred as African Americans moved to the suburbs West of the Ashley and whites moved to Mt. Pleasant and Dorchester County. In 1981 the Justice Department brought a lawsuit to further desegregate the county's schools which had been desegregated in the late 1960s and 1970s. Controversies over whether the schools were, in fact, desegregated, the quality of education for both black and white children, taxes and the management styles of school boards and superintendents were major political issues of the 1980s and 1990s. In 1990 the federal courts found the public school system to be "unitary," that is, no legal vestiges of segregation existed, but Charlestonians of both races continued to see public education as a controversial issue.

Explosive growth and affluence also brought new problems. As in many other cities, the highway system could not handle the increased traffic, and the dramatic uncontrolled loss of the natural environment shocked many Charlestonians. Concerned citizens founded a number of environmental organizations including the Low Country Open Land Trust and the South Carolina Coastal Conservation League. Dana Beach became active in the environmental movement as a member of Save the Wando, a group opposed to the expansion of the port on the Wando River. Beach later became director of the Conservation League. Jo Humphreys spoke for many Charlestonians when she wrote about urban sprawl in *Rich in Love*:

"In the distance the highway appeared to flare suddenly into the air; that was the bridge to Charleston. But before the bridge, just beyond the television station, was an opening in the shopping strip and a nondescript road that cut back behind the import repair shop. That was my road. It led to my town, Mount Pleasant, which huddled secretly behind all this new development. In Latin class . . . I had studied the town of Herculaneum, buried by hot mud in the year 79 A.D. My

town had been similarly engulfed, not by mud but by overflow from the city of Charleston, which had erupted and settled all around, leaving Mount Pleasant embedded in the middle."

In the historic district, opposition to unlimited growth grew. As early as the Charleston Place debate in the 1980s, preservation organizations and neighborhood groups saw growth as a negative force rather than a positive one. While the overwhelming majority of Charlestonians, including the venerable Historic Charleston Foundation, supported Riley's plans for King Street, the Preservation Society and an *ad hoc* advocacy group, the Save Historic Charleston Foundation, opposed him. Opposition to growth rose in the 1980s and 1990s. The Charlestowne Neighborhood Association was organized to represent residents of the historic district as were other louder groups. Controversies about the historic district continued into the 1990s over the building of the new judicial center on Broad Street, the number of hotels, the height of buildings and the future of tourism generally. Mayor Riley responded to these concerns with major planning initiatives including tourism management plans, historic preservation and neighborhood plans, height limits, public transportation, hotel zoning restrictions, and an emphasis on waterfront access. A tourism commission was established in 1984 to address problems arising from the dramatic increase in tourism. Neighborhood councils were officially established by city council, and by January 1999 Riley said in his State of the City Address: "I am very proud of our 65 neighborhood councils . . . I hold regular meetings with the presidents of our neighborhood organizations . . . "

Riley's interest in urban planning and redevelopment was particularly evident on the Cooper River waterfront. The old State Ports Authority wharves located along the Cooper River were destroyed by fire in the 1950s. Given the weak economy of the period, the wharves were never rebuilt and the land remained in public hands. In the late 1980s, the city began planning a waterfront park on the site. Financed by public and private funds, including a $3.3 million federal Urban Development Action Grant (UDAG), of the Waterfront Park opened in May 1990. It contains twelve acres including the huge Pineapple Fountain, a four hundred foot long wharf and fishing pier, and plenty of Battery benches. Next came the Maritime Center between Concord Street and the Cooper River. Completed in 1997, the Center is home to a marina and facilities for special events.

In the late 1990s Riley convinced the General Assembly and the voters of Charleston County to help fund the South Carolina Aquarium on the Cooper River at the foot of Calhoun Street where Christopher Gadsden's Great Wharf once stood. The Aquarium cost $69 million and was paid for by state, county, city, and private funds. It opened in May 2000. The National Park Service built a major $15 million facility next door to the Aquarium in 2002 to orient and transport visitors to Fort Sumter. In recognition of the area's significance in the Revolutionary period, the city named the adjacent open space Liberty Square. In his inaugural address in 2000, the mayor proposed the building of a major African American Museum on Calhoun Street near the Aquarium and on other occasions called for the building of a symphony hall in the area.

By 2003 "Aquarium Wharf" included the Aquarium, the Fort Sumter tour boat facility, restaurants, offices, and an IMAX theater.

The full participation of African Americans in the civic life of the community continued. The city launched a black

112

The waterfront park on the
Cooper River opened in 1990.
This twelve-acre park was built
on the site of former wharves.
Photograph by Michael Levkoff
and Barbara Baker

The South Carolina Aquarium,
built with state and local funds,
lost $69 million. Photograph by
Michael Levkoff and Barbara
Baker

The Fort Sumter Visitor Center
is located at Liberty Square.
Dockside condominiums are in
the background. Photograph by
Michael Levkoff and Barbara
Baker

arts festival in 1979 and sponsored the MOJA (a Swahili word meaning "One") Festival beginning in 1984. Designed to showcase, explore, and celebrate black music, theater, and the arts, MOJA was the city's first effort to recognize its African American cultural heritage. Major events included opera, film, jazz, the Dance Theatre of Harlem, African, and Caribbean artists, poetry, storytelling, and Gullah plays.

The Avery Institute for Afro-American History and Culture opened at the College of Charleston in 1978. The Avery Research Center for African American History and Culture opened in 1985. Housed in the building, which once was home to a black school, The Avery Normal Institute, it is the only research center of its kind in the Southeast region of the United States.

The affluence of the late twentieth century brought Charlestonians a heady fare of cultural activities. The Charleston Symphony Orchestra, under the able leadership of its renowned maestro, David Stahl, had forty-six members by 2002, a season beginning in September and lasting until May, and a budget of over $2 million annually. The 1905 Gibbes Museum of Art was renovated and a new wing provided increased gallery space. A new Charleston Museum was built on Meeting Street in 1980.

The city made extensive use of the Dock Street Theater, and it too was renovated and modernized for use, not only for the Spoleto Festival, but as a year-round facility. The Footlight Players moved to Queen Street and created a new playhouse. The "Spoleto Effect" raised expectations and the festival's rising tide raised all arts boats.

One of the most destructive hurricanes in Charleston's history, and one of the most costly hurricanes in America's twentieth century history, hit the city near midnight on September 21, 1989. Hurricane Hugo was a calamity to the Caribbean Islands and to the South Carolina Low Country. Riley and County Council Chairman, Linda Lombard, took to the local television airwaves to urge Charlestonians to evacuate the city beginning the night before the hurricane hit. At midnight, twenty-four hours before Hugo swept ashore, the traffic was bumper-to-bumper on Interstate 26 and remained so well into the afternoon of the hurricane. Hun-dreds of thousands of people left the coast for inland areas. The governor and Mayor Riley ordered an evacuation of low lying areas.

By 10:30 p.m. on September 21 powerful winds battered Charleston. The city was pounded by rain and sheets of water. Tides rose. The city went dark. By midnight, winds were 130 m.p.h. The eye of the hurricane passed over the city at 11:50 p.m. Trees and utility poles cracked. A twelve-to-seventeen-foot wall of water hit Fort Sumter. Many homes were badly damaged. The courthouse on Broad Street was so badly damaged that the courts moved temporarily (for twelve years!) to North Charleston. Many of the homes at Folly Beach were destroyed. The damage was devastating on Sullivan's Island and the Isle of Palms. Nine people were killed in Charleston County. Nearly every house and building in the city was damaged. The *Wall Street Journal* reported the storm as the costliest in history to the insurance industry to date. The *New York Times* reported $3.7 billion in losses. Hugo totally destroyed 3,785 homes and 5,815 mobile homes.

Massive numbers of trees were knocked down by the storm and the loss changed the look of parts of the city and surrounding areas. Power was out for a month in some places. After the hurricane, Mayor Riley, who had remained at city hall throughout the night, invoked a curfew. The governor sent in 2,500 National Guardsmen to prevent looting.

Hugo, author Dorothea Frank wrote, "forced Charleston to clean herself up. While Charleston was always a beautiful city, now she is a stunner, cherished all the more for her near death experience." Many of Charleston's churches and steeples needed extensive repair. St. John's Lutheran Church at Archdale and Clifford was closed for repairs for more than thirteen months. First Baptist Church was closed for fourteen months, while $1.6 million in repairs were made. "The sight of church steeples dangling from cranes turned many heads upwards," the *Post and Courier* reported in 1990. It took the city a year to clean itself up. But by 1991 many Charlestonians believed that Hugo had been a blessing in disguise. Houses in the historic district and Sullivan's Island were repaired and looked better than before the hurricane. The new judicial center on Broad Street owes its existence to Hugo.

The Charleston Museum at John and Meeting Streets, built in 1978, houses a variety of collections in its 80,000 square feet. Photograph by Michael Levkoff and Barbara Baker

African-Carribean Market Vendors at the MOJA Arts Festival in Hampton Park, produced by City of Charleston Office of Cultural Affairs. Courtesy of the City of Charleston

The day after Hurricane Hugo in Charleston. Photograph by the Post and Courier

Hurricane Hugo may even have woken up the staid, conservative *News and Courier*. In 1990 it named Barbara S. Williams, a well-respected journalist, its first woman editor. The two Charleston daily newspapers, the *News and Courier* and the *Evening Post*, merged in October 1991 to form the *Post and Courier*, and Williams was its first editor.

Special events proliferated after the success of the Spoleto Festival. The biggest such event, the Southeastern Wildlife Exposition, which features wildlife art of all kinds, began in 1983 and has grown to over 500 artists and exhibitors from around the globe who present their offerings to over 40,000 attendees. One of the biggest women's tennis events in the world, the Family Circle Cup, came to Charleston in 2001. The Family Circle Tennis Center, located on Daniel Island, includes a 10,200-seat stadium and has made Charleston a major tennis destination.

The United States won the 29th Ryder Cup match at Kiawah Island Ocean Golf Course in September 1991. The worldwide media event, which included continuous coverage on NBC, established Kiawah Island, the Low Country and Charleston as a premier golf destination. By 2002 the Charleston area was home to a plethora of golf resorts and courses. By1971 several suburban developments had been built around golf courses: Shadowmoss on Highway 61 West of the Ashley and Snee Farm on Highway 17 East of the Cooper. In addition to Kiawah, Seabrook Island, and Wild Dunes, golfers teed up at the Charleston National Golf Course in Mt. Pleasant on Daniel Island, Stono Ferry, Patriot's Point, and Coosaw Creek Country Club in North Charleston among others.

In 1991 Riley called a special meeting of city council and annexed Daniel Island. The 4,500-acre island, purchased by Harry F. Guggenheim in 1947 as a hunting preserve, was suddenly made a part of the Charleston metropolitan area by the construction of Interstate 526 which crossed the island. Dramatically demonstrating how powerful the building of highways can be in modern American cities, a remote rural island with few inhabitants, previously an hour and a half drive from downtown Charleston, was, by 1993 (when Exit 23 opened), a five-minute drive from Interstate 26. The Guggenheim Foundation wanted to properly dispose of the huge tract, and, in 1989, the original "Daniel Island Concept Plan" was released. Situated in Berkeley County and adjacent to both Mt. Pleasant and North Charleston, the city of Charleston's annexation provoked a firestorm of controversy and a lawsuit by the Guggenheim Foundation. In the end, however, the Guggenheim Foundation's confidence in Mayor Riley and the city's history of sound land-use planning led to a resolution when the Foundation voluntarily annexed into the city. Bishop England High School relocated to Daniel Island in 1998. By 1999 Exit 24 of Interstate 526 opened directly onto the island.

But progress in the 1990s did not follow a straight line. The banner headline in the *Post and Courier* on March 13, 1992, read, "A Direct Hit." The Defense Department had just announced the closure (or "realignment") of forty-three major military installations across the country. "Charleston was among the worst hit," the *Post and Courier* reported, "with nearly every naval command targeted for closure." Senator Hollings called the plan, which meant closure of the Charleston Naval Station (or Base), the Naval Hospital, the Naval Supply Center and other facilities, "an economic disaster." The Charleston Naval Shipyard, a fixture in the local economy for ninety-two years, would also close. Shipyard workers,

116

Barbara S. Williams, editor of the Post and Courier. *Rising through the ranks as a political reporter, Williams brought a breath of fresh air to the* News & Courier, *long known as "The Old Lady of Broad Street," for its stodgy, conservative opinions.* Photograph by the Post and Courier

engineers, naval personnel, business and political leaders were surprised and worried. The *Post and Courier* called the announcement "shocking news." The Charleston Naval Weapons Station near Goose Creek and several related military activities would remain.

The reaction of community leaders was swift. Facing millions of dollars in lost revenue, $4 million in payments annually to school districts alone, local governments banded together to fight the closure. D. E. "Sis" Inabinet, president of the Trident Chamber of Commerce, led an effort to lobby the Defense Base Closure and Realignment Commission to reject the recommendation. The chamber estimated the Navy's total impact in the Charleston economy at $3.2 billion ($1.1 billion in Navy and civilian payroll alone). Riley compared the loss of the Navy to the devastation of Hurricane Hugo. Inabinet insisted, "We can win this if we're in the fight together." Riley was "confident we can reverse this decision." Rallies and meetings were held, delegations went to Washington, black leaders and Democrats lobbied President Clinton. A committee, In Defense of Charleston, was organized. Military consultants were hired.

The Base Closure Commission met in Charleston on May 1, 1993, and thousands of Charlestonians, many wearing yellow "In Defense of Charleston" buttons, came to the Gaillard Auditorium to hear Governor Carroll A. Campbell, Jr.; Riley; Inabinet; and others make an impassioned plea for the base. "Closing the base," Riley told the commissioners, "will rip the heart out of the region's economy," causing a depression; 37,000 jobs would be lost immediately, 10,000 jobs were already gone and 22,000 additional civilian jobs would be lost in the future. The mood of the meeting was somber.

Despite the massive community effort, on June 25, 1993, the commission voted to close the base and the shipyard. "SCUTTLED" screamed the headline in the *Post and Courier.* "Two hundred years of naval history came to an abrupt, gut-wrenching halt," the newspaper announced, "when a federal panel voted to close Charleston's Navy base and shipyard." "This is probably the worst disaster that's happened to Charleston in my lifetime," Senator Strom Thurmond lamented. The Navy could have downsized the Norfolk base, but "closing Norfolk is like moving the Pope out of Rome," Senator Hollings quipped. "It's devastating," Inabinet said. "What more can you say?" "This community," the *Post and Courier* editorialized, "has a . . . calamity on its hands."

But Riley had more to say: "We're not going to be crying in our soup and beer. We've got to roll up our sleeves and get to work." The base was scheduled to close on April 1, 1996. On March 16, 1996, an assistant secretary of the Navy handed a gold key to South Carolina Lieutenant Governor Bob Peeler, turning the Naval Base over to the state. The future of the base was turned over to the Charleston Naval Complex Redevelopment Authority, a state agency.

Despite the widespread and deeply felt concern about the impact of the base closure, the loss of the naval facilities did not, in fact, impact significantly on the local economy. Construction was booming; the population of the metropolitan area increased dramatically; suburban areas expanded. The tourist industry, the port, all services, and especially health services, manufacturing, construction, educational institutions, and transportation all grew. The city's accommodations tax revenue doubled from 1990 to 1998. Patriot's Point Naval and Maritime Museum in Mt. Pleasant became a major tourist attraction. Even with the base closing, government jobs declined only slightly from 1990 to 1998. There was a 40% increase in services likely due to the increase in tourism in the region. There was a 5.8 percent drop in the government sector from 1990 to 1998 due to the closure of the base. Unemployment rates were highest in 1993 and 1994, but by 1998 the unemployment rate declined to its pre-closure (1990) level. Increases in local and state government jobs offset the decline in federal jobs. The Medical University remained the city's largest employer, and local hospitals (Roper, St. Francis, VA) provided many jobs.

Although manufacturing did not make a dent in Charleston's public image, the area's manufacturing sector expanded substantially in the late twentieth century. A huge Amoco plant was built at Cainhoy. Westvaco expanded its operations on the banks of the Cooper River. By 2000 fifteen hundred people worked for Bayer Corporation and Jacobs Applied Technology at the Bushy Park industrial park in North Charleston. Alcoa (formerly Alumax), JW Aluminum, Nucor Steel, Mikasa, Robert Bosch Corporation, even high-tech software maker Blackbaud located in the metropolitan area.

The Mark Clark Expressway (Interstate 526) opened in June, 1992. Twenty-six miles long at the time it was opened, Charleston's version of a "loop" around the city allowed

Patriot's Point Naval and Maritime Museum, established in 1975, the museum consists of five ships, including the aircraft carrier Yorktown, the nuclear merchant ship Savannah and the destroyer Laffey. Courtesy of Patriot's Point Museum

Charlestonians to drive from West Ashley to North Charleston, across the Cooper River to Daniel Island, across the James B. Edwards Bridge over the Wando River to Mt. Pleasant. The James Island Expressway opened in 1993 after thirty years of planning and controversy. The venerable architectural reporter for the *New York Times*, Ada Louise Huxtable, had reported in April 1971 that there "is a truce in this city this week that is almost as welcome as the end of the Civil War. The threat of a controversial bridge [into the historic district] . . . has been temporarily stayed."

The Spoleto Festival was rocked by the departure of its 82-year-old founder and chief prima donna, Gian Carlo Menotti, in October 1993. "The time has come for me to take my festival away," the maestro threatened. Riley and civic leaders, determined to hold on to the prestigious festival despite its financial difficulties, politely disagreed with Menotti and let him depart—but without the Spoleto Festival. Indeed, Menotti's departure strengthened the festival, and, under the direction of Nigel Redden, it has flourished. Regularly featured in national and international media, the Spoleto Festival has put Charleston on the world's cultural map. "Through the years," the *New York Times* noted in April 2001, "Spoleto has featured not just great art, but also the city itself . . . This year, Spoleto encompasses more than 130 performances of opera, dance, music, and theater in a dozen historic sites."

The State Ports Authority (SPA) expanded its container ship operation during the 1980s and 1990s making Charleston the nation's fourth busiest port and the busiest container port along the Southeastern and Gulf Coasts. Docks and huge cranes were built in Mt. Pleasant on the Wando River, but only after substantial opposition from citizens groups such as Save the Wando. In the early 1990s, the SPA bought 800 acres on the Cooper River side of Daniel Island to build a "Global Gateway" to accommodate newer gargantuan container ships. These plans floundered as environmental and neighborhood groups protested.

It was clear by 2002 that Charleston's Depression-era mentality—the desperate search for any industry and any job—had been replaced, or at least neutralized, by Charlestonians who were willing to fight businesses, such as the port and tourism, which they viewed as harmful to the environment and the historic scale and pace of the city.

The mayor responded to growing criticism from residents of the historic district with a Tourism Commission to regulate the tourism industry and other reforms. The Visitor Reception and Transportation Center on Meeting Street (between John and Mary) was designed to orient tourists and get them out of their automobiles. It opened in May 1991 at a cost of $13 million. By 1999 Riley agreed that development had its limits. "I am working with the Coastal Conservation League to develop ways to create Greenbelts," he said in his State of the City address. "Now, before it is too late, we must act to preserve farmland, forests, and vistas for future generations . . . We are aware of the danger of a city having too many hotel rooms."

The affluence of the 1980s and 1990s led to other civic improvements. The Community Foundation was established and led by a dynamic director, Madeline McGee. Other civic achievements included the building of a modern new airport in 1985; construction of the North Charleston Coliseum in 1993; and an $11-million library on Calhoun Street in 1998. In 1997 the city built a new $19.5-million, 6,000-seat baseball park on the banks of the Ashley River, and city council promptly named it the Joseph P. Riley, Jr., Park with one dissenting vote: Riley's. The park is home to a professional baseball team as well as The Citadel Bulldogs.

Suburbanization and urban sprawl meant that more people were living in unincorporated areas of the county. New towns were created at Kiawah and Seabrook. Kiawah Island, in particular, has attracted new residents to the Charleston area. Developed over a period of twenty-five years starting in 1976, the island is a private residential and resort community sprawling over 10,000 acres. Mayor Riley sought to annex James Island, but many James Islanders resisted and sought to establish their own town. A referendum to establish a town was favorable but the city sought dissolution of the town in court and won. New legislation allowed the town of James Island to be reestablished, but its legality was still contested by the city in 2003.

The City Market was re-invented between 1975 and 2000. Prior to the Riley administration, the market was a warehouse district for the distribution of produce and groceries, butcher shops, and port-related businesses such as bars, nightclubs, and a red light district. It was leased to tourist-related businesses in the 1970s and 1980s, and gradually the area has become a tourist Mecca. Henry's restaurant at 54 North Market Street, for example, was a fixture of old Charleston from 1932 to the 1970s. It was sold and "updated" in 1985.

The leaders of the Civil Rights movement passed on. Younger black leaders emerged. Esau Jenkins of Johns Island died in 1972; J. Arthur Brown, the leader of the NAACP in Charleston, died in 1988; Septima Clark in 1987; Bernice V. Robinson in 1994. But James Clyburn of Charleston was elected to Congress in 1992 and became the leader of the Congressional Black Caucus in 1998. In December 2002 he was elected vice chair of the Democratic Caucus which made him the highest-ranking African American in the House. McKinley Washington and Herbert Fielding were leaders in the South Carolina Senate. Robert Ford went from City Council

Container ship at the Port of Charleston. Photograph by Michael Levkoff and Barbara Baker

to a leadership role in the South Carolina Senate. Lucille Whipper became a leader in the South Carolina House of Representatives.

The tourism industry began a serious effort to include black history. Black tours and tour guides emerged in the late 1980s and early 1990s. Plantations began to highlight slave quarters and discuss the contribution of African Americans to the success of the Low Country economy. "Charleston has been trying hard to promote African American history in its tourism offerings," the State newspaper reported in May 1993. "Since 1985, city guides have been required to study African American history to get their licenses."

The nature of downtown Charleston changed over the last quarter of the twentieth century. Restored to perfection, with Sunbelt weather, a cultural renaissance, resort islands, golf courses, superb restaurants, one of the most popular "getaway" destinations in the nation, Charleston attracted newcomers to the historic district. Many purchased a second or a third house in Charleston and are part-time residents. Like Palm Beach, Santa Fe, and Nantucket, Charleston is now a place for the rich to own "trophy" houses. Indeed, the autumn 1999 issue of Art World News claimed: "Charleston: the Time Is Right . . . It's Being Hailed as the Next Sante Fe." These new Charlestonians have contributed substantially to the success of civic and cultural organizations, but some old Charlestonians grieve for the loss of continuity and tradition in the historic district. The Palm Beachification of old Charleston (or "Hamptonization" for New Yorkers) is, however, a fact of life in the twenty-first century.

The Citadel attracted national attention in 1995 when Shannon Faulkner brought a federal lawsuit to force the military college to admit her and other women to the Corps of Cadets. Faulkner could not cut the mustard and dropped out after six days, but other women succeeded. Nancy Mellette intervened in the federal suit. Riley and Hollings, both Citadel graduates, urged their alma mater to admit women. The Citadel surrendered to the inevitable in June 1996 after the U.S. Supreme Court ordered the Virginia Military Institute to accept female cadets. The case generated a great deal of controversy—and humor. Pat Conroy supported Shannon Faulkner, but he could not abide politically correct, anti-Citadel feminist rhetoric. Of one feminist writer who interviewed him about the case, Conroy wrote, "her questions . . . were remarkable for their shallowness and lack of importance." One bumper sticker urged: "Save the Males" (a parody of "Save the Whales"). "We have come a long way since 1995," Citadel President John S. Grinalds wrote in January 2000, noting that The Citadel's first female cadet had graduated in May 1999 and that female cadets were winning honors. The "unheralded story is that The Citadel has emerged from its troubled beginnings with co-education and can be proud of the success we have achieved."

Charlestonians vigorously debated the issue of gentrification as dramatically rising property values in the peninsula made dilapidated but historic houses much more valuable. Black property owners could sell their homes at a handsome profit and, like white Charlestonians before them, move to the suburbs. But black tenants were dispossessed as their rented homes and apartments were sold to more affluent homeowners. Major controversies swirled over the displacement of the residents of Shoreview Apartments on the Ashley River in 2000 to accommodate an upscale development and about what should be done with the site of the

Congressman James E. Clyburn. First elected in 1992, Clyburn represented the sixth district and became the first black congressman from South Carolina since Reconstruction. Courtesy of the Post & Courier

former Ansonborough public housing projects near the Cooper River waterfront. The unmistakable trend at century's end was the loss of African American neighborhoods on the peninsula.

Riley was reelected in 1995 defeating Republican State Representative Ron Fulmer and again in 1999 when he defeated a black candidate, Maurice Washington. The city later switched to non-partisan elections at Riley's instigation.

Riley earned a national reputation in urban planning. "There is no reason," Riley told the Washington Post, "for government ever to build something that is not beautiful." He was president of the United States Conference of Mayors and a founder of the Mayor's Institute for City Design. In July 2000, he was the first recipient of the Urban Land Institute's Nichols Prize ($100,000) for Visionary Urban Development. He also won the first President's Award from the United States Conference of Mayors. Riley even demanded creative designs for parking garages. He staunchly defended the building of the new judicial center on Broad Street despite opposition from neighborhood groups opposed to any further development on the peninsula. Riley praised the County's decision to pursue "the difficult, costly, complicated, controversial course to preserve and reinvigorate" the courthouse complex area.

Beginning with the construction of an elegant replica of the 1853 Mills House Hotel on Meeting Street in 1970, numerous hotels and inns have sprung up, many with the help of the city government and use of federal support, such as UDAG grants: Charleston Place in 1986, Lodge Alley Inn in 1982–1986, and the Francis Marion in 1996. The Lodge Alley Project, led by the city in the late 1970s, spurred the revitalization of East Bay Street. Built in 1924 the Francis Marion had closed in 1989. Riley's efforts at revitalizing upper King Street led not only to the reopening of the Francis Marion but to the renovation of the old Citadel building on Marion Square and its use as a unique Embassy Suites Historic Charleston hotel. In May 1998, Rick Widman opened the magnificent Wentworth Mansion. In 2001 a new six-story hotel, the Renaissance Charleston, took the place of an abandoned bus station on Wentworth Street. In 2002 the French Quarter Hotel opened in the Market.

Charleston celebrated the millennium by going about its business as usual. The year 2000 was advertised by many doomsayers as a potential technological disaster, but according to the *Post and Courier*, "It was a flag-furling, sub-raising, tax-capping kind of year." (The tax cap was designed to give residential property owners some relief.) A bitter controversy over whether or not the Confederate flag should fly over the South Carolina Capitol boiled over. Mayor Riley, accompanied by black and white Charlestonians, joined the protest against the flag and marched all the way to Columbia. The Confederate flag battle was ultimately moved to a monument on the Statehouse grounds.

Ironically in the very same year, the Confederate flag was lowered from the statehouse in Columbia, and the Confederate submarine *Hunley* was raised from the depths of the Charleston harbor. The small vessel, a desperate measure designed to keep the Union navy out of Charleston harbor during the Civil War, was the first submarine to sink an enemy ship in battle. It also sank in the attack and divers searched for it for years. A team funded by author Clive Cussler found the *Hunley* in 1995 and a recovery effort, led by State Senator Glenn McConnell, a Charleston Civil War buff, was successful in raising the submarine in August 2000. Thousands watched from the shore of the Cooper River, and people all over the world saw images on television, as the relic was raised from the ocean floor and was carried by ship to the Naval Shipyard.

In 2001, after two decades of debate and explosive growth east of the Cooper, the state approved a $531 million contract to build yet another bridge over the Cooper River. By 2001 Mt. Pleasant had 49,000 residents, a 52 percent increase from the 32,000 in 1992. The Arthur Ravenel Bridge, named for the congressman and state senator credited with securing its funding, is expected to cost in excess of $531 million and will be eight lanes wide for automobile traffic and will also include a pedestrian/bicycle lane. The bridge will be two and a half miles long; the main span towers will stand five hundred seventy feet above the water; and the bridge will rise one hundred eighty six feet above water and will have the longest cable-stayed main span in North America.

The historic district had a stable population in the late twentieth century. In 1940 the peninsula contained 71,000 residents. By 1990 it was less than 39,000, the lowest since 1850, and it remained at approximately 40,000 through 2000. The decrease was due to the move to the suburbs in the 1950s and 1960s and the restoration of homes which formerly housed many low-income people into homes for the affluent. The decrease was offset somewhat by the increase in the number of students at the College of Charleston (11,665 as of 1998), MUSC, and Trident Technical College. Retirees and absentee owners also affected the population figures as numerous homes in the historic district are now second homes. The city is also older because of retirees. Indeed, 78 percent of the population growth in Charleston County between 1990 and 2000 was attributed to residents age fifty-five and older.

Charlestonians were rarely successful in the late twentieth century in achieving state-wide political office and Charleston's influence in the state legislature waned. With

Top photo: The first two bridges over the Cooper River: The John P. Grace Memorial Bridge and the Silas N. Pearman Bridge. Construction of the new Arthur Ravenal Bridge is also visible. Photograph by Michael Levkoff and Barbara Baker

Bottom photo: One of several new architecturally interesting parking garages. This one is on King Street. Photograph by Michael Levkoff and Barbara Baker

Lodge Alley Inn. These buildings were restored with the use of Federal (UDAG) grants. Photograph by Michael Levkoff and Barbara Baker

The Old Citadel, which is now a hotel, is where The Citadel, the Military College of South Carolina, was founded in 1843. The original arsenal, or "citadel," was built as a result of the Denmark Vesey slave conspiracy of 1822. It fronts on Marion Square, named in honor of Francis Marion. Photograph by Michael Levkoff and Barbara Baker

the exception of Senator Hollings and Dr. James B. Edwards, who served as governor, and Nancy Stevenson as Lt. Governor, from 1974 to 1978, Charleston candidates did not fare well statewide. In 1994 Joe Riley failed in his bid to become the Democratic nominee for governor, and former GOP congressmen Arthur Ravenel and Tommy Hartnett were unable to win the Republican nomination. But by 2002, Charlestonians had returned to power in state government. Republican Mark Sanford of Sullivan's Island, formerly a congressman from the Charleston area, was elected governor in 2002; Senator Glenn McConnell had risen to the position of President Pro Tempore of the Senate. Representative Robert Harrell was Chairman of the House Ways and Means Committee.

By 2003 Charleston's historic district had been dramatically transformed from its appearance of only thirty years before. Riley's strenuous efforts at urban revitalization included the rejuvenation of upper and lower King Street, the rebuilding of the Calhoun Street corridor, the renovation of Market Hall and Marion Square, the Waterfront Park, and the building of the South Carolina Aquarium and Liberty Square. After Hurricane Hugo in 1989, County government contributed to this transformation by restoring the Charleston County Court House to its 1792 appearance and building a new Judicial Center at the Four Corners of Law at Broad and Meeting Streets. The debate over the court house and the restoration and construction work took more than twelve years. The Federal government contributed by building a modern annex to the Federal courthouse named in honor of Senator Hollings. It was said to be the most expensive federal courthouse per square foot in the United States. The South Carolina Historical Society restored the Fireproof Building. St. Philips and St. Michael's Churches were both restored, as were the French Huguenot church on Church Street, Mt. Zion Church on Glebe Street, and K.K. Beth Elohim Synagogue and St. Mary's Church, both on Hasell Street. The continued expansion of the College of Charleston and the Medical University also contributed to the revitalization of the historic district.

The value of private homes in the historic district soared. "Taxes, Tourism alter City's Face," a Post and Courier headline told its readers in November 1991. Property taxes also rose dramatically. Between 1980 and 1990, the average value of a home south of Broad increased more than 300%. The Simmons-Edwards House (or Pineapple Gate House) at 14 Legare Street was purchased by a corporate executive for $3.1 million in 1997. The Sword Gate house at 32 Legare Street was next, purchased for $3 million in 1999.

The tourism boom brought with it an explosion in restaurants. "How does one small city lure so many sophisticated travelers?" Conde Nast Traveler magazine asked in August 1997. One answer was Charleston's cuisine. New restaurants with nationally recognized chefs abounded: Robert's and Garibaldi's in the Market in the 1970s; Phillipe Million at McCrady's Long Room on Unity Alley in the 1980s; Louis's, Anson's, Carolina's, Magnolia's, and Slightly North of Broad in the 1990s; and 1886 at the Wentworth Mansion, Cypress, Fish, High Cotton, McCrady's, Hank's, and the Peninsula Grill set new local standards. Seafood restaurants multiplied in Mt. Pleasant, West Ashley, and on the island. Eclectic restaurants such as Brett's on James Island and the Mustard Seed and J. Bistro in Mt. Pleasant sprang up. The elegant Woodlands opened in Summerville. Charleston became a

restaurant destination as more visitors came for the dining than seeing old dining rooms.

In November 1999, R. W. Apple, Jr., wrote a travel piece on Charleston in the New York Times entitled "A Southern Legacy and a New Spirit." "You can't say it about many cities," Apple wrote, "but you can say it about this one: One man changed its destiny. His name is Joseph P. Riley, Jr. He is Charleston's mayor. He halted its long decline, which lasted for a hundred years after the Civil War, turning it from a proud but rotting relic into a model modern city." Michael Shnayerson writing in Conde Nast Traveler described Charleston as "the town that Joe rebuilt." The Post and Courier concurred. It consistently supported Riley for reelection, stating in 1995 that "Joe Riley is no ordinary mayor, and this is no ordinary city."

Future historians might not agree completely. After all, the general affluence of the nation and of the Sunbelt South (other Southern cities reinvented themselves in the late twentieth century), a revolution in race relations, an influx of new wealth, massive federal and military spending, all had something to do with Charleston's economic and cultural revitalization. Riley has not been without his critics. Neighborhood and environmental activists complain that he is too pro-development, that the historic district is too crowded, and taxes are too high. Some Charlestonians lament the loss of family businesses on King Street. Riley's Republican opponents vigorously criticized his use of federal funds. "We said all the time," Nancy Hawk recalled in 1996, "we've survived wars and hurricanes, but can we survive federal money?" John Bourne, the former mayor of North Charleston said in a 1992 interview: "Nobody's perfect, even Joe. He has been progressive, but at the same time he really has created a very big and expensive government." Republican Representative Ron Fulmer ran against Riley in 1995 and criticized Riley's alleged massive spending and big municipal debt, but the voters did not agree. Riley garnered 75 percent of the vote.

"First elected in 1975," Walter Edgar wrote in South Carolina A History, "Mayor Joseph P. Riley led a city government that transformed the old port city . . . For the first time in its history, Charleston became a livable city for most of its residents, not just those south of Broad Street." It is undeniable that Joe Riley's vision of a racially inclusive community, a multi-faceted, lively and busy downtown, his insistence on excellence in urban design (best exemplified in the Waterfront Park), and his emphasis on the cultural life of the city (Spoleto, MOJA, the symphony, and ballet) have fundamentally altered Charleston. The "standard itinerary" to Charleston prior to Spoleto, Cecily McMillan wrote in the New York Times in 1988 was old houses, Fort Sumter, a souvenir, and she-crab soup. "It took an arts festival of international importance to break the spell."

"Joe Riley has done a remarkable job since he became mayor," the Post and Courier editorialized in 1995, "and he retains an infectious enthusiasm for the task ahead." In the aftermath of Hurricane Hugo in late 1989, Jesse Jackson, the Civil Rights leader, compared Riley to Moses saving his people. A few months later, Prince Charles visited Charleston to discuss urban preservation and called the mayor "a remarkable man." Thus, Riley's promise of "a new age of tolerance, harmony, and creativity" was, according to a broad consensus of Charlestonians and a wide variety of visitors, a promise he had kept.

Prince Charles at a press conference during his visit to Charleston, where he lauded Riley's preservation efforts and called him a "remarkable man." Photograph by Bill Murton

French Protestant (Huguenot) Church, 140 Church Street, designed by Edward Brickell White. The present structure was built from 1844 to 1845. The original congregation was organized on this site in 1687. Photograph by Michael Levkoff and Barbara Baker

Mount Zion A.M.E. Church (1847-1848) 7 Glebe Street. Originally the Glebe Street Presbyterian Church, the building was sold to the A.M.E. church in 1888. Photograph by Michael Levkoff and Barbara Baker

Edward B. White was superintending architect for the Custom House, the design attributed to Ammi B. Young of New England. Begun in 1853, the Civil War delayed its completion until 1879. The foundations were laid just outside the line of old fortifications, and remains of Craven Bastion were discovered during excavation.

Chronicles
of Leadership

In a sense, when promoters of Low Country tourism adopted the slogan "Charleston: America's Best Kept Secret," the slogan was true. Until quite recently, relatively few strangers had "discovered" this old port city, noted chiefly in history books as the cradle of the war that rent the nation in the 1860s and in the pages of *Gone With the Wind* as the home town of the infamous Rhett Butler, who cared not a damn what would become of Miss O'Hara.

Strangers were long unaware of Charleston's Old World charm, of the architectural gems rescued from the savagery of demolition and now handsomely restored to their pristine state. They were equally unaware of the beauty and elegance of Charleston's gardens, landmarks known throughout the botanical world; Middleton Place, for example, is the oldest landscaped garden in America, with lawns and terraces that remain as they were designed years before the Revolutionary War.

These features, perhaps, were little known. But, "Charleston: America's Best Kept Secret"?

Hardly. Business, industry, and commerce have known about Charleston for a long, long time.

As agriculture in the area waned with the disappearance of rice and indigo, and with Sea Island cotton the victim of the rapacious boll weevil, the Low Country labor force took on an added dimension. Workers were plentiful, the wage scale was relatively low, and tax incentives made locating in the area overwhelmingly attractive.

Charleston's magnificent harbor and port facilities, constantly expanded to meet the demands of export/import commerce, have been other compelling reasons for industry to locate here. As trade in South Carolina burgeoned after World War II, the administration of former Governor Ernest F. Hollings (a Charlestonian) had the foresight to plan for a highly skilled work force. To this end, technical education centers were established throughout the state and have proved an invaluable training tool for South Carolina workers. At the same time, they have served as an additional lure to industry, which is relieved of the training burden.

For example, while a given industry is establishing its base here—a process that may involve months-prototypes of its machines are already in use for training at the local Trident Technical Center. When the plant is officially opened, a skilled work team can start work immediately.

In one instance, a luxurious hotel was proposed for the historic section of the city, planned as a very posh hostelry. While construction proceeded, the training of personnel was underway at the technical center. When the inn's doors were opened to the public, the entire staff, from bellhop to bartender, from chef to chambermaid, was able to offer superb service befitting the opus lent atmosphere.

Further inducement to newcomers is Charleston's recognition as a center of education and the arts. Splendid preparatory academies, four colleges, a medical university, and a number of excellent business schools are all easily accessible to scholars; the artist colony is populous and active; local theater, symphony, ballet, and opera companies play to packed houses; and touring theatrical and musical groups are booked regularly onto Charleston stages.

For others not so artistically inclined, who favor more the activities of the outdoors, Charleston again has much to offer. Splendid beaches are nearby; the area is dotted with challenging golf courses, and tennis courts abound. Nowhere is found better sailing and fishing, and the countryside is legend among discriminating hunters.

Altogether, it is no surprise that industry chooses Charleston. It could not find a better host.

ABRASIVES-SOUTH, INC.

Jim Carter, owner of Abrasives-South, Inc., had no idea that his part-time job while in college would lead to a lifelong career in the abrasives industry. Today the North Charleston-based company earns annual sales of about $5 million and is a major supplier of abrasives and related products throughout the Southeast. But Carter credits much of his success to a mentor who recognized his potential and gave him the opportunity to prove himself.

During his years at Assumption College, Carter worked at night and during the summer at Norton Company, an abrasives manufacturing plant in Worcester, Massachusetts. His jobs ranged from "floor sweeper to dust collector to mixer." Following graduation, he entered the company's sales training program and was later transferred to Jamestown, New York. While working in Jamestown, he struck up a friendship with Tom Pembridge, a man whose parents sold chemicals and plating supplies to the same customer base as the abrasives industry. Don and Rosalie Pembridge soon became like family to Carter, and included him in personal and business outings.

Rosalie (Ro) and Don Pembridge, founders of Abrasives-South, Inc., and mentors to Jim Carter.

Jim and Kim Carter with Madison, 3; Adam, 6; and Alec, 3.

In 1978 the Pembridges expanded their operations into South Carolina, opening a chemical company in Columbia and an abrasives company in Charleston. It was here that Abrasives-South, Inc., was born. Don Pembridge found that his abrasives plant was struggling, however, and realized he needed an experienced salesman to draw more business. He immediately knew the right man for the job.

"I was only 25 years old and excited and surprised by this generous offer. Also, I had very little or no money at the time," says Carter. "Don and Ro offered to lend me the money to buy 1/3 of the business if I would move down and work to turn the company around. Their payback plan was also a gift in that they only wanted me to begin to repay when the company was successful. There was no predeter-

mined time or obligation. It was all based on trust and knowing that eventually the company would be running well."

Carter jumped at the opportunity, and in January 1982 he relocated to Charleston to begin a career with Abrasives-South, Inc., as 1/3 owner. Two years later Pembridge and Carter became 50/50 partners. Eventually Pembridge sold all of his shares of the business to Carter, making him the sole owner.

Today Carter continues to follow the example set by the Pembridges. His wife, Kim, is the vice president and secretary of the company and is part-owner. The couple's three children call Don and Rosalie "Poppi" and "Nonni."

"After seeing the model of success that Don and Ro have, we are living the dream that I had early on in my career. What better success, a loving wife and family to share a good business and future with," Carter says.

Under his leadership, Abrasives-South has blossomed over the past two decades. In 1978 the company had three employees and $250,000 in sales. Currently there are 16 employees. The company moved from its original location to a 10,000-square-foot building on four acres on Rourk Street in North Charleston. In 1999 they added on another 12,000 square feet.

Abrasives-South, Inc.'s product line.

Abrasives-South, Inc., specializes in the coated abrasives conversion of belts, sheets and discs. The company buys jumbo rolls of abrasive material, such as sandpaper and sanding cloth, and then slits, cuts and joins the product into various sizes. Their full range of products include bonded abrasive wheels, non-woven belts and wheels, superabrasives, automatic equipment, high-energy finishing systems, and cleaning equipment and supplies.

In the early years, the company supplied products and services primarily to the hand-tool industry. Today its diverse market has expanded to include the automotive, steel, foundry, furniture, glass, fittings, hardware, tool manufacturing and aerospace industries.

Abrasives-South, Inc., assists customers throughout the process by supplying a total package. Abrasives South examines the customers' raw forging or casting and recommends the best way to achieve a high quality finished part. As an example, the company can help a customer develop a system for finishing from turnkey equipment installation to supplying all the abrasives and chemicals needed to achieve the desired finish. The company manufactures or converts the coated abrasive belts and sells the

Jumbo roll slitter.

equipment to help automate the plant. It also provides chemicals needed for plating and finishing. Lastly, the company helps implement process improvements.

In fact, what sets Abrasives-South, Inc., apart from its competitors is its ability to offer a complete solution to customer needs. Many of its customers turn to Abrasives-South, Inc., to help them reduce their manufacturing costs and improve productivity.

"Most of our competitors sell abrasive belts or grinding wheels for a specific job. We like to say we sell the finish that our customer wants and the products we provide are the tools to get there," states Carter. "We try to offer a full solution by asking is this

problem or application best served by a coated abrasive solution or by a chemical solution? This causes creative thinking at both our level and the customer's, not something you can pull out of a catalog."

Although this route may be a slower way to establish a customer base, Carter says he finds it more rewarding. He enjoys partnering with companies to develop process improvements and cost savings ideas. Often this leads to satisfied, long-term customers. This unique approach to complete customer service is one of the keys to the success of Abrasives-South, Inc., over the years.

This same commitment to service was instilled early on by the organization's founder, Don Pembridge. In 2001 the man who made all this success possible passed away. And although Carter and his family miss Don Pembridge, Carter says he hopes to pass on his mentor's generosity to others.

"He has influenced my life in so many positive ways. I am truly better as a person for knowing him," Carter reflects. "He believed in me as a young man and gave me the chance to become what I dreamed of. I could never repay that except I hope someday I can be the mentor and the guiding light for a young person who is trying to find their way."

Abrasives-South, Inc.'s warehouse.

ATS LOGISTICS, INC.

To most people, lost luggage spells a guaranteed headache—but to the Gianoukos brothers of Charleston, South Carolina, it spelled the opportunity of three lifetimes and the seed idea for their parent company, ATS Logistics, Inc.

When Jimmie, Andy and Tony Gianoukos started Atlantic Transportation Services in 1986, they had no office space, no warehouse space and no trucks. What they had was a plan and a will to succeed rivaled only by their enormous energy. Andy, working at the time for Piedmont Airlines, heard that Piedmont was less than happy with the company in charge of delivering lost luggage to customers. The brothers decided to pick up on that need and formed a transportation services firm, working from a tiny apartment with one extra employee and one van. They put 100,000 miles on the van the first year, delivering lost luggage for several airlines serving Charleston International Airport. "We got another van that year and put 100,000 miles on it, too," said oldest brother Jimmie, company president.

Luggage delivery soon turned into delivery services in general, with the fledgling company taking on the handling of small packages and documents, as well as deliveries for local department stores and appliance companies. The small company was wrestling stiff competition in that arena: heavyweights like United Parcel Service and Federal Express had already carved out a pretty good niche for themselves. "We didn't want to battle those guys," said middle brother Andy, the firm's chief executive officer. So the brothers decided to diversify.

Customers encouraged them to consider the warehousing business. Research showed that there was a need in that area, and in 1988 the Gianoukos brothers branched out again. They created ATS Warehouse with $40,000 in capital and the unqualified support of their parents, who took a second mortgage on their home to provide their sons with start-up

The Gianoukos family members outside, on the front porch entry with ATS sign. Left to right: Andy; Katherine; Tony, Jr.; Tony, Sr.; and Jimmie Gianoukos.

money for their new venture. "We couldn't have started the business without it," Jimmie said of his parent's generous gesture. "We needed equipment. We paid them back in a year."

Within that year, the new division also quintupled its square footage. "We filled it up in three months," Tony said of the division's original 10,000 square feet of leased warehousing space, located on West Montague Street in North Charleston. At the end of its first year, ATS Warehouse was able to purchase the entire 50,000-square-foot West Montague warehousing structure. Between 1988 and 1994, the warehousing operation grew to include 500,000 square feet in 10 different locations. The division has since downsized to 300,000 square feet in three buildings, a figure which efficiently meets its requirements.

In 1996 the brothers sought new markets. They found them with the formation of ATS Express. This division served as a liaison between local businesses and local truck carriers for

efficient transfer of freight. It succeeded admirably, and by the year 2000, the division had contracts with 500 different carriers making deliveries throughout the United States and Canada. Andy noted that "this allows us to match the right cargo with the right carrier, which better serves our customers."

Matching the right cargo with the right carrier would open up another line of pursuit for ATS. In 1998 the company acquired Evergreen America shipping lines as a client, and started providing local transportation of shipping containers to and from Evergreen vessels. From this foundation, ATS has since developed an intermodal division and expanded its services as a regional carrier, covering the entire

The Gianoukos brothers beside an ATS Intermodal truck. Left to right: Andy, Tony Jr. and Jimmie Gianoukos. The driver is Wesley Cox.

Southeast of the United States with its own fleet.

Close proximity to the Port of Charleston has proved a boon to ATS, as most of the international cargo it handles comes through the port. The company also benefits from its proximity to interstates I-26, I-526 and I-95, and to CSX and Norfolk Southern railway lines. The benefits of hard work and a well-thought-out business plan manifested in 2000, when the Gianoukos brothers brought the three divisions of ATS Warehouse, ATS Express and ATS Intermodal together under the umbrella of ATS Logistics, Inc.

It would be hard to overstate the importance of family loyalty in this particular American success story. Tony and Katherine Gianoukos, the brothers' parents, have watched their initial $5,000 start-up loan to ATS grow into a multi-million dollar warehousing and transportation company. Both Tony and Katherine have also worked in the business, with Katherine maintaining the books and Tony, Sr., overseeing equipment and maintenance matters. Brother Tony serves as the firm's chief financial officer and also handles its warehouse division.

ATS extends a similar loyalty to its employees, whom it prefers to regard as associates. The firm provides its workers with as much flexibility as possible in such matters as work schedules and use of benefits. "People have legitimate family needs," Jimmie recently told a *Charleston Regional Business Journal* reporter for the article "Family Friendly Practices Boost Employee Loyalty." He cannot stress firmly enough that the firm's success depends strongly upon the contribution of every ATS associate.

Both local and national sponsors have recognized the firm's excellence. The City of Charleston's Metro Chamber of Commerce honored ATS Logistics in 1996 with its "Top Award"

for outstanding performance by area businesses. In March 2003 the South Carolina Truckers Association presented ATS Intermodal with its Award in the State for Industrial Safety and its Award for Truck Safety. In 1996 Mass Mutual and the U.S. Chamber of Commerce awarded ATS with its Blue Chip Enterprise Initiative Award "for demonstrating innovation, determination and courage, and for serving as a powerful and inspiring example for other small businesses."

On September 21, 1989, Hurricane Hugo struck the South Carolina coast at midnight at Sullivan's Island, just southeast of Charleston, with recorded winds of 135 mph and the highest storm surge ever recorded on the East Coast. The eye of the hurricane passed directly over Charleston. Damages created by this monster of a storm totaled $7 billion in the United States, with an insurance claim rate in Charleston of 20 percent. The Gianoukos brothers and associates from the firm worked through the weekend to get their clients' cargo under cover before the rains started. They incurred an insurance claim rate of only .5 percent. This statistic alone seems to tell the story of ATS Logistics, Inc.

ATS Logistic's associates working at the warehouse dock door. Left to right: Randolph Mood, Uly McDonald and Dawud Shaheed at the dock door.

129

INSTITUTE OF RELIGION AND HEALTH

What place should religion have in the training of medical students and in the physician's practice? This was the topic of discussion in 1985 between James B. Edwards, president of the Medical University of South Carolina, and Don C. Berry, former pastor of Charleston's Citadel Baptist Church located at Calhoun and Meeting Streets.

Since studies show the well-being of the patient (and the physician) is influenced by matters of faith and religion, ought this be a part of the curriculum for medical students? The physician and the clergy hold a unique "healing" role in the lives of individuals and their families. Each understands the value of treating the whole person as essential to health and healing. But how should these matters be introduced, and how could connections be made between the medical and religious communities in benefiting medical professionals, patients and the community-at-large? How can the physical, emotional, mental and spiritual well-being of the individual become an integral part of medical and religious education?

This meeting was the inspiration for the Institute of Religion and Health. Twelve years later, on September 11, 1997, Dr. Edwards; Dr. Berry; Dr. and Mrs. Louis Costa III, a reconstructive

Don C. Berry, Th.D./Ph.D., president and principal founder.

Donald C. Mullen, M.D., M.Div., first chairman and initial founder.

Cindy Costa and Louis Costa II, D.M.D., M.D., initial founders.

surgeon; and Dr. Donald Mullen, a cardiac surgeon hosted a group of physicians, clergy and business leaders to consider a center to provide resources and research in relating the converging matters of medicine and ministry, faith and health. They would become the initial founders of the future Institute.

Edwards grew up in Charleston and attended the College of Charleston and the Medical University of South Carolina. After practicing dentistry as an oral surgeon, he ran for governor of South Carolina and won—becoming the first Republican governor since Reconstruction. Later, he was President Reagan's Secretary of the Department of Energy and served as the president of MUSC from 1983 through 1999.

Berry, a Charlestonian by birth, is a graduate of Baylor University, holds a master's of divinity and a doctorate in

theology and philosophy, and has taught in several colleges, in addition to serving as adjunct seminary professor. He is the principal founder and president of the Institute in Charleston and Augusta, Georgia.

The Harbor Club dinner of September 11 garnered support and commitments. The initial advisory persons meeting with Berry included Costa; Mullen; Arnold Prystowsky, a local clothier; Richard Sosnowski, M.D., Ob-Gyn physician and long-time and honored faculty member of the Medical University; Dr. Kenneth Caldwell, orthopedic surgeon; William Warlick, architect; Nedah Haden, development consultant; Reverend Donald Fail, rector of Grace Episcopal Church; and Nancy Smythe. Two months later, the Institute of Religion and Health opened its office at the Maritime Building on East Bay Street, where it remains today.

Dr. Mullen, founding chair, helped Dr. Berry energize and guide the Institute's beginnings. Donald Mullen, M.D., holds a master's of divinity from Princeton University and serves as a lay minister. He is also board chairman for the Philadelphia Foundation, which is committed to building a Christian state-of-the-art hospital for the 2004 Olympics in Athens, Greece.

The vision and financial support of Reverend Woodrow W. Richardson, retired minister, and Tommy Bozard, layman and president of Bozard Enterprises, both of Orangeburg, South Carolina, have enabled the Institute to fulfill much of its mission.

The Institute's aim of providing emotional and spiritual support to those who are ill, injured or dying is being accomplished through its programs of research in addition to the resources of conferences and materials. It is presently conducting research on the effect of the religious and faith perspectives of the physician-nurse upon the patient and their families and the multi-faceted benefits of faith-centered support. The concept of integrating religion and health is being implemented in most medical schools by including issues of spirituality as a part of their curriculum.

The mission of the Institute is to become "a national resource and research center dedicated to the health and healing of persons founded upon the uniqueness of the biblical faith and worldview."

Some of the various projects sponsored by the Institute include: presenting conferences and seminars led by nationally known leaders on medical and scientific issues relating to faith, religion and health; establishing within communities of faith a healthcare network to minister to persons within their faith community while supporting a congregational/parish nurse program; training in identifying, understanding and addressing complex ethical issues from the Judeo-Christian perspective;

Chaplain Joseph Dukes of Albany, Georgia, entertains children at the Medical University Children's Hospital in between sessions of the Institute's national conference.

establishing a Grace Corps, an on-call, trained and certified volunteer organization to assist, upon request, hospitals, chaplain and clergy in the emotional and spiritual support of the patient and their families. The Grace Corps also fulfills a supportive role in community emergencies.

Recent and projected publications include *Healing Prayers, The Physician's Calling, The Nurse's Calling, The Hospital Experience, The Healing Community;* "Re-Collections," a video series for hospital patients; and a 1-800 support-line for medical professionals.

The Institute opened a second center in Augusta, Georgia, co-sponsoring a regional conference with the Medical College of Georgia in October 2002. Another office is expected to open in Dallas, Texas, sometime in 2004.

Two national conferences convened in Charleston in March 1999 and October 2000 at the Baruch Auditorium of MUSC. Participants from thirteen states consisted of physicians, nurses and allied health persons, chaplain, clergy and laity. Presenters included Dr. Harold G. Koenig of Duke's Center; Dr. David B. Larson, president and primary founder of the National Institute for Healthcare Research; Dr. Dale A. Matthews, Georgetown University School of Medicine; and Dr. Francis MacNutt, co-founder of Christian Healing Ministries, Inc., Jacksonville, Florida.

Charles Fennessy and Dr. H. Biemann Othersen followed Dr. Mullen as chairpersons. Donald

Kenneth Caldwell, M.D. (left) and Donald Morillo (right), with Don Berry, sharing the Healing Prayers *booklet.*

Time out for a picture during one of six Board of Directors planning sessions. Left to right: William Warlick, Amy Corder, Bill Eaton, Nancy Smythe, Daniel Massie, Fleetwood Hassell, M.D., Don Berry, Biemann Othersen, M.D., Alan Rashford, M.D., and Woodrow Richardson.

Morillo and Dr. Kenneth Caldwell serve as chair and vice-chair respectively. In addition to those named earlier, Frederick Reed, M.D., assists the following board members, who lead the Charleston Institute: Alan Rashford, M.D.; Daniel Massie, DMin, DD; William Eaton; and Amy Corder, RN.

The Institute of Religion and Health— www.instituteofreligionandhealth.com www.faithandhealthmatters.com— also seeks to play a strategic role in acknowledging the calling of those who are in the ministry of health and healing. "The church, the medical community and the business community join hands . . . reminding people that life, in all its stages, is valuable, and that God's presence is here in the midst," states Berry.

Dr. Harold Koenig, director and founder of the Center for the Study of Religion/Spirituality and Health at Duke University Medical Center, says that "the Institute is unique in its perspective and mission of providing both resources and research in the vast arena where faith connects with healthcare and healing." From its inception the Institute has sought to be a listening ear and an enabling presence in this vast arena.

KALMAN CONSTRUCTION CORPORATION

Kalman Construction Corporation of Charleston, South Carolina, was founded in 1987 by Kevin and Betsy Kalman. For seven years they developed their business by building high-end custom homes, renovating older homes and contracting work on Massachusetts's Nantucket Island. In 1996 the Kalmans moved to Charleston, and for three years Kalman Construction operated both there and on Nantucket before building exclusively in the Charleston area.

Kevin and Betsy Kalman work hard at creating a business marked by quality and professionalism. Their company consists of employees that take pride in their work, people who have come to join the company from all over the country. This firm has builders and cabinetmakers on staff that bring with them years of experience, as well as a wide range of

Betsy and Kevin Kalman.

Curved barrel vault hallway: "an art gallery surrounded by a house," the client exclaimed.

educational backgrounds. One member of Kalman's staff has a degree in marine biology, while still another has a degree in electrical engineering. With all his staff, he's embedded the philosophy, "If you don't have time to do it right, when will you have time to do it over?"

Kevin learned the construction trade from his father and older brothers. He especially learned the importance of preparation and time management from his father. "Construction is in my blood," he says. From an early age, Kevin worked with his family learning the ins and outs of the business by working on site. Construction has been the only work he's ever known. Kevin remembers watching his father sit at the kitchen table after

dinner, planning and preparing the next day's project. Because he was so exact with his planning, he could pre-cut every piece of lumber in his workshop—and then bring that wood on location, ready to use. His father's construction approach was revolutionary, because he wasted little time on the construction site planning, measuring and cutting materials. In this way, Kevin says, "the men working for you are more productive, and the job is completed in better time."

Besides his construction upbringing, Kevin has the "islander" mentality. Born and bred on Nantucket, he explains that people who live on islands are "independent, resourceful and thrifty." Living on an island means "you live where you work. There is no 20-minute commute back to one's home from work. If you mess up a job or can't service customers, you can't hide. You have to deal with the consequences," explains Kevin. Also, learning the construction trade on an island and operating a successful business there for years demonstrates his ability to do some exceptional planning. "On Nantucket there are no chain Home Depot's or Lowe's you can rely on as back up. If you don't plan for it, you don't have it, and work can be delayed."

One of the milestones in Kalman Construction was when it was awarded the contract to build a summer home for an internationally recognized architect and his family. The work they did led to them building a home—which was featured in *Architectural Digest* in June 1998—for renowned architect Graham Gund. This opportunity opened even more doors for Kalman Construction. One such door was with Bob Villa's *Home Again* television program. They built the "Lifespan House" in I'On, South Carolina, that was filmed and included in a 13-part series. Kalman Construction's extensive website, www.kalmanconstruction.com, shows

The "2003 American Home of the Year" (HOME Magazine) in Daniel Island, South Carolina, celebrates the Barbados/ Charleston connection.

own families, a chance to get off campus and enjoy a home-cooked meal.

All in all, Kevin describes his life and work simply as "battles and blessings." As the company grows, he will continue to work hard in hiring the right people, and letting go of the reins a little more. His son, Alex Holdgate, who has been working with the company since age 11, is taking a bigger role in the business, as well. With a talented staff steeped in a responsible work ethic, Kalman Construction Corporation has a future of continued growth and prosperity, positively affecting all those involved—from the homeowner to the community of Charleston.

many pictures of their award-winning projects including new homes, remodeled rooms and outdoor spaces. The company's history and detailed biographies of the staff can be found on their site as well.

Besides having their work featured in *Architectural Digest*, it has also been seen in *Home*, *Country Kitchen & Bath Ideas*, *House Beautiful*, *Better Homes & Gardens* and *Southern Living*. Kalman Construction has won national awards from the National Association of Home Builders and American Society of Interior Designers. They have also earned ten PRISM awards for their work in Charleston.

Having recently opened a new bath and kitchen showroom, Kalman Construction offers its clients a wide range of custom cabinetry options. This showroom will enable them to work with their customers to create a custom design using a variety of door styles and wood finishes.

Along with building quality homes for the Charleston area, Kevin and Betsy's devotion to Charleston can also be seen in the many ways they give back to the community—through their church, East Cooper Baptist; by encouraging their employees to give of their time and resources; and helping the elderly with home repair through the Methodist Relief Organization. The Kalmans are also very much involved in supporting the college students that attend the many Charleston colleges. Every Sunday afternoon they have about 125 co-eds come to their home for lunch. It gives many of these students, who are away from their

Custom staircase with carved newel post.

133

LIFE CYCLE ENGINEERING, INC.

Born and Bred in the Low Country.

Life Cycle Engineering, Inc. (LCE) is a privately held, full-service engineering company with offices nationwide. LCE was born in the low country and still has its roots firmly planted in low country soil. The principle owners—LCE is 37 percent employee-owned—Jim Fei and George Thornley, CEO and president, respectively, first met while working at the Naval Ship Engineering Center, NAVSEC (now NAVSEA) in Washington D.C. The fledgling young engineering company that they set up began its operation from an office in the back of a pharmacy in Holly Hill, South Carolina, primarily due to a paucity of venture capitalists to allow anything more luxurious. The partners incorporated in South Carolina as Life Cycle Engineering in October 1976.

That name was chosen for two reasons: first, because Fei and Thornley wanted a company name that was representative of the field of engineering they intended to specialize in, and, second, because they wanted a name that would have a catchy, three-letter

Oil Refining.

acronym to represent it; something that clients and potential clients could easily recall—and so LCE was born.

The Charleston area was chosen as home to LCE primarily because Thornley was from the South Carolina low country as well as an engineering graduate of the University of South Carolina. Fei, on the other hand, had to emigrate from the D.C. area to the low country in "a well-used station wagon" (his description). Besides, it was a shorter trip to South Carolina than to his alma mater, the University of Southern California. Fei had serious doubts that the well-used station wagon was capable of that trip.

The two struggled, but with enthusiasm, to bring work into the company that first autumn and winter. By the spring of 1977 there was a glimmer of light at the end of the tunnel in the form of paying work, and in June they opened the first "official" LCE office in the King and Queen building in downtown Charleston. They also hired their first employee—who served as receptionist, secretary, bookkeeper, draftsman and general jack-of-all-trades.

LCE's corporate headquarters, which is now located at 4360 Corporate Road in North Charleston.

By November 1977 the two had enough money coming in that they were able to draw their very first paychecks. LCE was a success! By the end of 1977, their first full year in business, LCE had a staff consisting of five employees and yearly revenues of $103,000. One of Fei and Thornley's mutually agreed-on objectives was to have a staff of fifty employees some day. Another objective was to carve out a specialty niche in the engineering field. LCE had begun to define that niche—maintenance engineering—one that was already beginning to be recognized within the Navy's engineering community.

As a result of steady growth, by the summer of 1981 LCE had outgrown their offices in downtown Charleston and relocated to an office building on Wesley Drive in West Ashley. Coincident with the move, LCE began to venture into commercial markets, their first work that was not strictly for the U.S. Navy. The first major market to benefit from LCE's particular brand of maintenance engineering expertise was the offshore oil and gas drilling and exploration industry, a market segment in which LCE continues to play a significant role in the twenty-first century.

It was also during this period, the early 1980s, that LCE was awarded several competitive, multi-year contracts from the Department of the Navy. The nature of much of the work made it more economical to open offices closer to the work sites, and as a result LCE established offices in the Washington, D.C. area; Portsmouth, New Hampshire; Philadelphia, Pennsylvania; Norfolk, Virginia; and San Diego, California. In turn, the LCE presence in these areas provided greatly expanded markets for commercial maintenance engineering opportunities. As the headquarters division, the Charleston operation also continued to steadily grow. In 1986 LCE had outgrown its Wesley Drive location and moved to the Park Shore Centre in West Ashley. In their tenth year, LCE realized total revenues of more than $14 Million—a long way from the initial year's $103,000.

Bearing replacement in progress on a large motor.

The decade of the 1990s was witness to continued growth at LCE, as they became internationally, as well as nationally, recognized as a leader and innovator in Maintenance Engineering applications. Sustained growth led to their move in 1996 to their present location on Corporate Road in North Charleston. Today the company's revenue is approaching $50 million per year.

The Charleston area has proven to be an ideal location for LCE. Central to a large part of the Southeast's premier engineering aca-demia, the University of South Carolina, The Citadel, Clemson, Georgia Tech, etc., and also home to Trident Technical College, the Naval Shipyard and to many separating or retiring Naval-trained technicians, the Charleston area provides a wealth of personnel resources. Resources that are highly trained, highly skilled and highly motivated.

Electrical generator is repaired on a submarine.

Fei and Thornley are both of the school that taking good care of your employees provides employees who will take good care of the company. This has certainly proven to be true at LCE. The partners attribute LCE's success to the dedicated employees that they have had throughout the years, as well as a company culture that encourages, supports and rewards employees for doing what is right. Supporting this premise is the fact that LCE still has a number of employees who have been with them since the first five years of the company's existence.

LCE has provided hundreds of jobs, not only to low country residents but also to residents across the U.S. over the years since incorporating in South Carolina. They have certainly met and exceeded their original objective—to have a company of fifty employees. Fei and Thornley, without prompting, are both quick to state, "LCE *is* its employees."

LIOLLIO ARCHITECTURE

Charleston is rich with stories of people who have come in search of prosperity for themselves, but have then devoted their lives to the prosperity of their community. In 1957, when Demetrios "Jimmy" Liollio came to Charleston and worked as D.C. Liollio,

Above: SouthTrust Bank of Charleston.
Below left: Avery Center, circa 1967.
Below right: 288 Meeting Street.

architect, he was attracted not only to the prosperity of a new world, but to a sense of place that reminded him of his native island in Greece. The people of Charleston exuded a spirit of independence and self-confidence that caused Jimmy to make it his home. He worked with dedication as a careful listener and a good steward of his clients' time and budgets—and built a name for Liollio Architecture.

Today, Liollio Architecture has evolved into a multi-disciplined organization, offering architectural design services, structural and civil engineering services, master planning and construction administration. Nearly 50 years of practice has matured the firm's philosophy to reflect the various people and communities that have been integral to its accomplishments. With Jimmy's values, Liollio still cares for every commission, and is proud to call its projects thoughtful, respectful and creative solutions.

Liollio Architecture's portfolio includes public, commercial, educational, multi-family and retail projects both in Charleston and across the Southeast, and the firm's depth of experience in the design of public education facilities is at the core of the practice. Liollio Architecture's educational design work has been recognized by the American Association of School Administrators, American Institute of Architects, National School Board Association and the Council of Educational Facilities Planners International. Liollio design solutions reflect a history of experience joined with a creative willingness to introduce new ideas.

Liollio has also cultivated a wealth of experience in historic preservation. The "Restored South" is a testament that it is more than bricks and mortar that hold old walls together; by preserving buildings, we preserve our shared memories. Liollio Architecture's approach to preservation is driven by research of buildings, places and people: first, finding the history of a building to tell the story of the structure, and then asking the community to help discover the architectural and social features significant to that story. During "town hall" design charettes, people present old photographs, letters and memorabilia, revealing the memory of the place and explaining the building beyond the bricks.

Designing commercial spaces has also become a cornerstone of

Liollio's success. The firm understands the need to place a structure within its context, whether that context is a historical streetscape or a rural community. Liollio's commitment to context-driven design has on several occasions been recognized by the SC AIA.

The firm's work has grown from the lessons learned in every project in which they have participated. After almost 50 years of practice, Liollio Architecture's philosophy has matured to reflect the various people and communities integral to their accomplishments.

Above, top to bottom: Hilton Head Elementary, Beaufort College building, circa 1852 and Bond Hall, circa 1920.

Right, top to bottom: Atlantic Transportation Services, INC., SCDNR Composite office building and Bluffton Elementary.

LIVINGSTON ANTIQUES

Renowned for its 18th- and 19th-century fine English furniture and accessories, Livingston Antiques has been a Charleston tradition since 1969.

John Ashe Livingston, Jr., inherited his business sense from his ancestors, who for generations were involved in the auto salvage industry. John opted not to follow in his family's footsteps, however, and decided to try his hand with antique furniture. In 1969, with financial help from his father, a 19-year-old John purchased a piece of land along a largely undeveloped section of Savannah Highway 17. A 5,000 square-foot building became his headquarters. The business was named Livingston and Sons Antiques.

Using an old pickup truck, John would traverse the upscale, historic downtown neighborhoods as well as the surrounding countryside, scouting out old pieces of furniture in need of repair. After purchasing his discoveries, he stacked them in the back of his truck and transported them to his workshop. Once there, he began the painstaking process of mending broken chair legs and refinishing chests of drawers and tables. He would then offer the restored items for sale.

Success came relatively soon for the young man, who was fortunate to set up shop in a city flourishing with a sense of history, fine taste and tourism. His reconditioned furniture sold so quickly he could barely keep up with the demand for it. It wasn't long before John had to enlarge his operation. And with the growth of his clientele, he found it necessary to travel to England and Continental Europe to acquire the most sought-after antiques from their source.

After the death of his father in 1998, John Livingston III and his mother, Elizabeth, obtained ownership of the business. The company's name was shortened the following year to "Livingston Antiques."

Livingston Antiques is still headquartered at its original site on Savannah Highway and has expanded to 30,000 square feet. In 1983 an addi-

John Ashe Livingston, Jr., 1990, founder of Livingston Antiques.

tional building was acquired and opened as a showroom at 163 King Street in the downtown district.

Today the company is one of the largest sole proprietorships of 18th- and 19th-century antiques in the United States. From stately English furniture to Japanese and Chinese export porcelain and ceramics, Livingston Antiques—which also has a website, www.LivingstonAntiques.com—offers an extensive inventory of quality merchandise. Its solid reputation has led to market expansion into the nation's largest cities—New York, Boston, Chicago, Charlotte, Atlanta, Dallas, San Francisco and Los Angeles.

Livingston is quick to acknowledge Charleston's crucial role in the establishment and continued prosper-

ity of the business. "We owe a great deal of our success to our local community. Without its patrons, Livingston Antiques could not have earned its popular reputation," he said. "However, Livingston Antiques is making a conscious decision to not expand to the point of sacrificing quality of inventory or customer accommodation."

The company's select inventory of antique furniture and decorative items includes such distinguished names as Chippendale, Sheraton, Hepplewhite, Wedgwood, Canton, Mason, Copeland, Spode, Staffordshire, majolica and Imari. Paintings and sculptures are also available for sale.

Complete with pictures and brief descriptions, the online catalog showcases an array of ceramics, metalware, glassware, furniture and miscellaneous items. There are ironstone plates, jugs and dishes circa 1820 from England. A willow pattern tureen, also from England, dates back to the mid-1800s. A majolica owl jar, circa 1860 to 1870, came from France.

Among the treasures are such items as brass candlesticks from England and France dating back to the 1700s, a Chinese porcelain bowl, circa 1800, and an assortment of Imari plates, bowls, dishes and vases from the 1860s in Japan. There are unique items, such as the English fireman's bucket, circa 1850. This brass-studded leather water bucket was the kind used in bucket brigades. Also available are a gentleman's toiletries box and a footbath, both from early to mid-nineteenth-century England.

For avid readers of history and literature, the company sells rare books from bygone eras in England.

The collection includes the 1815 edition of *History of the War,* and *The Complete Works of Robert Burns,* published in 1850.

The clientele of the company includes private collectors, other antiques dealers and interior designers. While some very fine quality antiques can cost as much as $100,000 to $1,000,000 per item, Livingston says he prefers to keep his prices at reasonable rates in order to reach a larger market.

"Our basic philosophy is to provide a larger market with authentic period antiques by offering them at more affordable prices," he says. "Our goal is to provide good quality items without immoderate expense."

Fine period antiques are significantly more expensive than contemporary reproductions, but they retain their historical value. As with other markets, supply and demand fluctuate and play a large role in both buying and selling prices of fine antiques.

"We are not dealing with a perishable commodity. We are dealing with investments," Livingston explains. "The items in our inventory have survived and succeeded for approximately 100 to 300 years. They generally do not depreciate in value."

Livingston says a popular misconception exists among newcomers to the period antique collecting market. Some feel that antiques are overpriced; however, there is a great difference between "overpriced" and "expensive," he counters. Livingston cautions his prospective customers to remain objective and to realize that his prices are indeed reasonable.

Steeped in history, Charleston seems the ideal location for the antiques business. And Livingston's business is very much about history and the importance of preserving it.

"I hope that people will not lose sight of the history of their community

A circa 1800 English secretaire chest in mahogany, with splayed feet and brass knob pulls.

and the contributions that my business hopes to provide them," says Livingston. "In a world that is constantly evolving technologically, it would be a regrettable shame to forget the craftsmanship of the artisans of the past."

A mid-18th-century Irish lowboy in carved mahogany, with claw and ball feet adorned with a pair of 19th-century Imari vases.

MIDDLETON PLACE

For generations Middleton Place has been an icon of garden design. Its geometric precision and formality reflecting the architectural style of great European gardens of the 17th and 18th centuries are testimony to the ambition and success of colonial planters in South Carolina's Low Country. Perhaps of even greater importance, Middleton Place is a National Historic Landmark, in recognition of its possessing "exceptional value to the nation as a whole rather than to a particular state or locality" in interpreting our historical heritage.

Henry Middleton established Middleton Place in 1741 as a family seat and business headquarters for his several properties. He was a successful rice planter, but also an active political figure. Prominent in the British-controlled colonial government, in the final days before the break with the mother country, England, he was a delegate to the First Continental Congress where he served briefly as that body's second president.

Middleton Place was the birthplace and home of Henry's son, Arthur Middleton, who succeeded his father as delegate to the Congress, a radical patriot who in 1776 signed the Declaration of Independence. Later, Middleton Place was the home of Arthur's son, another Henry, who served his state

Visitors step back in time on carriage rides to experience the history of Middleton Place, including Eliza's House, a freedman's dwelling built circa 1870.

and his country as legislator, governor, congressman and minister to Russia.

In 1846 ownership of Middleton Place passed to Henry's son, Williams, who, despite the political beliefs of his father, a leader in the Union party, was a member of the South Carolina's Secession Convention in 1860 and a signer of the Ordinance of Secession—thus helping set in motion events that led to the eventual destruction of Middleton Place.

The spirit of Middleton Place is alive and strong, having survived the Revolution and Civil War, earthquake devastation, ravaging hurricanes and numerous economic challenges. It is this spirit that has allowed the plantation to remain self-sustaining, calling on every aspect of the property to play a role in helping save this most important American landscape.

The Gardens at Middleton Place have been a notable attraction to Charleston visitors since the 1920s. The Gardens follow the principles of André Le Nôtre, the master of landscape architecture who laid out the gardens at the Palace of Versailles. In 1941 the Garden Club of America awarded Middleton Place the Bulkley Medal, declaring that the Gardens at Middleton Place were not

Middleton Place, America's oldest landscaped gardens, has inspired generations of the Middleton family and their guests since 1741.

only the oldest surviving landscaped gardens in America, but also the most interesting and important. Today, rare camellias bloom in the winter months while over 65,000 azaleas create a blaze of color in the spring. In the summer, magnolias, crepe myrtles and roses accent the formal landscape that now blooms year-round.

The House Museum was opened to the public in February 1975. Originally a gentleman's guest quarters, the House Museum is the only remaining building of the once grand three-building residence, and contains many Middleton family possessions from the 18th and 19th centuries, including family silver, furniture, paintings, books and documents, each interesting and important in their own right, but all more important as they enhance each other.

Beyond its significance as a National Historic Landmark or its historically important gardens, Middleton Place brings to life the world of South Carolina rice planters. Out of necessity plantations were self-contained worlds, where African-American slaves produced the essentials of daily life from food to furniture to candles and cloth. These slaves had everything to do with growing rice and, before the

Revolutionary War, the indigo that brought wealth to their masters. Today, the Plantation Stableyards at Middleton Place tells the story of those workers, as blacksmiths, potters, weavers, coopers and carpenters discuss slavery and plantation life from colonial days through the Civil War, Emancipation, Reconstruction and the early 20th century. Plantation-made crafts are available at the Museum Shop.

Located next to the Stableyards, the Restaurant at Middleton Place was built in 1933, originally designed and used as a guesthouse. Today, guests enjoy authentic Low Country cuisine influenced by renowned Southern chef Edna Lewis, who was chef-in-residence for several years.

To provide an elevated perspective of the historic landscape, carriages take visitors around the periphery of the gardens. The carriages tour through a virtual forest of bamboo and scenic woodlands to the banks of a rice field alive with wading birds, ducks, herons, ospreys, nesting bald eagles and alligators.

Now some 85 feet tall, with a circumference of over 37 feet and a limb spread of 145 feet, the Middleton Oak, designated a Constitution Tree in 1989, marked an Indian trail long before English settlers came to the Low Country.

The Inn at Middleton Place, a recipient of AIA's highest national award, is a cluster of austerely beautiful modern structures secluded among tall pines and majestic live oaks on the banks of the Ashley River.

At the south end of the Garden Rice Field, a demonstration crop of Carolina Gold rice not only tells the story of the first great one-crop economies that made all of this possible, but also is a cornerstone of the daily African-American focus tours. The tour also incorporates Eliza's House, a freedman's dwelling built in the 1870s in the original form of a two-family slave house, the restored plantation chapel, rice mill and slave cemetary.

While there are several Middleton antebellum houses in downtown Charleston, the Edmondston-Alston House, at 21 East Battery, is a fine example of a planter family's Charleston residence. Built in 1825, the Edmondston-Alston house was one of the first dwellings built on Charleston's High Battery. Many pieces of the Alston family's 19th-century furniture, books and other personal belongings remain in the house, now also a museum.

Middleton Place Foundation owns the 110-acre landmark encompassing the Gardens, House Museum and Stableyards and administers the Edmondston-Alston House. The Foundation, a 501(c)(3) non-profit educational trust established in 1974, relies on membership fees, donations, gifts and admission fees to continue in its mission to preserve these historic sites.

The continuing effort to preserve and interpret Middleton Place also includes land uses surrounding the National Historic Landmark. As a counterpoint to the 18th- and 19th-century architecture and landscape of Middleton Place, the 20th-century Middleton Inn received in 1987 the highest award that the American Institute of Architects confers nationally. Its 55 rooms are only a short walk from the Butterfly Lakes. Its outdoor program offers kayaking, birding and horseback trail rides coordinated through the nearby Middleton Equestrian Center.

It is the synergy created by all the above contributing parts that today makes possible the survival of Middleton Place. Working together, each part supporting the other parts, creates a sense of history and a sense of place that attracts tens of thousands of visitors each year.

MORELLI HEATING & AIR CONDITIONING, INC.

Morelli Heating & Air Conditioning of Charleston, South Carolina, not only has a slogan,"The Problem Solvers," but proven customer service to back it up. For more than 20 years, Morelli Heating & Air Conditioning has been providing the Low Country area with the best comfort solutions and a 100 percent satisfaction guarantee.

In 1981 James "Jim" Morelli and his son Anthony "Tony" opened the doors of the full-service heating, air conditioning and ventilation company in the offices of Charleston Oil. With only six employees and Jim's vision to be a success through superior customer service, they set to work.

The father and son team had extensive experience in the industry with careers at Charleston Oil, the South's oldest oil distributor. Jim joined the local company in 1954, and Tony was employed there to work for his father in 1975. When the heating and air conditioning division of Charleston Oil became available for purchase, the men recognized the opportunity to realize the dream of owning a family business.

The company quickly grew and the Morelli's niche evolved. Charleston boasts some of the country's most el-

Tony Morelli.

egant and stately historic homes and mansions. These structural testaments to the area's culture presented special restoration needs. In many cases, these needs evolved into problems until Morelli Heating & Air was called to help. Over time and through many historic restorations, the company became known for its highly technical problem-solving abilities for the complex projects.

Morelli Heating & Air Conditioning has been credited with outstanding work on several of the area's historic preservation projects including the Nathaniel Russell House, Miles Brewton House, SC Society Hall, Fire-

proof Building and the Sword Gate House. Morelli's work was also featured on *Home Again* with Bob Vila as the show chronicled the restoration of the private residence known as the Isaac Motte Dart House.

But Morelli doesn't limit its services to historic efforts. The company provides heating, air conditioning and ventilation for residential, commercial and industrial clients as well.

The Morellis realize that people's comfort depends on their prompt and dependable service—a factor they do not take lightly; therefore, the company features a service department that provides emergency support 24 hours a day, seven days a week. This benefit, for both commercial and residential needs, is one of the many reasons Morelli's maintains a long-term relationship with its customers.

Customer satisfaction is also extended through the offer of estimates for projects at no cost. That means if a client has a new installation for a structure, or simply routine service, the trained Morelli experts will provide a free estimate for the customer's consideration.

Over the years, as Morelli has grown, the family participation has grown. Jim chose to retire in 1992, turning over the reins to Tony, who now

Corporate offices at Bridgeside.

serves as president and chief executive officer.

Another of Jim's sons, Andrew Morelli joined the company part time in 1981, as a helper when he was a high school student, and was later promoted to mechanic. By 1989 Andrew had worked his way up to the residential sales division and had earned the title of vice president.

Jim's daughter, Angela Morelli Prince, currently serves as secretary/treasurer/comptroller for the company. Angela graduated from the University of South Carolina with a baccalaureate degree in business administration, with an emphasis in finance. She joined the company in 1988 as a bookkeeper.

As a founding partner in the business, Tony Morelli's initial responsibilities included not only managing, but also performing all the service and installation work. Tony, who studied at the College of Charleston, grew to be well respected by those in the industry for his ability and forward thinking.

An active member in the area, Tony gives back to the community that his company calls home. He has served as president of the Charleston Chapter of Air Conditioning Contractors of America, is a past board member of

Chiller process renovation-GEL.

the Coastal Chapter of the Carolina Constructor Training Council and is a member of the Charleston County Vocational School Marketing committee. He was also elected into the *Who's Who* of U.S. Executives in 1994.

Through Tony's commitment to the Charleston area, the company has followed his lead in taking part in charitable, non-profit and civic activities. Over the years, Morelli's has sponsored soccer and baseball teams, participated in local business chapters and assisted in the preservation of the community.

The company also prides itself on its goal to provide the highest standard in employee relations. Specialized continuing training, proactive direction and comparable benefits are just a few of the reasons so many of the staff members have been with the company for many years.

Morelli Heating & Air Conditioning is a member of ASHREA, SC Association of Heating and Air Conditioning Contractors and South Carolina Mechanical Contractors Association, and has grown from a modest start to a viable business since opening. The company now employs more than 60 staff members, utilizes a fleet of 35 trucks and operates with a residential and light commercial division, a com-

mercial and industrial division, as well as a mechanical division.

The company hires only certified and trained service technicians who possess extensive knowledge with all makes and models of heating and air conditioning equipment. Morelli provides service on any type of residential, commercial or industrial systems ranging from home-type systems to boilers, chillers, large commercial VAV systems and DDC controls.

From office buildings, medical centers, retail centers, manufacturing facilities, churches and schools, to specialized design for industrial processing & laboratories, Morelli Heating & A/C can provide clients with full design-build solutions including engineering, mechanical drawings, construction management, installation and service with complete customer satisfaction.

For more than two decades the Morelli family has been building a solid reputation and well-deserved trust from area residents and businesses. Their dedication to quality work and customer satisfaction will keep this company growing for many years to come.

Miles Brewton House.

NATIONAL CRIME VICTIMS RESEARCH AND TREATMENT CENTER

The National Crime Victims Research and Treatment Center (NCVC) is a division of the Department of Psychiatry and Behavioral Science at the Medical University of South Carolina (MUSC). It was formally established on April 1, 1977, by Dean G. Kilpatrick, Ph.D. and Lois Veronen, Ph.D. Both of these individuals were also among the founding members of People Against Rape (PAR), a Charleston, South Carolina-based crisis center that was established in 1974. Through their work with PAR, Dr. Kilpatrick and Dr. Veronen recognized that little research existed about how rape influences the victim's mental health and about the best ways to assist rape victims after the rape. They collaborated with colleagues at PAR to write a large research grant application that received funding from the National Institute of Mental Health, thereby establishing the NCVC.

Originally, the NCVC consisted of two clinical psychologist faculty members, one secretary, and five research assistants and was housed in four small offices. Its sole mission was to conduct research with a large group of recent rape victims and to evaluate the effectiveness of procedures for treating rape-related mental health problems. Over the years, however, the NCVC's

The faculty of the National Crime Victims Research and Treatment Center, Medical University of South Carolina.

mission, staff, budget and space have expanded dramatically. Its mission now includes teaching, providing specialized mental health services to crime victims of all ages and types of crime, consultation with public policy officials at the state and national level, as well as a greatly expanded research portfolio. Today, the NCVC houses 10 faculty members, approximately 11 full-time graduate-level students, and approximately 15 support staff and research assistants in its offices located on the MUSC campus at 165 Cannon Street. Since its inception, the NCVC has generated over $15 million in research, training and service grants.

The mission of the NCVC is unique because of its emphasis of integrating teaching, research, specialized mental health services, collaboration and public policy consultation focused on the mental and physical health impact of violent crime and other traumatic events. The clinical treatments developed at the NCVC are considered to be state-of-the-art

and are used as model treatments for crime and psychological trauma patients at other centers throughout the country. The NCVC's educational programs have helped attract and train a large, nationally competitive group of tomorrow's trauma researchers and clinicians. Its research has contributed substantially to what is known about the scope, nature, impact and treatment of violent crime, terrorism and other traumatic events. The NCVC collaborates with numerous criminal justice system and nonprofit victim's service agencies throughout the local community, state and nation.

Because of its unique mission and the quality of its services, the NCVC and its faculty have received considerable national recognition. The NCVC was identified by the U.S. Department of Justice's Office for Victims of Crime as an innovative Model Program in its 1998 landmark report, *New Directions from the Field: Victims' Rights and Services for the 21st Century.* Two faculty members, Dr. Dean Kilpatrick and Dr. Connie L. Best, have received the nation's highest award for service to victims of crime, the President's Award

Dr. Connie L. Best receives the President's Award for Outstanding Service on behalf of victims of crime in 1996 presented by President Clinton and U.S. Attorney General Reno.

for Outstanding Service to Victims of Crime. President George Bush presented this award to Dr. Kilpatrick in 1990, and President Bill Clinton presented it to Dr. Best in 1996. Many of the NCVC faculty have played leadership roles on the boards of several local, state and national organizations. Because of their expertise, NCVC faculty have provided invited testimony to numerous public policy groups including the South Carolina General Assembly, the U.S. House of Representatives, and the U.S. Senate.

The basic philosophy of the NCVC has always been the same. Crime victims and victims of other traumatic events deserve nothing less than high quality services, and good research is the best way to find out which services work best. However, just conducting the research is not enough. Good research is of little value unless it is shared in understandable fashion with those who serve victims, public policy makers, and the general public. This philosophy has guided the NCVC's educational outreach efforts to victim service agencies as well as its extensive utilization of the news media to disseminate information. Information about the NCVC and its programs has appeared repeatedly in literally every major national print and electronic news vehicle including all the morning news programs, all the network evening news programs, C-Span, CNBC and CNN.

The NCVC's success is attributable to three factors. First, it always had the support of the Department of Psychiatry and Behavioral Sciences and the Medical University. Dr. Layton McCurdy, first as Chairman of the Department and then as Dean of the College of Medicine, had the vision to support the NCVC when it seemed far from mainstream mental health. His successors as chairman, Dr. George Orvin, Jim Ballenger, John Oldham and MUSC presidents Dr. James Edwards and Dr. Ray Greenberg have been equally supportive. Second, the NCVC has been successful in recruiting an outstanding group of students and faculty, all of

whom share a commitment to the NCVC's mission. Any organization's success is built on the quality of its people, and the NCVC has been fortunate to have some of the very best. Third, the NCVC's success partially results from it having provided services that became more relevant because of America's increasing concern with the problems of violent crime. The NCVC has had many successes, but it is especially proud of its recent work addressing the issue of violent crime due to terrorism. Prior to the September 11, 2001, terrorist attacks, the NCVC was commissioned by the Justice Department to evaluate services provided to family members of those killed in the terrorist bombing of Pan Am Flight #103 in Lockerbie, Scotland, in 1988. The information from this evaluation was given to governmental officials after September 11 and helped inform them as they developed services for the victims and survivors of those attacks. The NCVC also assisted colleagues at the New York Academy of Medicine in conducting studies addressing the mental health impact of

Dr. Dean G. Kilpatrick receives the President's Award for Outstanding Service on behalf of victims of crime from President George Bush in 1990.

the attacks on adults in New York City. The results of these studies were used by public policy makers and mental health authorities to design mental health services for victims. One major focus of the NCVC's current efforts is to develop new mental health interventions for terrorist attack victims and to evaluate their effectiveness.

The future of the NCVC holds both opportunities and challenges. Unfortunately, crime, terrorism, and other traumatic events are likely to be major problems for Charleston, South Carolina, and the United States in the foreseeable future. As long as they exist, the NCVC and its services will be needed. The chief challenge for the future is to obtain sufficient resources to support the NCVC's vitally needed services. The key to meeting this challenge is to improve public awareness about the unique and important services the NCVC provides.

RICHARD MARKS RESTORATION INC., ARCHITECTURAL CONSERVATION

Richard D. Marks III was inspired by his parents' love of old buildings at a young age. In high school, he worked on several historic houses with his father. At Clemson University, he formulated the idea of owning a restoration and design firm. While there, he studied Building Science & Construction Management in the College of Architecture. He completed the State General Contractor's exam in 1984 and undertook a six-month study of European architecture at Clemson's Daniel Center in Genoa, Italy. He graduated in May 1985 and formally began Richard Marks Restorations (RMR). In its first year of operation, RMR had one employee and one truck. The business philosophy was simple: concentrate solely on historic structures, learn from each undertaking and apply this knowledge to future projects. A primary goal was to gain a thorough working knowledge of the architectural history of Charleston, and to fully understand the evolution of the buildings and their technology. The goal remains the same today, and the company has prospered. RMR has consulted and worked on the finest structures in the Lowcountry, and continues to add to its resume. The core of the company's success is in its employees.

In 1986 Curtis Houston, a Clemson classmate of Richard's, moved to Charleston. The partnership of Houston-Marks General Contractors & Restorations was formed. Curtis concentrated on commercial and new residential construction, while Richard continued to specialize in restoration. In 1987 Houston-Marks incorporated and purchased two buildings on North Meeting Street. One served as an office and the other as a workshop. Houston-Marks operated in this location until 1991 when Curtis left to form Houston Builders. Richard kept the business and returned the name to Richard Marks Restorations Inc. In 1991 RMR purchased and renovated 12 Vanderhorst Street with Glenn Keyes Architects. In 1994 RMR moved the office from North Meeting Street to this location.

Isaac Motte Dart House, circa 1806. The house as it appears today after its 1994 restoration is pictured above, and in the bottom photo, prior to restoration, featured on Bob Villa's Home Again *syndicated television series.*

The wood shop remained on North Meeting Street.

In 1993 Richard moved with his family to Philadelphia, Pennsylvania, to study architectural conservation at the University of Pennsylvania. While attending classes in Philadelphia, he maintained the business via telephone, fax and frequent trips back to Charleston. RMR projects were managed locally by several key individuals. Robert Dempsey, David Holland and Hoyt Roberts oversaw the field work, and Patricia Jones ran the office. Richard returned to Charleston in 1995, and with the education from PENN, set up a small conservation lab at 12 Vanderhorst Street. This created the first analytical lab for historic building fabric in the city of Charleston. While

the company expanded its conservation services, it also increased its quantity of specialized trades. The hallmark of the business had been its skilled woodworkers, carpenters and brick masons. As the business grew, it broadened these trades to include carving, millwork, plaster, ornamental plaster, ceramic tile and stonework, as well as composition casting.

The most senior employees, Robert Dempsey and David Holland have worked for the company as carpenters, foremen and superintendents for the past seventeen years. Robert Dempsey has supervised numerous projects. Some of his most notable works include 54 Montagu Street, 14 Legare Street and 15 Legare Street. David Holland's most recognized projects include Rose Hill Plantation, 8 Bedon's Alley, and the William Alston House. Hoyt Roberts was hired in 1992. He has managed some of the more unique projects, such as the bells at Stella Maris Church, restoring the 1710 Powder Magazine and rebuilding the windmill at Oakhurst Plantation. Mike Gore came to work at RMR in 1993. He is a very talented and seasoned framer, trim carpenter and cabinet maker. R. Lee Hutto attended North Greenville Jr. College and began working at RMR in 1996. He is now adept at all aspects of trim work and traditional carpentry. Chris Simmons started as an apprentice car-

Drayton Hall, a circa 1742 neo-Palladian structure owned by the National Trust for Historic Preservation, underwent a complete window, shutter and great hall floor system restoration in 2001, carried out by RMR. The historic 1824 double-hung sashes were carefully removed, rehabilitated and reinstalled. Special care was taken to preserve virtually all of the original fabric of the sash.

penter in 1997 and has become a very vital part of the restoration team. Larry Jeffcoat attended Spartanburg Methodist College and has worked in the building industry for over 23 years. He brought a great deal of finish work experience to the company, when he joined in 1998. He has supervised extensive work at Drayton Hall, 39 East Battery and the Nathaniel Russell House. Ronald Simmons, Aaron Janes, Donald Bozman and Alan Shumaker complete the carpentry crew.

James "Monty" Hinson studied engineering and architectural drawing at Trident Technical College. He is a well-known Charleston furniture maker and joinerman who started with the company in 1999. His abilities added a great deal of depth to RMR's furniture restoration, cabinetry, millwork and fine woodcrafting capabilities. He has been joined by two other seasoned millwrights, Stephen Fielding and A. Robert Voorhees. Steve attended Florida Presbyterian College in St. Petersburg and has been a boatwright and woodworker in Charleston for the past thirty years. Bob Voorhees is a true old world craftsman and wood carver who prefers traditional hand tools to modern machines. He worked for the National Park Service from 1960 to 1998 as a wood and stone carver, millwright and craftsman. Joe Ioerger and Joel Russell have also become part of the team of woodworkers.

In 1995 Jack Ackerman and John Blandford joined the company to head up a masonry division. Jack unfortunately passed away in 2002, but his legacy will live on in the company and in the buildings he restored. John is still plying the trade, now with Doug Scott, a very talented preservation stone and brick mason.

In 1999 Michael Plate, a decorative plasterer, came to work full time. He had apprenticed under one of the great masters of the trade, Earl Felber. Justin Hettich joined Mike as an apprentice in 1999. Mae Hutto started working in 1998 as a composition ornament restorer. Together, these artisans have worked on such buildings as the Pineapple Gate House, The Swordgate House, The Aiken Rhett House and the Nathaniel Russell House. A plaster and composition ornament studio was added to the North Meeting Street workshop in 2000.

The circa 1714 St. James, Goose Creek Church project included complete exterior and interior conservation. The highlight of the interior work was the restoration of the hand-molded decorative plaster reredos with a rare surviving King George I seal and Gibbs family cartouche.

Patricia Jones graduated from the College of Charleston with a fine arts degree. She began as the in-house bookkeeper in 1991 and has since risen to office manager and chief financial officer. She has wonderful insight as a life-long resident of the Historic District, and knows many of the Charleston buildings and neighborhoods intimately. Jeff McNeely began working

in 1998 after graduating from Georgia Southern University with a bachelor's in business administration. He has continued classes in historic preservation at the College of Charleston. Some of Jeff's many duties include ordering & purchasing, material and equipment coordination, and documentation. In 2000 Larry Leake moved to Charleston and joined RMR. Larry studied design and preservation at Massachusetts College of Art and The Savannah School of Art and Design. He ran his own restoration and remodeling business in Savannah, Georgia, from 1987 to 1990 and then attended graduate school in American Studies at The College of William & Mary. He is well-versed in computer aided drafting, preservation theory, research and documentation. Jim Wigley began his remodeling and restoration career in 1988, after many years as a shipwright and architectural millworker. In 1991 he started J. Wigley Construction (JWC). JWC specialized in preservation and restoration of historic structures and decorative building components. In 1996 he was hired by the County of Charleston to act as the Architectural Conservator and Preservation Field Manager for the Courthouse Restoration as well as half-a-dozen other historic structures and archaeology projects. The courthouse restoration was a five-year, 11-million-dollar undertaking. Jim joined RMR in 2001 as a project manager and preservation consultant who specializes in restoration, conservation and technical preservation issues. He has added a great deal to RMR's consulting, documentation and management abilities.

RMR has maintained its traditional trade and craft expertise, but now provides a much greater range of services in research, documentation, analysis and conservation. The knowledge and data gleaned from Charleston's built environment over the past 18 years is quite impressive. The primary mission of the company is to provide a qualified resource for individuals seeking services or advice on historic structures.

SKATELL'S MANUFACTURING JEWELERS

Anthony J. Skatell III, president and C.E.O. of Skatell's Manufacturing Jewelers, knows from experience where determination and hard work can lead. Skatell, who grew up in Greenville, South Carolina, watched his family run its own jewelry business, Skatell's Jewelers. Eager to join in, he started working there when he was 14 years old. For a small wage per hour, he cleaned the store, handled some repairs and polished the jewelry. As precise as a finely cut diamond, Skatell began to carve out a great reputation for himself that carries on to this day.

Having a sense of responsibility and a knack for business at a young age helped motivate Skatell in other areas of his life, too. While at Wade Hampton High School, he was elected both class president and president of his WH fraternity. Not one to rest on past achievements, he went on to earn a bachelor of arts degree in administrative management from Clemson University, where he was on the dean's list and was a member of the Kappa Sigma fraternity.

What's interesting, though, is that Skatell began college intending to pursue dentistry. Though seemingly different, the same type of casting is used by both dentists and jewelry

Skatell's Manufacturing Jewelers, Mount Pleasant, South Carolina.

manufacturers. During his studies, however, his love for his family's business won out, and he switched majors—but before Skatell's freshman year ended, he thought his school days were over, when his family's store in Greenville was robbed. Wanting to make sure his mother, Helen, and father, Tony, would be all right and that their business would survive, Skatell went home to help. After a while, his mother insisted that he return to college and finish his degree. "She's a great inspiration!" he said.

Skatell's mother is also the person who encouraged him to get his gemology degree, telling him that if he was going to go into the jewelry business, he needed to know everything about it. So, soon after college graduation, he headed off to New York City to study at the Gemological Institute of America. There, he found the course work all-encompassing and rigorous, but he, and his roommate from Cartier in Paris, France, worked hard. Skatell, taking courses from 9 a.m. to 5 p.m., had managed to put four years' worth of classes into one year. To pass the final exam, the students had to have a score of 100 percent. "When you passed the test," said Skatell, "you felt like you were the best in the industry."

Tiffany's soon offered Skatell a position with its company, but Skatell wanted to move back to South Carolina, a place where he found the people to be polite and charming. The most charming person to catch Skatell's eye, though, was Laura Hoke, also from Greenville, and whom Skatell had met at Clemson, where she was the 1974 homecoming queen. "She's friendly, beautiful and smarter than any

Skatell's Manufacturing Jewelers, Charleston, South Carolina.

woman I've ever known," he said, also adding that she is a community leader, who's involved with many charitable organizations, most notably the Susan B. Komen Race for the Cure Foundation, which raises money to fight breast cancer.

During the early part of their marriage, both worked in the retail industry. Laura was employed by Mercantile, also known as "J.B. White Department Store," serving in several capacities, from clothing buyer to fashion director. Skatell, while studying toward his builder's license, worked at his parents' Greenville store. Both he and Laura worked hard, both in their retail positions and subcontracting the building of five homes, but, after ten years—and now with three children, Kristen, Joey and Alex—they started re-evaluating their career goals. They knew that they both had a passion for work, but their greatest passion was their family. They made it a priority that they would work toward one of them able to be at home when their children arrived from school every day. They had to make some changes to

Tony receiving the "Order of the Palmetto" from Governor Beasley in 1998.

After a buying trip in Vicenza, Italy, Tony enjoyed family time with his two sons and father.

make their plans happen.

"We decided we wanted more for our family, so we started looking for other business opportunities," Skatell said.

Skatell and his wife found themselves perusing the back of trade magazines for ads pertaining to the sale of jewelry stores and jewelry operations, and then began calling the ones that interested them, businesses whose owners wanted to retire and sell their operations.

After much research, the couple found two favorable opportunities. One was a jewelry manufacturer in Manhattan, and the other was a jewelry store located in Charleston. "After several more months of negotiations

with both operations, we came to the conclusion that the opportunity in New York made the most sense. Once we agreed upon a price with the then present owner, we started looking for financing at local banks. After being turned down by three banks, we refused to give up or be discouraged. We were lucky that the third bank was a member of the Business Development Corporation.

"The Business Development Corporation was, and still is, the largest SBA-backed lender in South Carolina," Skatell explained, "but to go before a BDC, you had to be turned down by three banks and recommended by one of those banks. Luckily, for us, the last bank liked our business plan and business model and recommended us to the BDC. The BDC approved our loan."

Skatell said that their business plan was simple. They would buy the existing New York City jewelry manufacturer and then move the operation to South Carolina. South Carolina was chosen for its Southern appeal and because, in order to qualify for a BDC loan, the operation had to be located somewhere in South Carolina. "Not wanting to compete with my family," Skatell said, "I knew I couldn't open this new operation in Greenville. Only two other cities in South Carolina were large enough to start such a new concept. I had two choices: Charleston or Columbia. We had fallen in love with the beauty and charm of Charleston while spending time there in negotiations, so it was not a hard choice."

Their plan, however, was thwarted at the last minute when the owner decided he wanted more money than was originally agreed to. Undaunted, the couple turned this disappointment, and what seemed like a huge obstacle, into a time of innovation. A great influence and a great man, Skatell's father-in-law, Harold Hoke, through unlimited support and encouragement, and with the blessing of his wife, Alice, helped guide them toward their new goal.

"Laura and I went back to the drawing board and came up with a new business plan and a unique model, which called for a new operation and a new concept called Skatell's Manufacturing Jewelers," Skatell explained. "The concept was quite simple. We would manufacture jewelry. Instead of making and selling jewelry to other jewelry stores, we would sell it directly to the public. The BDC liked our idea and arranged to lend us the money. The original note had a pay off of ten years. Due to the early, fortunate success of our business plan and model, we were able to repay the loan in eleven months."

The board of directors of the BDC was so impressed with Skatell's success, that they invited him to join them.

Laura and Tony at a Kappa Sigma fraternity formal, Clemson University, 1974.

The Skatell's three children: Alex, a senior at Bishop England High School; Kristen, a senior at UNC at Chapel Hill; and Joey, a rising sophomore at Auburn University.

Skatell accepted and has been a member of the board ever since, and has expanded to a sister company, the Certified Development Corporation. As an original board member of CDC, he serves on the loan committee with various bankers and business people around South Carolina.

Since the company's founding on November 5, 1988, Skatell's Manufacturing Jewelers has grown to include two Charleston stores and one in Charlotte, North Carolina, but even the growth of this company had its setbacks. In its first location in a small shopping center overlooking Northwood Mall, with a staff of six, including Skatell and his wife, the new jewelry store, as well as the entire Charleston area, endured the wrath of Hurricane Hugo. Hugo, which almost leveled Charleston, was, at that time, one of the worst natural disasters, in terms of monetary amounts, to hit a U.S. city.

"I never lived on the coast, so we were unfamiliar with hurricanes and their destructive force," Skatell explained. "I had two concerns, first was my family's safety and second was the survival of our new business. We'd put everything on the line. We had borrowed to the max. And, if the business didn't make it, I'd be out on the street looking for a job."

The stakes were high. Skatell sent Laura and their children to his in-laws' house in upstate South Carolina, where he knew they would be safe. He then contacted his insurance company, which gave him some suggestions, and told him he would need a security guard in place in case the alarm system went down; otherwise, that insurance company would not cover anything. So, Skatell took their advice, hired someone, and stayed up all night helping to guard his store and his family's future from potential looters.

"That," Skatell said, "turned out to be one of the scariest nights of my life." Amazingly, though, his store suffered minor damage, compared to the neighboring businesses. Both stores on each side of his were gutted out and destroyed by the storm. Skatell described the trees that were snapping around the shopping center as sounding like bombs exploding. "We survived the night with water up to our knees," he said. "After that night, I knew that I would never do such a stupid thing as wait around during a hurricane."

After the city began recovering from the devastation, Skatell worried that his business would not survive. He thought

150

The family celebrates opening day in Mount Pleasant, South Carolina.

Skatell's Manufacturing Jewelers in Mount Pleasant, South Carolina.

that the last thing on people's minds would be to buy jewelry. Fortunately for his business, he was wrong. "People wanted some things to get back to normal in their lives," he said. "We ended up with a great first year. Engagements were up as people began to realize what was really important."

There were many reasons why the people of Charleston wanted to purchase merchandise from Skatell's. First, and foremost, was the special emphasis it placed, and places, on the customer. "Our basic philosophy has been the same since our founding,"

says Skatell. "Give the people what they want when it comes to jewelry. That's the reason we do so much custom manufacturing, and always remember we are here because of our customers."

Skatell's is unique in that, not only does it sell jewelry, it creates it. When customers walk through the doors of a Skatell's store, they can feel confident that the merchandise will be of high quality. On the premises, experts in the field of jewelry-making work diligently—designing, cutting and polishing, among their other skills. "Our people are very well-educated in the jewelry and gem field and know how to treat the customer," said Skatell, whose staff consists of master jewelers, certified gemologists, and diamond and colored stone graders. Four diamond appraisers work with Skatell's so that customers have confidence in what they purchase, and all of their gemologists have certificates from the Gemological Institute of America, where they, too, had to pass with flying colors.

From diamond and jewelry appraisals, to custom design and manufacture, Skatell's offers a wonderful array of services. Customers can expect nothing but the best from this manufacturer. Whether the jewelry is specially designed, or whether its created from copyrighted designs purchased from Italy or California, the outcome is the same: perfection. This company searches the world over to find just the right gemstones to place in just the right settings.

It even offers the tradition of hand-engraving—especially popular in the Charleston area—by personalizing wedding rings, bracelets and lockets, for example. Jewelry repair is another popular service, as well as cleaning and polishing—using an ultrasonic polisher and Skatell's Manufacturing Jewelers brand jewelry polish.

Also, if customers have a diamond that is chipped, or one that they want placed in an antique setting, or if their diamond has lost its brilliance, Skatell's has a diamond faceting machine that will bring back its sparkle.

More goes into creating jewelry than what meets the eye. First, an individual piece, such as a bracelet, is made of wax, cast in investment, which is then heated in a steel cylinder in a special type of kiln. This process creates a mold. Next, little gold pellets are melted down, inserted into the molds, then placed into cylinders, which are submerged in water. The plaster then cracks, releasing the almost-finished piece, and the stones are placed, set and buffed.

One way Skatell's designs its jewelry is by using a state-of-the-art, computer-aided design and manufacturing system, known as CAD-CAM. With this machine, designs can be cut to exact specifications, which makes details extremely clear.

To help his customers—especially those interested in engagement rings—Skatell holds diamond seminars. Since no two diamonds are alike, the information imparted gives the customer knowledge to make wise decisions. In his seminar, Skatell stresses the importance of cut, color, clarity and carat—with cut referring to the diamond's

Laura, Tony and the boys in Florence, Italy, visiting Kristen in a summer abroad program.

shape; color, rated from D to Z; clarity, the diamond's level of purity; and carat, the weight of the diamond.

Along with custom-designed jewelry, Skatell's features items from such top designers as Tacori, Joey Clapper and Cyma. Fortunately, for customers who live outside of Charleston, purchasing Skatell's merchandise is made simple by visiting the store's website at www.skatells.com. Here, customers can find help if they just aren't sure

what to give for that special occasion, such as a first, fifth, fifteenth or fiftieth anniversary!

Skatell sees the jewelry business as an important industry. "It's an honor to have a small part in helping someone celebrate or begin a family tradition," he said. "It's where people can pass down a ring, for example, from generation to generation. It's an industry where people's lives are celebrated. When customers come into the store, they are happy to be here!"

In 1999 the Smithsonian National Museum of Natural History acknowledged Skatell's in its "development and enhancement of the museum's Janet Annenberg Hooker Hall of Geology, Gems, and Minerals." In that same year, both Skatell and his wife were each listed as an "Honored Professional of National's Who's Who in Executives and Professionals."

Eventually, Skatell would like to expand his three-store business. So far, with his builder's license, he's already developed three shopping centers and built eleven houses. His first priority, though, is his family, and, until the youngest child is in college, which

Laura and Tony celebrating 25 years of marriage.

will be soon, the expansion will have to wait. For now and for always, whether the occasion is a holiday, an engagement, or a company event, Skatell's offers some of the best choices in gift-giving. Customers may choose from an already available item, or have their own design implemented, while a knowledgeable staff with excellent store managers waits to assist them. Whatever the customer chooses is what Skatell's delivers. That's why they keep a steady client base, with new clients coming in all the time.

With some Charlestonians, Skatell's has become a tradition. "We're involved with thousands of people's lives throughout Charleston in a positive way," says Skatell, "whether it's with their wedding or their anniversary, Christmas or through the dozens of civic organizations that we help every year."

Organizations that Skatell's donates to include Rotary International, the Susan Komen Foundation and the American Heart Association. He also served as vice president of the church council for the St. Matthews Lutheran Church of downtown Charleston and is a member of the Mt. Pleasant Rotary Club, serving as a State of South Carolina Constable for several years, and had the "The Order of the Palmetto," the highest award given in the state, presented to him by Governor David M. Beasley.

In addition, Skatell is a life member of the 100 Club, a law enforcement organization, is on The Board of Governors of The College of Charleston and donates to countless numbers of children's organizations, such as the Medical University of South Carolina's children's hospital, Camp Happy Days, and sponsors numerous baseball and basketball little league teams.

Since 1997 he has been involved with a volunteer mentoring program, through the Auxiliary Probation Service, which originated from the Department of Juvenile Justice, for at-risk teens. This service proclaimed him a "Hero of the South Carolina 2001 Year of the Child" by then-governor Hodges, who said

Joey and his sister (not pictured) were both honored to work with Senator Strom Thurman in Washington D.C.

that "thanks to people like you, the citizens of our state can be a source of inspiration, information, and ideas for others across the United States and around the world."

As evidence of the governor's confidence, through Skatell's intervention, several teen-agers decided to change the course of their lives. One young man that Skatell mentored, chose to become a police officer, and another, who had been involved in carjacking, has now graduated from a technical college. Others come from families with little supervision and no motivation. "Each family has its own set of problems," Skatell acknowledges. On a lighter note, Skatell remembers the time when he promised a young teen, who wasn't doing well in school, that for every *A* he earned, he'd give him twenty dollars. Well, not only did that student make *A*s, but so did his siblings—and, yes, Skatell paid them all!

Skatell is adamant about letting

these children know —as he does with his own children—that they are precious and have value, that there are people who care about them, and that they can reach goals they've never even thought about achieving. The encouragement he offers others is a reflection of the encouragement he received when he was struggling with his own hopes and dreams, as well as the support he receives from his wife and children.

Through determination and a strong work ethic, Skatell has made a difference in his home, profession and in his community. He is a family man and a businessman with a heart— one who sees the beauty in both his manufactured jewelry and, more importantly, in people. Skatell's perception is that the jewelry he manufactures only enhances the beauty that's already there.

Joey, Kristen and Alex—summer 2002.

THE CITADEL

Established in 1842, the Citadel is perfectly placed. Set in Charleston, South Carolina, the Citadel's mission of excellence in honor, leadership and pride fits right in with the city's southern charm.

Known as The Military College of South Carolina, this public institution that sits on the banks of the Ashley River requires undergraduates to take ROTC in one of the three service branches—Army, Air Force or Navy/Marine Corps—while studying toward a baccalaureate degree. Degree programs are offered in 20 disciplines, and range from political science, criminal justice, education and engineering to the humanities, science and business administration.

Another side to The Citadel experience is its College of Graduate and Professional Studies. This civilian evening program is geared toward working adults. It offers the Lowcountry nationally accredited bachelor's, master's and specialist degrees scheduled around students' lifestyles. For study toward the master's degree, there are 20 programs available,

Corps of Cadets at the original Citadel on Marion Square, 1892.

General Mark Clark, president of The Citadel, 1954–1965.

with concentrations in business, psychology, education and computer science. Of note, The Citadel is the only college in South Carolina that offers an evening civil and electrical engineering bachelor's degree program.

Says J. Emory Mace, retired brigadier general and class of 1963 alumnus, "At The Citadel, the education comes first; the military experience come second. You'll have the opportunity to learn about leadership in the barracks. You'll have positive role models who insist on high standards, and you'll learn how to make things happen. The Citadel is a great educational value."

Those cadets who complete the four years of study will develop qualities that will be with them forever—that will make them well-prepared to handle life outside the college, whatever their chosen fields.

Former U.S. Senator Robert Dole once said: "Citadel graduates have

become successful leaders in both the public and the private sectors . . . . Thanks to its effective teaching techniques, The Citadel has earned an enviable reputation as one of the best public colleges in the United States, and there is not a better military school anywhere in this nation than The Citadel."

Notable Citadel alumni include Major General Lewis G. Merritt, who was a pioneer in Marine Corps aviation; Ernest F. Hollings, U.S. senator from South Carolina; Joseph P. Riley, Jr., mayor of Charleston; Dr. Charles B. Hammond, president of the American College of Obstetricians and Gynecologists and former chair of Ob-Gyn at Duke University Medical School; Alvah H. Chapman, Jr., former chairman/CEO of Knight-Ridder, Inc.; Paul L. Maguire, ESPN sports analyst and former professional football player; and Pat Conroy, author, who wrote such novels as *The Lords of Discipline, The Great Santini* and *Beach Music.*

Leadership is strongly emphasized at The Citadel, where it is believed that a leader should motivate others, see the future optimistically, demonstrate loyalty, be a good role model, respect others' rights, treat people with dignity, have the courage to act responsibly, strive for excellence, have unwavering integrity and be devoted to honor and duty.

Graduates of The Citadel have fought in every American war since 1846 and hundreds have died defending their country. The first casualty of the War with Iraq was a Citadel graduate, 1st Lt. Shane Childers.

Each year, cadets get to put their leadership skills into practice by holding leadership conferences for middle-school students. Additionally, they volunteer their time helping programs such as Habitat for Humanity, Crisis Ministries, the Footlight Players, the Junior League, the city's Clean City Sweep and the American Red Cross.

Approximately 1,900 students make up the Corps of Cadets, with an average 600 students entering each year—

The South Carolina Corps of Cadets preparing for the parade.

Chemistry and biology majors receive comprehensive training for medical school.

and almost every state is represented, along with over 20 countries.

Life at The Citadel is only for those who persevere, however. It takes courage and determination to complete the school's rigorous four-year program.

Upon entering as freshmen, or "Fourth Class Cadets," new students will find their first year—called "the Knob year,"(because their shaved heads resemble doorknobs) full of trials and challenges. They will learn from upperclassmen about how to follow, and will live in barracks, following a daily regimented schedule from Reveille to Taps.

Respect, discipline, time management and attention to detail are all mastered during the first year—as well as learning to live by the honor code, which is a standard at The Citadel. The honor code states: "A Cadet does not lie, cheat, or steal, nor tolerate those who do." Considered the moral backbone of the cadets, this code has been a guiding principle for over 150 years.

At the end of the first year, the fourth-class cadets take part in Recognition Day, a symbolic celebration signifying the conclusion of the most difficult year they will experience at The Citadel.

Along with studies and military training, every cadet has the opportunity to worship in the Summerall Chapel, where the words, "Remember Now Thy Creator In The Days Of Thy Youth" grace the facade of the building. Various faiths and denominations all share this chapel for their own worship services.

Sports play a big part in the cadets' lives, too, as The Citadel offers something for everyone. The college fields nine men's and seven women's varsity teams. A variety of intramural sports are avail-

able, too, such as racquetball, weightlifting, billiards, croquet, triathlon and swimming.

Athletics at The Citadel have garnered recognition and awards, with individual Southern Conference championships in javelin and shotput, five Southern Conference Tournament championships in baseball and four All-America honorees in football. The school has also been the host for the All-Academy Wrestling Championships.

In August 1996 The Citadel broke tradition and welcomed the first women cadets. Now, six percent of the Corps are women.

By the time the cadets are ready to graduate, there is a strong bond between them that will last a lifetime. Symbolic of this, on graduation day, they all take off their Citadel rings, which they've been wearing backwards, and turn them around, to face the world. Together, as a family, they leave The Citadel, united with each other and committed to excellence in their chosen fields—with honor, leadership and pride.

More than a third of each graduating class pursues military careers.

TRIDENT TECHNICAL COLLEGE

A powerhouse of productivity, Trident Technical College (TTC) is a public two-year college that works—on three campuses, seven days a week. With more than 11,000 credit students enrolled in 150-plus programs and registrations in continuing education numbering close to 30,000 annually, TTC provides quality education and flexible scheduling to suit a diverse range of student needs.

TTC began life in 1964 as part of the statewide system founded by Gov. Ernest F. Hollings to meet the education and training needs of South Carolina's citizens. In the early 1960s, the challenges of an agrarian economy, the emigration of young people to other locales, and the lack of industry prompted South Carolina's leaders to draft legislation to implement technical training programs that led to the development of technical centers and two-year colleges.

The Berkeley-Charleston-Dorchester Technical Education Center opened in North Charleston in 1964 with two

Offering both food preparation skills and field experience, the College's culinary arts program provides a quality labor force for South Carolina's multi-billion dollar tourism industry as well as Charleston's renowned restaurants.

Responsive to the needs of business and industry, Trident Technical College prepares its 11,000+ students to meet the high-performance demands of the work place.

buildings, 20 full-time instructors and 226 students. As the tri-county area grew, so did the center, developing new academic programs and receiving initial accreditation by the Southern Association of Colleges and Schools.

With demand for services increasing, the center merged in 1973 with Palmer College, a private business college, and became Trident Technical College. The merger also provided the College with a campus in downtown Charleston. By 1982 a third campus south of Moncks Corner in Berkeley County had been completed; four years later the Palmer Campus was relocated to a more spacious site in Charleston at 66 Columbus Street.

Trident Technical College's Foundation was established in 1975, creating a framework for major financial support to supplement state funding for TTC. The Foundation's first fundraising campaign garnered $88,000 over three years. The Foundation sets its sights higher these days, but still

continues to enjoy great success, with a staggering 90 percent+ employee participation rate for 11 consecutive years in the annual campus campaign. The TTC Alumni Association, formed in 1980, funds scholarships and college projects.

In 1973, another event occurred that would prove very significant in TTC's history when Dr. Mary Thornley took a part-time faculty position with TTC. Through a series of increasingly responsible faculty and administrative positions, Thornley would become the driving force behind TTC's innovation and ability to adapt to changing workplace needs throughout the 1990s and into the 21st century.

Born in the small mill village of Concord, North Carolina, Dr. Thornley recognized early in life that change, whether in industry or education, would be the agent behind creating a good quality of life for families. During her early work with industry, she studied quality management and communication strategies that empower every individual in an organization.

After being appointed president of TTC in 1991, Thornley personally implemented an intensive quality management training program for all of TTC's employees. Her egalitarian approach continues to create an atmosphere of open communication and data-based decision-making that makes TTC responsive to student, business and community needs.

Under her leadership, TTC continued its development both in programs and buildings. In 1997, the Complex for Industrial and Economic Development on the Main Campus at Rivers Avenue opened with a Continuing Education Center, the Center for Accelerated Technology Training and the Advanced Manufacturing Center. Phase Two of the complex is targeted for completion in late 2004.

This $30 million, 143,000-square-foot facility will house an Information Technology Center, an Electro-Mechanical Skills Laboratory, a Culinary and Hospitality Training Center and the future Learning Center. With Sen. Ernest F. Hollings and his wife Peatsy as honorary co-chairs of the Foundation's capital campaign, one of South Carolina's most prominent legislators has come full circle to further develop the endeavor he first established more than 39 years ago.

"This is the single most exciting and visible project ever undertaken by this institution," says Thornley. "Phase Two will help meet the needs of our growing student body and the workforce demands of the region."

Locally, the extra job-training capacity will be a strong asset in economic development. "It really supports our sales message that this region, with Trident Tech's support, can provide the workforce that leading-edge companies need," says David T. Ginn, president and CEO of the Charleston Regional Development Alliance. H. Ross Boyle of Growth Strategies Associates agrees: "Workforce training provided by Trident Technical College is one of the region's strongest assets."

Along with Thornley, TTC faculty members are constantly looking to the future for ways to improve programs to keep their students one step ahead on the technology curve. More than half of TTC's programs have been added in the last five years with 30 percent of new programs focusing on technology—something that Thornley

Students have a choice of more than 150 programs of study, ranging from business technology to nursing.

President Mary Thornley has led the College for more than a decade, overseeing extraordinary growth in student enrollment, program offerings and facilities.

recognizes as essential to meeting the future needs of South Carolina's students and businesses.

"The needs of employers now and in the near future must be understood so that classes can be kept current. The input we receive from the 400 business and industry representatives who serve on our 40 academic advisory committees provides critical information we use to evaluate current programs and to develop new curricula to train students," says Thornley.

TTC currently offers programs in allied health sciences; business technology; community, family and child services; engineering technology; hospitality, tourism and culinary arts; humanities and social sciences; industrial technology; law-related studies; nursing; and science and mathematics.

TTC's president has received numerous awards for her quality management approach and the promotion of economic development in South Carolina. But what makes Mary Thornley most proud are the awards and the accomplishments of TTC's students. "What our students do will determine the reputation of the college," says Thornley.

Not only are TTC students essential to tri-county businesses and organizations, but they are also stars at the national level. TTC students compete with the top institutions in the country, as evidenced by the team sent to Harvard University to compete in the 2001 annual simulation of the United Nations. The team of 11 students took top honors for representing the country of Peru. Participant Lavenia Anderson exemplifies the TTC philosophy with her words, "I learned you can achieve anything if you try."

Through the Alpha Epsilon Omicron chapter of Phi Theta Kappa, TTC students actively participate in the honor society founded in 1918 to recognize academic achievement in two-year colleges. Members recently finished in the top 25 chapters for fellowship and service.

TTC's innovative learning environment equips ambitious young students and mid-career professionals with the skills to excel in a complex global marketplace.

TTC is a member of the State Board for Technical and Comprehensive Education System and is accredited by the Commission on Colleges of the Southern Association of Colleges and Schools to award associate degrees, diplomas and certificates.

THE VENDUE INN

Walk into the Vendue Inn in Charleston, South Carolina, and you will find yourself surrounded with true "Southern hospitality."

The elegant property is located in the heart of Charleston's Historic District in the French Quarter area by the beautiful Waterfront Park at the harbor. The Vendue Inn is the chosen home-away-from-home for visitors and celebrities from all over the world, and 19 Vendue Range is the city's finest address.

Each of the 65 elegant guest-rooms and suites is individually decorated with 18th-century-style English or French furnishings, oriental rugs and antiques. Some guestrooms have king-sized, four-poster, canopy or sleigh beds. In a junior or deluxe suite, guests will have a sitting area near the fireplace and can enjoy a Jacuzzi with a separate shower in their large marble bathroom. Soft bathrobes, French-milled soaps and pleasantly scented toiletries are provided.

Guests arriving at the Vendue Inn are greeted with a choice of refreshments—lemonade, iced tea or cucumber water—to quench their thirst. As cars and luggage are attended to and their registration is completed, the friendly bell staff explains to guests all the features and amenities of the Inn. The bell staff and front desk staff are always available to answer questions about the variety of local attractions, which include the nearby historic homes and churches, the Old City Market, the antique shops and art galleries and the lovely parks—all within close walking distance. Guests will find also that bicycles are available for their use for touring the city.

Mornings at the Vendue offer a complimentary newspaper and either a scrumptious Southern Breakfast Buffet or an in-room Continental Breakfast. Each afternoon at 4 p.m., a Wine-and-Cheese Gathering is available to all the guests in the Music Room—an informal, relaxing time and an opportunity to talk with fellow guests or challenge each other to a game of chess or Chinese checkers or even to work

Charleston's finest address, 19 Vendue Range, in the heart of the historic district.

a puzzle together. Edmison recalls the time a young man and woman planned to be married quietly on the Roof Top by a justice of the peace. Before the ceremony, they attended the wine-and-cheese social hour and ended up inviting the entire group of guests to witness their marriage. Everyone was delighted to attend, and the group had a wonderful time.

Every evening at 8 p.m. after-dinner cordials are offered in the lobby area, and for those who wish an evening snack, freshly baked cookies and milk are served in the Music Room.

When guests return to their rooms at night, they will find the turndown staff has tidied their room and left a gift of fine chocolates on the pillow.

At the Vendue Inn, guests can dine under the stars on the Roof Top, or in intimate, Charleston-style dining rooms in The Library.

The Roof Top Restaurant and Bar, located on the top of the Vendue Inn, is the place to go for lunch or dinner. Guests and locals can visit the ever-popular Roof Top for a casual meal or refreshing beverage from 11:30 a.m. until 11:00 p.m. daily and dine in an open-air or covered seating area. Diners can enjoy a variety of appetizers, salads, sandwiches, wraps and side dishes. Be sure to try the traditional Lowcountry favorite, She-Crab Soup.

Group events and parties are held in the Crow's Nest dining area or in private sections of the Roof Top. Guests always have a wonderful view of the city's picturesque rooftops, church steeples and gorgeous sunsets. From the Bridge Bar, one can savor the 360-degree view of the Cooper River, ships and sailing craft in Charleston Harbor, and the entire Historic District.

The Library, another restaurant at Vendue, hosts special events throughout the year in its private, intimate dining rooms. Rehearsal dinners, wedding receptions, private dinners, buffets and business functions are offered a variety of excellent menu choices by the Executive Chef.

The name, Vendue, which means "to sell," invokes a time when the six buildings that comprise the Vendue Inn were once part of a row of merchant warehouses. During the 18th and 19th centuries, many French Protestants and Catholics escaped religious persecution in their homelands and settled in Charles Town to establish businesses as merchants and traders in their new country. The Vendue Inn was established by Morton and Evelyn Needle in 1972, in a small building in the old warehouse area. Beginning with eight beautiful guestrooms, over the years adjoining buildings were acquired and renovated. Today the Vendue Inn offers 45 wonderful guestrooms and covers the entire city block with Vendue Range on the north, East Bay Street on the West, Gendron Street on the south and Prioleau Street on the east.

In September 1998, Coyne and Linda Edmison acquired the Vendue Inn and began quietly renovating the Inn's guestrooms and public spaces. Linda, with Cindy Zimmerman, carefully redecorated the elegant interiors.

In April 2001, an additional 20 beautiful guestrooms were added across the street at 24 Vendue Range. Throughout the property, guests can observe the original hand-hewn beams and brick walls and the earthquake rods placed in support walls after the devastating earthquake of 1886.

Coyne Edmison began his career in the hospitality industry as a waiter in a fine dining restaurant. He was switched from food and beverage to Operations. He earned a bachelor of science degree in business administration from Central State University

Enjoy a beverage with a view—up on the RoofTop!

in Edmond, Oklahoma, with continuing education at Cornell University in Ithaca, New York. During his career, he has seen and done it all—from finding goat's milk for a celebrity's bath to cutting the boots off John Wayne after he had broken a toe.

Guests enjoy coffee by the fireplace in the lobby of 24 Vendue Range.

For the last two years, Coyne and Linda, who is a Board Member of the local S.P.C.A., have hosted a "Celebrity Chili Cookoff" at the Rooftop Restaurant as a fundraising event to benefit the S.P.C.A. Held during the first week of December, admission to the event guarantees "as much chili as a person can eat" and a lot of fun. Reuben Greenberg, Charleston's famous Chief of Police, and many other local celebrities and television personalities vie for a trophy by cooking their own "special" chili recipes which are judged by professional chefs. Helping others is part of the Vendue philosophy.

Edmison says he still enjoys his profession immensely and that the heart of his business is all about exceeding the expectations of his guests.

Visitors to the Vendue Inn will discover one of the most gracious inns the South has to offer, perhaps making them feel as though they were experiencing another world—one that they'll want to return to as often as possible.

W.H. WITHERS CONSTRUCTION COMPANY—
WITHERS INDUSTRIES INCORPORATED

It is no accident that Walter and Ardra Withers named their 53-foot Huckins Fairform Flyer *American Dream*. The boat represents one of many dreams they have realized during more than four decades together.

Walter has always been a dreamer. His nickname, Buzz, was attached to a child who was always working on a project. His mother—born on New Street in Charleston, the daughter of James Igoe, captain of the Charleston harbor—never quite knew what Buzz would be up to next. His father, a quiet, patient man, who worked as a chemist for DuPont, enjoyed his son's vigor.

Buzz's childhood, however, carried a complication: dyslexia. He battled this condition throughout school. With the help of a senior high school teacher, Olive Forbes, who recognized his talents, he not only graduated successfully, he went on to study at Augusta Military Academy. A member of its class of '56, he entered the Navy and served as an aviation structural and hydraulics mechanic and flew with the combat information center as a radar operator for the early warning squadron of the Atlantic Fleet until 1960.

Ardra and Walter met when he returned from the service.

She was a senior in the School of Nursing of the University of Virginia.

"Buzz" just out of the Navy.

The Withers family in 1980. Left to right, back row: Patrick, Randy and Robert. Front row: Paula, Ardra and Walter.

Born in northern Indiana, Ardra grew up in Richmond. She was a serious student with a passion for music. A cellist, she was a teen member of the Richmond Symphony for three years. Her father, a physician, who made string instruments as a hobby, made her a cello, now played by one of her grandchildren.

When it came time to choose a career, however, her parents' professional examples—her mother was a nurse—played a major role in her decision to pursue a medical career.

The couple married in October 1961 and settled in Richmond. They had little money, but their dreams were substantial and their energy was an incredible force waiting to be tapped; they had each other.

Ardra worked at the McGuires Veterans Hospital, and Buzz did sales, service, pick-ups and deliveries for the Standard Duplicating Company. They lived simply in an upstairs apartment on the west side of the city.

In 1962, the year son Patrick was born, Buzz accepted an apprenticeship with Crown Construction Company in Charlottesville. He learned the rudiments of home building and worked his way up to production manager. Ardra moved to the University of Virginia Hospital as an on-call nurse. They worked long hours and swing shifts to build their income.

In 1964 son Randy came along, and in 1967 they invested their accumulated savings in an old house and barn on 5 1/2 acres in Ivy. A year later, Buzz threw caution to the wind and followed his dream of having his own business. He left Crown with little more than a mortgage, a note on his truck; his two sons; a new baby daughter, Paula; and his contractor's license—with Ardra at his side.

With a greenhouse as his first job, Buzz opened W.H. Withers Construction Company. He did that job by himself, but the next one required taking on his first employees. Ardra took care of accounting, learning double entry bookkeeping and setting up the company's financial record system.

For the next 10 years, Withers Construction built big custom homes in Charlottesville and Albemarle County and remodeled buildings in Richmond. It grew to 26 people, mostly trim carpenters and laborers, and hired sub contractors for specialties such as roofs and heating. Withers Construction also volunteered to build small homes for the Farmers Home Administration.

In 1971 Buzz and Ardra completed their family with their fourth child, Robert. About two years later, they bought a 75-acre farm in Crozet, where they raised apples, nectarines and peaches, marketed the eggs from 300 chickens, had a cow, goats and a typical farm menagerie. The children were active in 4-H, with Ardra spending several years as a leader. Unfortunately, necessity awakened them from this phase of their dream in 1979.

With interest rates at unprecedented highs, the economy dragged. Buzz had begun supplementing their income by

James Igoe, Buzz's grandfather, was a harbor captain in the late 1880s–early 1900s.

making his own fine wood trim for the custom homes he was building. He realized there could be a market in restoration for early period moldings and his talent for duplicating pieces that had broken, but the Charlottesville construction market was drying up. As he looked at places where he could sell this product, family roots drew him to Charleston. His mother's history, deeply seated in his memory, gave him a rich connection to the low country, which proved to be just the

Buzz and Ardra Withers today.

market he was seeking. Yet, it was a difficult transition.

In 1980 the Withers sold their farm and headed south, buying a small house on Molasses Lane in Mt. Pleasant.

The move caught the Withers children at a range of stages. Patrick was a college-bound high school senior. In 1981 Randy joined the U.S. Navy. Paula was starting high school, and Robert was in third grade.

Ardra, who had earlier returned to school at Mary Baldwin College, added classes at the University of South Carolina to earn her master's

degree in psychology and counseling and her professional counselor's license. While working at St. Francis Xavier Hospital in a contract position, she started her own business, Professional Counseling Services, with offices in Mt. Pleasant and Georgetown, South Carolina.

Buzz began building a new identity for his business, renamed Withers Industries, Inc. He and Ardra bought property in a new industrial park on Long Point Road in Mt. Pleasant, near the Wando shipping terminal, and put up a 24,000-square-foot steel frame building. Buzz undertook the task of cutting steel bits for his machines so he could duplicate virtually any molding style brought to him for replacement. He went to work, handling everything: taking orders, making moldings, doors, windows and staircases, and delivering them. The Omni hotel and its exclusive shops became a major client. He recalls delivering there at all hours to meet demand. "Holy City" contractors and homeowners began seeking him out.

Buzz worked alone until 1983, when Patrick joined him. Shortly afterward, they hired another worker for the mill, the first woman to work in that capacity.

One of the storefronts manufactured by Withers Industries, Incorporated.

Shutters built by Withers Industries, Incorporated.

The Rosehill Plantation, Grace Episcopal Church, Florence Federal Court House, Lewis's Restaurant, Arizona's and the Miles Bruton House were among the many places where renovators called on Withers Industries.

A scarcity of good millwork created a steady demand for its products. The business grew and became more demanding, a good time, but one that required Buzz to seek additional help. "We added a person at a time as we saw the need," he says. Withers' workforce would number more than 50, before dropping back to 28 after the economy slowed after 2001.

All of the Withers children contributed their talents.

Patrick was a natural with machines and created new products as well as ensured the quality of product already in the market. Today, he is production manager and general manager.

Randy completed six years in the Navy and returned to the plant in 1987. He took an interest in marketing, office management and personnel management. Ardra, focused on her own business, was glad to relinquish the bookkeeping to him and Buzz. Today, Randy is sales manager, handles customer relations and teaches at installation schools for contractors and private customers.

Paula assisted in the payroll department and with accounting before she entered college to pursue a social work career. Today, she is employed by the state of South Carolina and is considering going back to school to study nursing.

Robert took charge of lathe work at Withers in 1990, turning all stair pickets, newel posts and fancy spindles. He had shown an artistic bent as a child; his interest in shaping wood grew. In 1993 he requested as his Christmas present a set of chisels. He began sculpting and in 1996 followed that dream, while working as a carpenter, doing trim for homes. He has exhibited at shows in the SoHo district of New York City and sold a number of his pieces.

Withers Industries, meanwhile, added a healthy diversity to its product lines. In 1988 its doors, windows and moldings were joined by interior shutters, Patrick's response to a customer's request. By 1993 the mill was producing all types of exterior and

Custom home in Charlottesville, Virginia, built by W.H. Withers Construction.

interior window coverings. Today, Withers ships them throughout the United States.

In 1994 the *Bob Villa Show* featured Withers. Villa filmed the shutter department as it prepared a set of shutters for display. Withers Industries has supplied shutters for Villa's home in Martha's Vineyard and for homes of other well-known figures.

In 2001 the company moved to larger quarters, taking an 80,000-square-foot former Broyhill Furniture factory in Lincolnville.

Today, Buzz and Ardra enjoy semi-retirement, boating and traveling while their sons serve as strong, efficient leaders of the company. "When Buzz starts dreaming, I get ready," Ardra says, "because I know something new is going to happen." They have sailed the East Coast from Jacksonville to New York, with frequent visits at the Baltimore harbor to visit friends and to explore the Chesapeake Bay.

Buzz and Ardra's partnership, both in life and business, fulfilled dreams of success for themselves and their children. Withers Industries continues strong, combining the integrity of old-world craftsmanship with the precision of modern technology. Its experienced craftsmen, with their respect for timeless design, turn the finest materials into the highest quality custom-made millwork and shutters. In addition to its shutter installation school, the firm offers decorating ideas for both wholesale and retail customers.

With their sons running the company, Buzz and Ardra find little to worry about. He consults when asked and visits when in town, but remains active at a distance. "We were once told, 'when you turn your business over, let them run it, and that's what we do.'"

A TIMELINE OF CHARLESTON'S HISTORY

1670 Charles Town founded on Albemarle Point (now Charles Towne Landing) August: First slaves arrive.
1680 Charles Town relocates to Oyster Point on the peninsula between the Ashley and the Cooper Rivers.
1680s First church built: St. Philip's (Church of England) where St. Michael's is now. Presbyterian Church established on Meeting Street. Huguenot Church established.
1700 First Baptist Church.
1718 Blackbeard's fleet attacks Charles Town. Colonel William Rhett captures the pirate Stede Bonnett who was later hung.
1715–1717 The Yemassee (Indian) War.
1719–1721 Revolt against the Lords Proprietor. Establishment of South Carolina as a Royal Colony.
Early 1700s Development of rice plantations, expansion of slavery and growth of city.
1727 St. Philip's Church built on Church Street.

John Rutledge House, 116 Broad Street. Courtesy of Richard Widman

The new brick St. Philip's, where the first services were held Easter of 1723, was described by Edmund Burke as "spacious and executed in a very handsome taste, exceeding everything of that kind which we have in America." This building burned in 1835, and was replaced the same year by the present structure on Church Street. Courtesy of South Carolina Historical Society

1731 First (Scots) Presbyterian Church built.
1730s Theaters on Dock Street.
1739 Stono Slave Rebellion.
1740 The Great Fire.
1743 Charles Town Library Society established.
1749 Congregation K. K. Beth Elohim organized.
1750 Charles Town, the fourth largest city in American colonies.
1751 Charles Town Baptist Association established.

1752 Cornerstone of St. Michael's Church laid.
1759 Construction of St. John's Lutheran Church.
1761 St. Michael's Church opened for services.
1765 Demonstrations against Stamp Act.
1772 Unitarian Church construction began.
1774 Revolutionary Executive Committee to resist Tea Act created. Delegates to Continental Congress elected.
1775 Revolutionary Assembly organized. American Revolution begins.
1776 June 28: Battle of Sullivan's Island. July 4: Date of Declaration of Independence. August 2: Declaration signed, four Charlestonians among fifty-six signers.
1780 Charlestown captured by British.
1781 August: Execution of the martyr Isaac Hayne. October: Cornwallis surrenders in Virginia.
1782 British troops evacuate Charlestown.
1783 City of Charleston incorporated. The city's name changed to Charleston.
1787 Cumberland Methodist Church established.
1787 Four Charlestonians attend the Constitutional Convention in Philadelphia. John Rutledge, Charles Pinckney and Charles Cotesworth Pinckney make major contributions.
1788 May: Constitution ratified by South Carolina at Exchange Building in Charleston.
1790 Founding of College of Charleston.
1791 President George Washington visits Charleston.
1800 St. Mary's Catholic Church founded.
Early 1800s Rise of cotton plantations. Expansion of city: Ansonborough, Wragg Borough, Radcliffe Borough, Harleston Village.
1804 City Market opens.
1812 War of 1812.
1820 Catholic Bishop John England arrives.
1822 Denmark Vesey slave insurrection conspiracy.
1830s White Point Garden laid out.
1831–1832 Nullification Crisis.
1833 Railroad to Hamburg, South Carolina.
1835 Rebuilding of St. Philip's Church.
1850 John C. Calhoun's funeral.
1848–1852 Battery built.

The Francis Silas Rodgers Mansion (1885-1887) now the Wentworth Mansion Hotel, 149 Wentworth Street. Courtesy of the Wentworth Mansion Hotel

1860 April: Democratic Party National Convention meets in Charleston. November: Election of Abraham Lincoln. December 17–20: Secession Convention meets in Charleston. South Carolina secedes from the Union.

1861 January 9: Firing on *Star of the West*. March 4: Lincoln takes office. April 12: Firing on Fort Sumter: First shot of the Civil War. December 11: Great Fire of 1861.

1863 April 7: Siege of Charleston begins. July 18: Assault on Battery Wagner by Union Army including Massachusetts 54th. August 29: Bombardment of city begins.

1864 February 17: *C.S.S. Hunley* attacks and sinks the *Housatonic*.

1865 February 18: Charleston occupied by Union Army. March 3: American flag raised over Ft. Sumter.

1865–1866 Race riots in city. Reconstruction era.

1868 Constitutional Convention writes Reconstruction Constitution.

1876 Election of Wade Hampton as Governor.

1877 Reconstruction ends.

1886 The Great Earthquake.

1890s Jenkins Orphanage Band.

1901 South Carolina Interstate and West Indian Exposition (at present-day Hampton Park). Navy Yard established.

1900s Era of Segregation which continues until the 1960s.

1920s Charleston Renaissance (Heyward, Allen, Bennett, etc.) "The Charleston" dance.

1922 Citadel moves to Hampton Park.

1925 Publication of *Porgy* by Dubose Heyward.

1929 Cooper River Bridge opened.

1930s Depression and New Deal. Burnet R. Maybank elected Mayor.

1937 Dock Street Theater opened.

This plan of Charleston shows the four corners of the law, the New Barracks, Gadsden's Middlesex, and the town gate. Courtesy of South Carolina Historical Society

1940 FDR visits Charleston.
1941–1945 World War II. Expansion of Naval Base and Shipyard. Growth of "North Area," now North Charleston.
1950s Growth of Civil Rights Movement.
1959 Election of J. Palmer Gaillard, Jr. as Mayor.
1960s Sit-ins, Civil Rights marches, desegregation of public facilities, restaurants, schools. Ansonborough Preservation Project of Historic Charleston Foundation.
1961 Civil War Centennial.
1969 Hospital Strike.
1970 Tricentennial (of South Carolina) Celebration: *Porgy and Bess* plays in Charleston for the first time.
1970s Development of Seabrook, Kiawah, Wild Dunes.
1972 Incorporation of City of North Charleston. John Bourne, first mayor.
1975 Joseph P. Riley, Jr. becomes mayor. The Age of Riley begins.
1977 First Spoleto Festival USA.
1979 First Piccolo Spoleto.
1982 Reuben Greenberg becomes police chief. Construction of Charleston Place.
1983 Southeastern Wildlife Exposition begins.
1984 MOJA Festival.
1985 *North and South* filmed in Charles-

ton. Movie industry discovers the city.
1989 Hurricane Hugo.
1990 Waterfront Park opens.
1991 Annexation of Daniel Island by City.
1992–1993 Closure of Naval Base and Shipyard.
1992 Opening of Mark Clark Expressway (I-526).
1996 Women admitted to The Citadel.
1997 Joseph P. Riley Park opens.
2000 *C.S.S. Hunley* raised from ocean floor.
2001 Construction of latest gigantic Cooper River Bridge begins.
2002 Opening of new Judicial Center.

The Holocaust Memorial at Marion Square, with a statue of John C. Calhoun in the background. Photograph by Michael Levkoff and Barbara Baker

Mayor Joseph P. Riley and Elizabeth Taylor. The great actress was in Charleston for the filming of John Jakes' North and South. Photograph by Bill Murton.

Bibliography

The basic text consulted was David Duncan Wallace, *South Carolina, A Short History, 1520-1948,* Columbia, S.C.,1951; also John and Isabella Leland, *Our Charleston,* Charleston, 1970.

Chapter I: Warren Alleyne, "A Barbadian Pirate," *The Bajan and South Caribbean,* June, 1973; Cheves, above; St. Julien S. Childs, "The First South Carolinians," SCHM vol. 71, p.101; Verner W. Crane, *The Southern Frontier, 1670-1732,* Durham, 1928; Alexander Hewat, *Historical Account of...South Carolina and Georgia,* in B. R. Carroll, *Historical Collections, I,* N.Y., 1836; Jose Miguel Gallardo, "The Spanish and the English Settlement in Charleston," SCHM vol. 37, p.131; Arthur H. Hirsch, *The Huguenots of Colonial South Carolina,* London, 1928, reprint, Durham, 1962; Shirley C. Hughson, *The Carolina Pirates and Colonial Commerce, 1670-1740,* Baltimore, 1894; Stefan Lorant, ed., *The New World,* N.Y., 1965; McCrady, above; Gertrude E. Meredith, *The Descendants of Hugh Amory 1605-1805,* London, 1901; H. Roy Merrens, ed., *The Colonial South Carolina Scene, Contemporary Views 1697-1774,* Columbia, S.C., 1977; Chapman J. Milling, *Red Carolinians,* Chapel Hill, 1940; Alexander S. Salley, Jr., *Narratives of Early Carolina, 1650-1708,* N.Y., 1911; M. Eugene Sirmans, *Colonial South Carolina, A Political History 1663-1763,* Chapel Hill, 1966; Joseph I. Waring, *A History of Medicine in South Carolina, 1670-1825,* Col., 1964.

Chapter II: Charles W. Baird, *History of the Huguenot Emigration to America,* Baltimore, 1966; Carl Bridenbaugh, *Myths & Realities,* Baton Rouge, 1952; Carroll, above; Hirsch, above; Ralph Julian, "Charleston and the Carolinas," *Harper's New Monthly Magazine,* January, 1895; *Charleston News & Courier,* June 27, 1960; Sidney George Fisher, *Men, Women and Manners in Colonial Times,* Philadelphia, 1898, Florence G. Geiger, ed., "St. Bartholomew's Parish as Seen by its Rectors 1713-1761," SCHM vol. 50, p. 191; Edward McCrady, *The History of South Carolina Under the Royal Government, 1719-1776,* N.Y., 1899; Merrens, above; Elise Pinckney, ed., *Letterbook of Eliza Lucas,* Chapel Hill, 1972; Walter L. Robbins, ed., "John Tobler's Description of South Carolina (1753)," SCHM vol. 71; George C. Rogers, Jr., *Charleston in the Age of the Pinckneys,* Norman Okla., 1969; Salley, above; Sirmans, above; *South Carolina Gazette,* January 8-15, 1731-2, July 5-10, 1736, July 17-24, 1736, August 8-September 6, 1736, September 6, 1740, November 19, 1766; Mabel L. Webber, "Peter Manigault's Letters," SCHGM vol. 31; George W. Williams, *St. Michael's, Charleston, 1751-1951,* Col., 1951; Peter H. Wood, *Black Majority,* N.Y., 1974.

Chapter III: Henry Steele Commager, *Documents of American History,* N.Y., 1948; Elisha Douglass, *Rebels and Democrats,* Chapel Hill, 1955; Fitchett, "The Status of the Free Negro in Charleston, S.C. and His Descendents in Modern Society," *Journal of Negro History,* XXXII, October, 1947; John

Fitzpatrick, ed., *The Diaries of George Washington,* vol. IV, 1789-1799, Boston, 1928; R. W. Gibbes, *Documentary History of the American Revolution,* N.Y., 1855-1857; "Journal of Josiah Quincy, Junior, 1773," *Proceedings of the Massachusetts Historical Society,* vol. XLIX (1915-16); Edward McCrady, *South Carolina in the Revolution, 1775-1780,* N.Y., 1901; Edward McCrady, *South Carolina in the Revolution, 1780-1783,* N.Y., 1902; William Moultrie, *Memoirs of the American Revolution,* N.Y., 1802; Rogers, above; *South Carolina Gazette,* September 28-October 5, 1765; William Willcox, ed., *Papers of Benjamin Franklin,* vol. XV, p. 201.

Chapter IV: Bridenbaugh, *Cities in Revolt,* N.Y., 1955; Thomas D. Clark, *South Carolina, the Grand Tour, 1780-1865,* Col., 1973; *Charleston Courier,* April 25, 1850, April 27, 1850; *Charleston Mercury,* July 30, 1835, November 3, 1860; *Charleston Yearbook,* 1883, 1886, 1893, 1894; John B. Irving, *The South Carolina Jockey Club,* Charleston,1857; Lionel H. Kennedy and Thomas Parker, "Insurrection of 1822, An Official Report of the Trials of Sundry Negroes...in the State of South Carolina," Charleston, 1822; John Lawson, *New Voyage to Carolina,* London, 1709, reprint, Chapel Hill, 1967; Robert Mills, *Statistics of South Carolina,* Charleston, 1826; Raymond A. Mohl, ed., "'The Grand Fabric of Republicanism' A Scotsman Describes South Carolina 1810-1811," SCHM vol. 71, p. 170; Alfred J. Morrison, trans. and ed., Johann B. Schoepf, *Travels in the Confederation,* vol. 2, Philadelphia, 1911; Beatrice St. Julien Ravenel, *Architects of Charleston,* Charleston, 1964; Mrs. St. Julien Ravenel, *Charleston, the Place and the People,* N.Y., 1906; Rogers, above.

Chapter V: E. Milby Burton, *The Siege of Charleston, 1861-1865,* Col., 1970; *Charleston Daily Courier,* August 24, 1863, September 1, 1863, October 13, 1862, July 21, 1863, *Charleston Mercury,* December 21, 1860, October 20, 1862, October 13, 1862, April 11, 1863; J. H. Easterby, *A History of the College of Charleston,* Charleston, 1935; Q. A. Gillmore, *Engineer and Artillery Operations Against the Defenses of Charleston in 1863,* N.Y., 1865; Elmer D. Johnson and Kathleen L. Sloan, *South Carolina, A Documentary Profile of the Palmetto State,* Col., 1971; Isabella Leland, ed., "Middleton Correspondence," SCHM vol. 63, p. 34; Walter Lord., ed., *The Freemantle Diary,* Boston, 1954; *Alicia Middleton correspondence,* unpublished, author's collection; *Post-Courier Centennial of the Civil War,* June 15-16, 1962; *Walker correspondence,* unpublished, Dorothy Gibbon Smith collection; Joel Williamson, *After Slavery,* Chapel Hill, 1965.

Chapter VI: *Charleston Courier,* June 2, 1865, June 29, 1865, September 26, 1865, December 20, 1865; *Charleston News & Courier,* October 3, 1874, October 5, 1874, August 28, 1893, August 30, 1893, September 8, 1893, June 23, 1894, December 28, 1964; Jonathan Daniels, *Prince of Carpetbaggers,* Philadelphia, 1958; Hampton M. Jarrell; *Hampton and the Negro,* Col., 1949; Johnson & Sloan, above; *Journal of Negro History,* vol. XXX, p. 93; *Middleton Correspondence,* Middleton Place Foundation; Isabella Leland, "Middleton Correspondence," SCHM vol. 65, p. 108; Francis B. Simkins and Robert H. Woody, *South Carolina During Reconstruction,* Chapel Hill, 1932; *Louisa McCord Smythe correspondence,* unpublished, Mrs. E. D. McDougal III collection; George B. Tindall, *South Carolina Negroes, 1877-1900,* Col., 1952; Alfred

B. Williams, *Hampton and His Red Shirts,* Charleston, 1935.

Chapter VII: *Charleston Evening Post*, March 25, 1976; *Charleston News & Courier*, October 16, 1915, July 30, 1967, March 26, 1976; *Post-Courier,* June 5, 1977; Charleston Negro File, John P. Dart Library, Charleston; *Charleston Yearbook,* 1902, 1906, 1910, 1914, 1923, 1930; Mayor Wm. A. Courtenay Collection, Charleston Library Society; "The Exposition," Charleston, 1902; Alfred O. Halsey Collection, South Carolina Historical Society; Hazel Ferri, "The Ivory Palaces of Charleston," *Art in the Lives of South Carolinians, Book II,* David Moltke-Hansen, ed., Charleston, 1979; Johnson & Sloan, above.

Chapter VIII: *Charleston News & Courier,* November 25, 1956; *Charleston Yearbook,* 1950; Letter, July 16, 1979, Historic Charleston Foundation; "Proceedings of Council, Regular Meeting, January 24, 1978," p. 711, Charleston, 1978; Elizabeth O'Neill Verner, *Mellowed by Time,* Col., 1953.

Chapter IX: The standard scholarly history of Charleston by Walter Fraser, *Charleston! Charleston!* (U.S.C. Press, Columbia: 1989) takes the city's story through Hurricane Hugo in 1989. See pp. 428-42. Walter Edgar's *South Carolina, A History* (U.S.C. Press: Columbia, 1998) brings the state's history up to 1998. Modern authors are described by David Aiken in his readable *Fire in the Cradle, Charleston's Literary Heritage* (Charleston Press, Charleston: 1999). Other useful works on recent history include: Robert N. Rosen, *A Short History of Charleston* (U.S.C. Press, Columbia, 2000); Jonathan H. Poston, *The Buildings of Charleston* (U.S.C. Press, Columbia, 1997); Brian Hicks and Schuyler Kropf, *Raising the Hunley* (Ballantine Books, N.Y., 2002); and Ted Phillips's introductory essay to *Charleston in My Time, The Paintings of West Fraser* (U.S.C. Press, Columbia, 2001).

The sources for much of this chapter were Charleston newspapers, *The News and Courier, The Evening Post,* and after 1993, the *Post and Courier;* the *New York Times, The [Columbia] State,* national and regional magazines and governmental and planning reports. See these citations in the order the information appears in the text: *Charleston* magazine (Winter, 1999, p. 38); *Post and Courier,* 4-6-02; *Post and Courier,* 11-7-95; U.S. v. Charleston County School Dist., 738 F.Supp. 1513 (D.S.C. 1990); *Post and Courier,* 1-23-00; *Newsweek,* 9-30-85; State of the City Address, 1-26-99; *Evening Post,* 9-30-91; *Post and Courier,* 3-13-92; *Post and Courier,* 3-13-93; *Post and Courier,* 5-02-93; *Post and Courier,* 6-26-93; *Post and Courier,* 3-15-96; City of Charleston Century V City Plan, July, 2000; *Post and Courier,* 2-28-99; *New York Times,* 4-22-01, "Travel"; *Post and Courier,* 11-21-91; *The State,* 5-30-93; *Post and Courier,* 10-17-99; *Post and Courier,* 1-30-00; *Post and Courier,* 10-10-01; *Post and Courier,* 9-9-01; *Post and Courier,* 4-24-91; *Post and Courier,* 10-4-99; *Post and Courier* ad, 11-5-95; *Post and Courier,* 9-1-96; *Post and Courier,* 5-10-92; *New York Times,* 5-1-88, "Travel"; *Post and Courier,* 11-5-95.

Index